THERE IS A BALM IN HUNTSVILLE

"Every time I share my story,
I heal a little bit more."

Ellen Halbert, crime victim survivor

THERE IS A BALM IN HUNTSVILLE

A True Story of Tragedy and Restoration From the Heart of the Texas Prison System

T. Carlos Anderson

WALNUT STREET BOOKS

LANCASTER,
PENNSYLVANIA

There Is a Balm in Huntsville: A True Story of Tragedy and Restoration From the Heart of the Texas Prison System is published by
Walnut Street Books, Lancaster, Pennsylvania
info@walnutstreetbooks.com

Cover design by Cliff Snyder and Mike Bond
Page design by Cliff Snyder

Also by T. Carlos Anderson: *Just a Little Bit More:*
The Culture of Excess and the Fate of the Common Good

*This book is dedicated to Dr. Linda White—
crime victim, Restorative Justice advocate,
college professor to prisoners, and
Victim-Offender Dialogue mediator*

Andrew Papke, by his own choice, does not benefit
financially in any way by the sale of this book.
T. Carlos Anderson is donating a portion of all book
proceeds to organizations that encourage healing and
restoration from drunk-driving crime and its effects.

Contents

This is a true story. Due to its sensitive nature, the names of some characters have been changed to protect their privacy.

List of Characters and Acronyms

The main characters are listed here in alphabetical order by first names, apart from the three lead characters in this true story.

PART I

THE ROAD TO HUNTSVILLE

Chapter 1

Andrew staggers into the dark apartment. He pauses, catches his breath, and tries to elbow the door shut. A second try produces a clumsy slam. He fumbles at a light switch and gets it to work. The sudden bright light dizzies him as he tries to focus on the kitchen clock—is it really 4:00 a.m.? This isn't the first time he's come home drunk and unreliable.

The previous year—his senior year of high school—he stopped going to class as fishing and drinking trumped biology and geometry. A smart kid, he still passed his tests, but the high school required class attendance for graduation. He dropped out. With no studies to worry about, he stepped up his drinking. This late night out with buddies is no different than the last six weeks of nights.

He shakes his head to clear it. From the kitchen he trudges to the hallway that leads to the bedroom he shares with his girlfriend Krista. She tries to sleep amid his commotion and the dread that prowls about in her mind. Yanking off the top blanket where Krista lies, Andrew drags it to the living room. He crashes on the couch and sleeps the few hours before daylight.

The sun will rise at 6:32 a.m. this Saturday morning in Austin, Texas. The temperature will climb to 91 degrees. The sun will set at 9:04 p.m., giving way to a night sky speckled with clouds underneath a nearly full moon. But none of this matters to Andrew, lying face-down on the couch. He has no inkling that this date—June 29, 1996—will indelibly mark the rest of his life, precisely at 10:41 p.m. As if a tattoo carved by the angel of death, this branding will scar and inflict many others as well.

"Hey, get up! It's time to go. We've got to do this today," Krista demands while kicking the couch where Andrew has crashed as if comatose.

She has an appointment at a clinic for 10:00 a.m. Last evening when she got home to their apartment, her entering call—"Hey, I'm here"—fell empty with no response. While Andrew was out with his buddies, she spent the evening alone, nervous and apprehensive about the next day and what it would bring.

This morning at the clinic, a doctor will administer pain medication to Krista. Someone will have to drive her there and bring her back home. Andrew promised to do at least that much.

Krista is almost three months pregnant. Neither of them has slept very well in the six weeks since they discovered their unplanned pregnancy. They don't know what to do.

High school sweethearts, they've been together for the better part of four years. Krista, at twenty, is a year older than Andrew. Could they raise a child responsibly? With this dilemma ever-present in her mind, Krista occasionally steals glances at him. She's looked into his deep brown eyes many times to catch a glimpse of his sweet soul. But in the last few months, eye contact has been rare between the quiet blonde and the guy who drinks too much and can't keep a decent job.

Toward the end of Krista's last year in high school, they promised each other that they'd marry and have a family. Krista was the good girl and Andrew the bad boy rebel. Together they had so much fun: hiking trips, swimming in rivers, hunting—things Krista never would have done on her own. Andrew bought Krista a gold ring with an emerald stone, and when things were good they told their friends they were engaged.

After graduating from high school, Krista moved to San Antonio to attend college with the goal of becoming a forensic scientist. She and Andrew, though, missed each other desperately. He spent as much time in San Antonio as in Austin, which didn't help either of their studies. She quit college after a year and moved back to Austin. They began to share an apartment when Andrew dropped out of high school. He passed the tests for his GED and began volunteering once a week at a local fire station with the hope of becoming a firefighter. Krista worked for a computer software company, and Andrew delivered pizzas and occasionally fixed cars for additional money. They scraped by. With Andrew's increased drinking and irritability in the last six weeks, however, they've seen much less of each other. When they do see each other, it only verifies for Krista that scraping by together is no longer worth it.

Scared, Krista hasn't said a word to her parents about the pregnancy. She reached out to a friend at work who knows Andrew. Woman to woman, the co-worker insisted that Andrew wasn't ready to be a father. Who knew if he'd be around after the baby came? Krista nodded, and then and there decided to terminate her pregnancy, telling her friend she did not want to raise a child with him. Her co-worker gave her a hug and called the clinic on Krista's behalf.

Three days before the appointment, Krista asked Andrew to sit down. She informed him that she had scheduled an abortion. Starting to cry, she told him of another decision she made.

"I'm thinking we're done as a couple." Her voice shook. He hung his head and looked away.

Unable to raise his head and look at her, Andrew said he wasn't ready to leave her. He told her he wanted to be with her at least during the procedure. They agreed to stay together through the weekend.

She awakes this Saturday morning with an overtaxed mind and a vague memory of Andrew having come in sometime during the night. Noticing the missing bed cover, she rises quickly and darts through the kitchen to the living room. There the young drunk slumbers on the couch, fully clothed with one boot hanging halfway off his foot. Kicking the couch, she demands that he get up—today's the day and it's time to go.

A ndrew rouses himself to drive Krista to the clinic. It's twelve miles north on a highway that parallels the old Missouri-Pacific rail line—the locals call the highway MoPac. Andrew's head hurts and his hands shake as he drives Krista's black 1991 Acura Integra. He wanted to take his pickup, but it was in the shop. When they pull into the clinic's parking lot, Krista touches Andrew's arm and holds it.

He half-cocks his head to look at her out of the corners of his eyes as she gives his arm a gentle squeeze and says nervously, "Andrew, if you can stick with me through this and turn your ways around, maybe there's still a chance for us." He nods and bites his lip. He doesn't want to say anything to upset her, not now.

In the clinic's waiting room, Andrew and Krista sit uneasily. Their grim decision hangs over their heads like a dull machete. Others also wait for their appointments. No one says a word. A nurse breaks the silence and calls Krista's name. Standing up, Krista nods goodbye to Andrew and slowly follows the nurse into a room to undergo a procedure that will unburden the young couple of some of their worries, if not all of them.

As soon as the nurse closes the door behind Krista, Andrew bolts from the clinic. His sour stomach churns from a combination of last night's drinking and thoughts of what the procedure will be like. He decides to go to Papa John's, a mile away, for some breadsticks to calm his stomach.

Halfway there, he pulls into a gas station and slams the transmission into park. Forcing the car door open with his shoulder, he stumbles out sideways and pukes out his guts on the concrete. He shakes uncontrollably. This isn't his first bout with delirium tremens, but this case bends him over and blinds his eyes with tears and sweat. There he is in broad daylight—for anyone who cares to see—a young man lost and reeling. Gasoline fumes and the smell of vomit choke him into a coughing fit. A recurring thought crosses his mind as he hacks: My life is a complete joke.

When Andrew stops drinking, the shakes come. This day is no different. Slumping back into the car, he curses under his foul breath and grabs the wheel. *Breadsticks? I need a beer.* He revs the Acura out onto MoPac and floors it to their apartment. The Acura skids as it enters the parking lot. He hurries inside and scours his usual stashes. He grabs a bottle of beer that he's hidden inside one of his cowboy boots. He twists off the top and takes a swig of the warm swill. Sinking into the same couch where he slept only hours before, he closes his eyes and cradles the bottle to his chest with both hands. A moment of apparent peace, it's simply one part of the enslaving cycle that has become his daily routine.

Anger is a hot flame in the center of his being, influencing most of his decisions and interactions with others. He doesn't know why, but anger fueled his decision to drop out of school, it led to a falling out with the captain and his dismissal from the firehouse, and it fuels his reckless driving and arguing with Krista.

Earlier this week, Andrew started a new job. *This is it.* Not some fast-food restaurant job but a decent paying one, finishing out custom homes. To keep the job, he knows he has to make some changes, starting with drinking fewer beers and controlling his temper. If he's ever to become a father, he knows he needs to change his ways. But not yet. Not now. Drinking beer is the only thing that seems to soothe his raging core.

It's time to get Krista. He drains the beer and rubs his eyes. He finds a clean shirt and makes his way out to the car. He fires it up. On his way to MoPac, he stops at a red light on the northernmost stretch of Brodie Lane. As he waits, he notices adolescent girls and their parents waving signs in the median—a fundraiser for a girls' softball team. Raising money for some type of trip, one of the girls approaches Andrew's car. Rolling down his window with his left hand, he reaches into his pants' pocket with his right hand and grabs every bit of cash he has. He stuffs it into the coffee can the girl holds. She smiles and says thank you. He doesn't acknowledge her but stares straight ahead. What does it matter? *My life is a wreck.*

Back on MoPac, Andrew holds it to the floor the whole way. The Acura tops out at 120 mph. He doesn't see any cops and neither does he care if any see him.

Two nurses guide the medicated Krista out of the clinic in a wheelchair. Andrew releases the passenger seat to full recline so Krista can lie down as he drives her home. At their apartment, he helps her into bed. She needs to rest. Intending to go to his mom's house to do laundry, he gathers up their dirty clothes. Andrew's parents divorced years earlier—messily—and he hasn't seen his dad much lately. His mom's house is less than ten minutes away. After asking Krista if she needs anything, he says he'll be back soon. After carrying out a second load, he slams shut the rear hatch. They haven't done any laundry in almost three weeks.

Andrew's folks divorced when he and his younger brother, Dave, were little boys. After two bruising custody battles, the boys lived with their dad and his new wife, Cathy. A few years later, when he was fifteen, Andrew got busted for shoplifting some music CDs and then for joyriding the car of a friend's mom. After his dad sternly let him know that type of behavior wouldn't be tolerated, Andrew and his dad stopped talking. Andrew moved out and went to live with his mom.

Peeling out of the parking lot, he heads two blocks north where he waits at a red light. To go to his mom's house, he needs to take a left. Instead, he turns right and heads east. It's not the type of turn Krista had in mind when, in the clinic parking lot, she gave him and their relationship one more chance. After making a few lights, he accelerates away from his problems. It's 2:00 p.m.

Chapter 2

Andrew has some friends Krista doesn't know much about. Younger girls in high school. They think Andrew's cool—he smokes, drinks beer, and drives fast. A cigarette in his left hand and a large cooler heavy with ice and beer underneath his bent right knee and boot, Andrew laughs with three girls—two of them sisters—at a rural property east of Austin. As Andrew takes a final drag of his smoke, he invites the girls to drive back into town with him. They shoot out on Texas State Highway 71. An open beer can, beaded with condensation, dangles in Andrew's right hand. Aggressively he weaves in and out of traffic, eventually getting stuck behind two cars. Tailgating the car in the left lane, he slams on the horn with his beer in hand. As beer suds drip off his forearm, the offending car moves over into the right lane. Finally in the clear, Andrew floors it. He calls out his speeds: "100! ... 105! ... 110! ... 115!"

The girls yell at him to slow down. Robbyne, the older of the sisters and seated up front, knows Andrew better than her younger sister and her friend in the back seat.

"Let me drive, Andrew!" she shouts as she digs her nails, more from instinct than spite, into his arm.

"No! This is Krista's car and I'm not letting anyone else drive it. What if something happens to it?"

Andrew slows down to 80 mph. He softens his approach and tries to reassure Robbyne, telling her that he knows what he's doing. "I can handle this," he manages to say before finishing off his beer.

Arriving in Austin, they exit off the highway. Late afternoon fades into early evening. They stop by a park with a creek. Staying in the car, the girls fight over which radio station to listen to as Andrew ambles down to the water with his troubled mind and a fresh can of beer.

He sits down on a rock at the edge of the creek. Staring blankly as water trickles past, he continues an internal conversation he's had ever since he dropped out of school: *You're such a loser. Can't you do better than this?* After draining the beer, he stands up and stomps the can under his boot heel. Kicking it into the creek, he curses and walks back to the car for another beer.

Krista stirs and wakens. With the medication still in her system, the numbers on the clock radio blur as she tries to figure out the time. It's a bit after 7:00 p.m. Andrew ... where is he? Is he in the apartment? He should be done with the laundry by now. She calls out to him. Again, like the night before—no response. Pushing herself up slowly from the bed, she stumbles out of the bedroom and inches toward the kitchen.

After finding a chair, she picks up the phone, its receiver heavy in her hand. She dials Andrew's mother, Jan, at her house, but there's no answer. Krista then calls Jan's parents' house and finds her there. Jan says she hasn't seen Andrew. Knowing about the appointment at the clinic, she asks Krista how she is doing. Jan, tall and blonde just like Krista, has always told her son that he's lucky to have Krista. The women talk a few moments longer, and Jan says she'll go home and see what's going on. As Krista puts down the receiver, she starts to worry. Something isn't right.

Just south of Austin, off Farm to Market Road 1626, the setting sun colors the scattered clouds crimson-orange as activity slows on the Kitchen Field baseball and softball diamonds after a full day of games. Moms, dads, brothers, sisters, and friends cheered on the boys and girls playing today. Concession stand volunteers, having sold all of their prized hamburgers, wipe the counter clean. The south wind flaps an American flag directly behind the stand.

The ballfield's lights, outshining the retiring sun, illuminate the diamond. Crickets chirp as one last game carries into the night. A scrimmage game, the competing teams are prepping for an All-Star travel tournament. Coach Bob Thonhoff and some of the other dads decide the teams will play two more innings. Their ten- and eleven-year-old boys will miss some sleep, the dads banter, but they'll learn something about the benefits of hard work and practice.

Bob's wife, Kim, seated in the stands, enjoys watching their son play baseball. Eleven-year-old Travis plays shortstop with flair. Kim, however, is ready to get home. Looking at her watch, she lets out a slow sigh. Two more innings means they won't get home until at least 10:30.

Faint starlight blinks through a few stray clouds. Andrew and the girls near the house of D.R.—Derrick Roberts—a friend Andrew knows from high school and pizza delivery work. They haven't seen each other in more than two weeks. D.R.'s mom told her son not to hang out with Andrew after the two of them got in trouble with the Travis County sheriff for vandalizing a car.

Andrew and the girls pull up close to the house, parking on the street. Robbyne runs up to the house while Andrew stays by the car. D.R. lies to his mother, saying he's going out with Robbyne in her car. His mom says to be home in an hour, no later than 10:30. The front door slams.

D.R. and Robbyne run to the car where Andrew stands by its hood, drinking a beer under the nearly full moon. Andrew tosses him a beer and slaps him a high-five. The three girls hop into the back of the car and the two guys in the front. As clouds veil the moon, Robbyne says something to Andrew about letting D.R. drive.

"Maybe," he replies, "but not yet."

They peel out, drive a few blocks, and then drop off the two younger girls at Robbyne's dad's house. While Robbyne's inside, Andrew kills the engine and tells D.R. about Krista's abortion, confiding that he's had more than twenty beers that day. As they talk, they empty the last of the beers from the cooler. Andrew says it's still early—time to make a beer run.

Robbyne and her stepmom walk outside together just as Andrew and D.R. return with more beer. The woman realizes Andrew has been drinking and states that Robbyne isn't getting into the car unless someone else drives. Andrew protests, saying that he can drive just fine.

"Well, you're not going to. You're going to let someone else drive." The woman is adamant.

Andrew and Robbyne slide into the back seat, and D.R. moves to the driver's seat. One block down the road, Andrew slaps his buddy's shoulder, eyes him in the rearview mirror, and nods for him to pull over. Andrew jumps back into the driver's seat, and the Acura squeals back onto the road, its tires spinning hot.

Krista can't sleep anymore. It's 10:00 p.m. She calls Jan at her house: "Has he been there?"

"I don't see any evidence of him being here."

Anguish threads through Krista's voice, "I feel like ... something's wrong."

Jan, a former Austin police officer, tells Krista not to worry and to get some rest. A photo of her oldest son hangs in her living room. Jan glances at it and turns away. She closes her eyes, takes a deep breath, and bites her lip.

With a contorted face, Robbyne yells at Andrew, "My stepmom is right. I want D.R. to drive me home now."

Slump-shouldered, Andrew tosses the keys to D.R. On the way, D.R. yanks the car into a ditch and then immediately brings the Acura back onto the road. He laughs, remembering an event two months ago when Andrew accidentally backed D.R.'s truck into a ditch. Tonight is payback time.

The prank revitalizes Andrew. One year older and much bigger than his friend, Andrew jerks on the emergency brake. "Stop—I'm not letting you tear up my girlfriend's car!"

The car stops. Andrew gets behind the wheel again. They drop off Robbyne at her mom's place.

The two drive to Railroad Barbeque on FM 1626 next to the railroad tracks. They park the car and fish a few more beers out of the cooler. As soon as they finish their beers, they will leave. D.R. needs to get home, and Andrew says he wants to see how Krista's doing. It's 10:25 p.m.

The last pitch, a strike, smacks the catcher's mitt at Kitchen Field. The coaches gather their players, talk them up one last time, and send them home. Two of the dads lock up the baseball gear in a metal trunk behind home plate on the outer side of the backstop fence. Kim Thonhoff walks to her Toyota and remembers that it's low on gas. Her husband says she shouldn't worry—he owes her for staying late and he'll fill it up. They trade car keys. Bob winks at her and says he'll race them home.

Kim starts the white Ford van with her eleven-year-old son in the passenger seat. While her husband drives off in the other direction for gas, Kim and Travis turn west onto FM 1626. They'll be home in twelve minutes, as long as no freight train runs through by the barbeque joint. Kim smiles as she thinks about laying her head on her pillow after a long day.

They cross the railroad tracks free and clear, but the traffic light ahead at the intersection of Manchaca Road is red. They come to a stop and wait. Pale moonlight reflects off the empty road's asphalt. The light glows green. Kim accelerates slowly, travels a half-mile, and then turns right on Brodie, a two-lane road. "Almost home," she says to her son with relief. She looks down and turns off her car radio.

Suddenly a jet-black Acura lunges from behind, its headlights flicking bright. Startled, Kim grabs the steering wheel with both hands. The black car's engine roars and its tires squeal as it accelerates aggressively. The car swerves and passes the van, its two occupants laughing and yelling. Kim sees the car gun forward, its red tail lights shrinking. Rattled, she shakes her head and raises her voice to her son. "It's kids like that who kill people!"

Immediately, headlights approach from the other direction where the road curves to the right. The black car doesn't slow down. Kim sees that it can't hold the inward curve at its speed. When it crosses over to the outside lane, Kim wants to close her eyes but can't. Real time converts to slow motion as the approaching car's headlights disappear.

Kim gasps as the two cars violently meld into the same space. A screaming explosion, followed by utter silence, chills Kim's heart. She trembles, instinctively reaching for her son.

It's 10:41 p.m., and what Kim has just told her son is true—terribly true, twice over.

Chapter 3

Sweethearts David Holland and Bethany Early, in the approaching car on Brodie Lane this moonlit night, are violently killed as they attempt to return to Beth's house—on time—for her 11:00 p.m. curfew. Both will be pronounced dead on the scene, just two-and-a-half miles from Beth's house.

Only hours earlier, David drove his immaculate red 1974 Volkswagen Beetle to pick up Beth at her family home just south of the Austin city limits. Beth's mom, Martha, was busy in the kitchen when the young couple waved goodbye, smiling and walking proudly to the Volkswagen. Martha, a self-described hugger, smiled back and waved to them from the kitchen window overlooking the driveway. Little did she know that she had already given her last hug to her only daughter.

David, nineteen, graduated from high school in 1994; Bethany, seventeen, looked forward to her senior year and graduating with the class of '97. They had been dating for one year, introduced to one another by mutual friends.

Curious and extroverted, David was the older brother of Benjamin and Lucas. The three boys were raised by their parents, Richard and Maria Soriano Holland, in Austin.

David was always on the move, much of the time on his skateboard. When roughhousing, the oldest brother used his favorite move, a bone-crushing bear hug, on his younger brothers. When David freed either of his brothers from his muscular grasp, he flashed a mischievous grin and let loose with wild laughter. He lit up a room with his trademark smile, showing his carefree and gregarious nature.

As young boys, David and Lucas decided to explore some backwoods close to their home. A tiny creek ran through the woods, rushing with runoff from recent rains. Lucas fell into the creek and became wedged underwater in a rock dam. David grabbed him and pulled him out of the water. Lucas said that his big brother saved his life.

The three brothers followed professional wrestling on TV. They were big fans of Rob Van Dam and Paul Diamond. David and youngest brother Lucas even plotted forming a professional wrestling tag team in the future. It was a dream Lucas never let go. Lucas would say about David: "He was the only one who fed into my fantasy as a kid."

A few years after David's passing, Lucas became a professional wrestler. Those watching Lucas perform in person or on video caught his mischievous grin and boisterous celebration, very similar to his older brother's, after executing a winning move.

Maria Soriano, originally from Mexico, often took her boys to her native country. She and her parents taught the boys to *hablar el español*—speak Spanish.

Richard and Maria divorced before David reached his teenaged years. But Maria continued living in Austin to be close to her boys.

After graduating from high school, David moved in with his mom. Maria enjoyed how David said goodbye to her before going to school—"I'm leaving, Mom"—in a tender and not obligatory way.

Maria deeply loved her oldest son and cherished the time they shared. Together they went to the park, the mall, the grocery store, restaurants, and the movies. He mowed the lawn and took care of other chores at the house. Later, after the wreck, she would tell friends about how she struggled not being able to be with him.

Bethany, the oldest of three blond-haired children born to Adrian and Martha Early, preferred to be called Beth. The Early family moved to the Austin area from Arizona just prior to Beth starting kindergarten. An animal lover, she wanted to become a veterinarian. With her brothers Aaron and Adam, Beth looked after and cared for the family pets: six cats, three dogs, and one turtle. She inherited her love of animals from both of her parents—Adrian had pets as a boy, thanks to his own animal-loving mother. Beth's mom, Martha, was raised on a dairy farm in Wisconsin and insisted that the children have pets.

Martha described her daughter as "full of life" and "very sensitive to pain." Most days, Beth was super-happy—giggly, chatty, smiling. Other days, sadness and anger crowded in, and she had no way to hide these emotions. But good days and bad days, she did her best to be true to the upbringing her parents gave her and her brothers: to accept and care about other people, no matter the situation.

For a couple of summers, she worked at a local animal kennel. Her brother Aaron later worked at the same kennel through his high school years. Beth fell in love with the pot-bellied pigs clients brought to the kennel. Her boyfriend shared her love of animals, too. When Beth talked about becoming a vet, David schemed right along with her, saying that he'd become a marine biologist.

Beth loved *The Lion King*, the animated Disney movie. Released in the summer of 1994 when she was fifteen, she watched its lush depictions of a diverse animal kingdom in Africa over and over again. The movie tells a story of redemption and second chances, and Beth knew all its scenes and songs by heart. On a family car trip to Colorado that same summer, she sang all the Elton John songs from a well-worn cassette tape as her brothers covered their ears in protest.

Just like David, Beth loved the outdoors. On a family trip skiing in the Rocky Mountains, her younger brothers nicknamed her "Frosty" when she came up covered with snow after a wipeout. Beth loved to fish with her dad at two nearby Texas state parks, both only thirty minutes away from their house. Zilker Park, just west of downtown Austin, was another favorite destination of father and daughter, where they'd walk near Barton Springs and count turtles.

She drove a dark blue Sterling sedan, a short-lived British model powered by a Honda engine, featuring interior wood trim and leather seats. Her dad found it in a used car lot for a good price. Beth helped pay for it with her earnings from the kennel. Sometimes Beth and David drove her car on dates.

Stuffed animals, especially teddy bears, filled her bedroom where she spent hours listening to music. David spent hours in his bedroom, too, his fingers buried in the controller of his Nintendo that he had hooked up to his TV. Or he'd be in the driveway keeping his red VW Beetle in primo condition. He adored classic cars—the VW had a new motor and he loved listening to its roar.

David and Beth both rocked their heads to music with hard basslines. He loved the heavy metal band Metallica and she loved rap. David wasn't a big fan of rap, but he'd play rap tapes in his car for Beth. David accessorized the inside of his white-vinyl Beetle with a sound system. He had completed a college level course in auto electrical systems, and he told Beth that one day he'd own a souped-up red Corvette just like the one on the poster hanging in his bedroom. Beth told him that one day she'd own a Mazda Miata convertible.

Richard Holland remarried after the divorce from Maria. He and his new wife Helen both worked as lawyers. They had a daughter together named Mindy. The whole family took vacations in Colorado—camping and hiking trips in the summers that included fishing and panning for gold in the cold mountain creeks, and ski trips in the winters.

In December 1995, a high school friend of Beth's was tragically killed by a drunk driver. David and Beth had been dating for half a year by that time. They confided in Helen, David's stepmom. Helen was affiliated with MADD— Mothers Against Drunk Driving—and assisted surviving victim family members with legal issues. Helen, nicknamed by her family "the wise owl" for her smarts, use of big words, and taste in professorial eyeglasses, gave David and Beth comfort and counsel. Drinking and driving, she said, was never a good option. Helen heard too many stories from victims and family members of drunk-driving's specific brand of pain and misery.

In May 1996, David and Beth went to the prom at Beth's high school, posing for pictures prior to the dinner and dance. David, handsome in a traditional black tux, sported light sideburns and combed his thick black hair back from the left side of his forehead. Beth wore a sleeveless red dress with matching red heels, her long, wavy strawberry blonde hair held back by barrettes, exposing her beautiful and radiant face. Beth wore her high school ring. On their photo that night, David and Beth look happy and content. David, as usual, wore his sly grin for the pictures.

After leaving the Earlys' house on the evening of June 29, David and Beth jumped into the red VW and drove to Austin for what would become their last date. They went out for Mexican food—Beth's favorite—laughing together, holding hands, kissing, and looking into each other's eyes. As darkness fell, David phoned his brother Benjamin, who was scheduled to fly out the next day for a weeks-long academic camp. David had a CD of Benjamin's and wondered if he'd like it before leaving. The two brothers agreed that David would take Beth home first and then stop by to give Benjamin the CD.

With Beth's curfew approaching, the young couple buckled up in the Beetle and headed south on Brodie Lane. Their hair blew in the summer night's breeze as the amplified music boomed to the outside world. The VW accelerated toward its destiny under the moonlight.

On the last stretch of Brodie Lane where it bends left, David and Beth never had a chance. The black Acura coming from the other direction didn't waver or swerve as it missed the curve and crossed over to the other lane. Neither car's tires darkened the asphalt with skid marks.

The initial silence that washed over eyewitnesses Kim and Travis Thonhoff is gone forever. A ferocious piece of hell has broken loose at 10:41 p.m. on Brodie Lane in far South Austin.

Chapter 4

The red Beetle, completely crushed from the impact, rests on its passenger side in the middle of the two-lane road. The Acura sits upright but crumpled in the southbound lane. Odors of burning rubber and charred plastic mix with the smell of gasoline.

Kim Thonhoff pulls her van to the side of the road and directs its headlights toward the two disabled vehicles. She switches on the brights and tells Travis that she fears another car coming up and slamming into the crash scene. The projection from the Ford's headlights floods the darkness and exposes a ghastly wreck.

Andrew comes to. The steering wheel is bent under his chin, and the motor has caved back into the console. D.R. gurgles and screams and wheezes for breath through a bloody mouth, his legs crushed and pinned under a tangle of metal and plastic. Andrew extricates himself and emerges from the driver's side where the window, now completely gone, had been. The smells of electrical shorts and gasoline cut through his inebriation and give him a short-lived alertness. He grips his way around to the passenger side of the car to free D.R. He can't budge the crumpled door, though. D.R. continues wailing in pain, additional blood spilling from his ears and nose. Andrew tells him they'll get some help.

He goes over to the VW. Reflected in the light, a reddish fluid oozes from the vehicle onto the asphalt—transmission fluid, he thinks. He sees David, seat-belted and hanging sideways. He looks dead, but Andrew doesn't believe it. He figures David will somehow revive. What Andrew doesn't see: Bethany, crushed by the weight of the whole car. She is dead, and her blood, not transmission fluid, covers the pavement.

Clutching for her car phone, Kim Thonhoff attempts to call 911. Her fingers shake and the call won't go through. Travis tries, gets the call through, and hands the phone to his mom.

Kim tells the 911 operator that there's been an accident. Travis asks his mom if they shouldn't go check on the people in the cars.

They walk gingerly toward the two mangled vehicles as if trespassing on private property. After a few steps toward the crash scene, Kim stops, holding her son back. Andrew is running around, yelling. He's torn off his shirt and is calling into the night.

"Who's a witness? Who's a witness? Did you see that car swerve into my lane?"

Kim's face fills with sadness and anger. She's a witness, but not the kind Andrew wishes for. She shields her son and takes him back to the van. Other cars arrive.

A barefoot man in swim trunks and a T-shirt comes up behind Andrew and grabs him by the arm. Andrew spins around and spits: "Are you the jerk who hit my car?" The alcohol on Andrew's breath causes the barefoot man to step back.

"Have you been drinking?" the barefoot man wants to know.

"No, I haven't been drinking!"

The man leaves Andrew and runs to the Volkswagen. He sees David and checks for a pulse. Nothing. Others say something about another passenger in the car. Someone gives him a flashlight. He shines the light inside the car and sees long blonde hair and an arm—Beth's. He tries to get into the car but can't. The barefoot man stands back, stunned. His own seventeen-year-old son is out with a girl tonight. This could have been him and his date.

An ambulance races down FM 1626. On her way to the store to get some cough medicine for her youngest sister, Robbyne waits at the stop sign for the ambulance to pass by. Listening to the siren's moan, she turns and pumps the gas pedal to follow it the short distance to Brodie Lane. She slows and parks her car as she approaches the accident. She gets out and comes upon a woman seated in a white Ford van, holding a phone. It's Kim.

Robbyne wants to know what happened. Are Andy and D.R. involved? As Robbyne listens, she looks again and sees two mangled cars. Turning back to Kim, she starts to shake and cry, saying that she tried to tell Andy not to drive. Between her sobs, she asks to use Kim's phone. She calls her mom, tells her what has happened, and asks her to please come and get her because she doesn't think she can drive anymore.

On the passenger side of the Acura, Andrew tries to console D.R., promising that help will come at any moment. Andrew's alertness, however, suddenly fades, and he sinks into a state of shock. His bladder and bowels release uncontrollably, and he slides down into a roadside ditch. He comes to rest, passed out, on a bed of swarming fire ants.

Police and sheriff deputies arrive, along with a firetruck. Cops and firefighters, sawing and twisting metal, work to cut D.R. loose from the car. A helicopter comes onto the scene, scattering onlookers, forcing them to turn their heads and cover their ears. Other cops with flashlights in hand, unfazed by the commotion, direct the chopper's landing on the road.

The chopper's lights revive Andrew as two EMS responders tend to him in the ditch. They move him out of the ant pile, scissor away his jeans, rinse him with water, and slide a spine board under him. A state trooper who has been dispatched to the scene approaches Andrew and asks him what happened.

"They hit me!"

Trooper Chris Brannen writes down what Andrew says to him, noting that Andrew doesn't ask about his passenger's condition or that of the other driver.

The helicopter lights continue to blaze and reveal a woman, stride by desperate stride, sprinting toward the wreck scene. Sheer terror wails from her face and eyes. Screaming incoherently, she arrives at the Acura just as the paramedics and firefighters rescue D.R. from the car. After seeing that the salvaged boy is alive, the woman collapses on the road.

With Andrew and D.R. strapped onto spine boards, the paramedics load and secure them in the helicopter. Nurses and doctors at the emergency room of Brackenridge Hospital in downtown Austin, fifteen miles away, await their arrival. Hospital police, in the emergency room's adjoining security office, also wait for them. Cleared for takeoff, the chopper lifts, its lights exposing a dust cloud created by its beating blades.

Near the crumpled Volkswagen, law enforcement officers take pictures and measurements. By radio, medical personnel confer with a doctor at the hospital and record the official pronouncement that the driver and passenger in the Volkswagen are dead at the scene. Firefighters assist in uprighting the VW and removing the two bodies. It's 11:17 p.m.

While waiting for her mom to come and get her, Robbyne asks Kim if she can use the phone once more. Robbyne has never met Krista, but she knows the phone number for the apartment Krista and Andrew share. She tells Krista that there's been an accident, and even though Andrew wasn't hurt very bad, he's going to the hospital. She doesn't tell Krista about the two people in the Volkswagen.

Krista calls Jan and tells her what she heard from a girl named Robbyne. As soon as she can, Jan says, she'll be by and they'll go to the hospital. Krista puts down the receiver and screams in frustration.

Jan calls the hospital. Eventually she talks with a social worker who tells her more details about the accident. When Jan hears that two people died in the wreck—apparently at the hands of her son—her knees buckle.

Trooper Brannen approaches Kim and asks her to give a witness statement. Because she and her son are the only eyewitnesses of the crash, he explains that she'll need to prepare a written statement as soon as she's able. She agrees and tells Travis not to look at the red car when they pass it.

Travis walks with his mom by the two crumpled cars. Broken glass, mutilated beer cans, and clothes are strewn over the asphalt like candy from a busted piñata. Travis can't help but look at the Volkswagen—it doesn't even look like a real car, but like an oversized red bumper car from a carnival ride, crushed and crudely sliced in half. On the side of the road, a large white blanket is spread out. He sees two shapes under it like two people in bed, completely under the covers. He doesn't say anything to his mom about what he notices.

Kim also sees the blanket and its covered-up contents. She has trouble giving the trooper her statement. What did she see? She can't say the words, much less write them down. Trooper Brennan says she can write her statement at home, but no later than the next day. Kim thanks him, assuring him that she will do it. He asks if she needs assistance getting home. She declines, saying they live close by, and grabs Travis's hand.

Bob Thonhoff arrives home after filling Kim's car with gas, but he doesn't see the van in their driveway. He goes inside, and his teenage son hurriedly tells him

37

that there's been a wreck on Brodie, but Mom and Travis are okay. Bob immediately calls Kim's phone but it rings unanswered into the night.

Kim and Travis cross back by the accident scene to their van. Travis looks at the black car this time, his plastic baseball cleats crunching broken glass underneath. The car looks as if it was struck straight-on by a huge wrecking ball. The big hydraulic saw that the firefighters used to cut through the steel grabs his attention. He stares at the saw so he doesn't have to look in the direction of the large white blanket.

They climb into the van. Kim takes a deep breath and turns the ignition key. She says a silent prayer for Travis and herself, asking that they get home safely. With Brodie Lane still blocked off, she cuts behind it on a side road. After traveling a few blocks, and less than a mile from home, she stops on the shoulder of the road. Travis looks at his mom and asks if she's okay. Shaking her head, she opens the door and steps out of the van. Travis reaches for the phone and calls home. "Dad, come and get us," he says. "Mom's not doing well." Kim bends over and vomits in the ditch.

When Bob arrives moments later, she breaks down and sobs in his arms, telling him about the complete horror she saw on the face of a woman running up to the wreck. Onlookers told her it was the mother of one of the injured boys. Two other mothers, she says, are going to be told the worst news imaginable this night, and no mother should have to face what she just saw.

Chapter 5

The cops press on with their work at the scene, their flashlights probing in and around the two demolished cars. A sheriff deputy pulled David's wallet from his pants pocket and discovered his license as David's corpse was removed from the vehicle. No identification was found on Beth except for a high school ring on her finger, engraved "Jack C. Hays High, Rebels, Beth, 1997." Eerily, its gemstone was missing. From the collapsed VW, one of the cops fishes out a mangled purse and calls out the find to his co-workers. A license in the purse reveals a last name and a home address for the girl wearing the ring engraved "Beth."

Two EMS responders leave the wreck scene to inform the residents at the address listed on Bethany Early's license. Just before midnight, they ring the doorbell and knock on the door. Martha and Adrian Early, anxious for Beth's arrival, come to the door. The visitors inquire if they are the parents of Bethany Early. When Adrian and Martha say yes, the visitors insist on coming inside. They ask the Earlys to be seated, and then tell them the news that Bethany has been killed in a car accident. Martha slumps in her chair, and the two visitors and her husband move to help her.

After the responders leave, Beth's parents decide not to wake her brothers. They'll wait until morning to tell them the devastating news. Neither Adrian nor Martha will sleep this night, the shock pummeling them like a recurring avalanche.

The chopper lands safely on the roof of Brackenridge Hospital's parking garage in downtown Austin. Medical personnel transfer Andrew and D.R. onto rolling stretchers and wheel them inside the emergency room. Two hospital police officers follow them closely. The two suspects end up in adjacent beds, separated only by a curtain. D.R. has lost two teeth, and X-rays will reveal that he also has a broken leg, a shattered ankle, and a ruptured spleen. Later, nurses will wheel him, with one of the police officers following, to surgery to have his spleen removed.

Andrew has lost a handful of teeth, and X-rays will show six broken ribs, two fractured vertebrae, and a broken tibia. These losses are just the beginning of a slowly revealed stockpile of losses for Andrew. A nurse, cold and brusque in manner, comes to his bedside under the watchful eye of a newly arrived state trooper and draws out a vial of Andrew's blood.

The trooper asks Andrew how much he drank that day.

"One and a half Budweisers, all day long."

The trooper responds with a nod, "We'll just have to see about that."

The trooper takes the vial from the nurse and proceeds to label, seal, and secure it for delivery to the Texas Department of Public Safety's crime lab. It's 12:15, early in the morning of June 30, 1996.

An hour later, at the home of Richard and Helen Holland on Austin's west side, a phone rings, shattering the household's middle-of-the-night quiet. The shocking news, communicated by a representative of the Travis County Sheriff's office, has to be a mistake of the largest proportions. How can such a message—horrendous and horrific, and so permanently intrusive—possibly be true?

The barefoot man finally arrives home after giving his witness statement to police. In a quiet voice on the verge of rage, he tells his wife and son all that he saw at the scene of the wreck, recounting the belligerence of the Acura's driver who showed little awareness of what he did. Tears flood his eyes when he talks about the two kids—similar in age to his son—who ended up dead on their date. He cries for them, and for their parents receiving the appalling news.

Her composure regained, Andrew's mother, Jan, gathers up Andrew's younger teenage brother, Dave. They stop by the apartment to get Krista, and the three speed to the hospital in the dead of night.

"Be prepared for the worst," Jan warns them. Andrew, she says, will be arrested because two people have been killed.

She also says D.R. isn't in good shape. Andrew is already handcuffed to a hospital bed with a police officer on guard, she explains, and will be going to jail as soon as he leaves the hospital.

When Jan parks the car at the hospital entrance, Krista starts to cry. Jan comes around to the passenger door to help her. The two of them walk into the hospital arm in arm.

Brackenridge is Austin's main public hospital, the destination of all serious trauma cases in Travis County. This night, as usual, its emergency room and adjacent waiting area are crowded and chaotic. Tragedy and sickness gather an improbable congregation of peoples, praying and cursing in languages diverse, but screaming and crying in a language universal. Jan has witnessed gatherings like this one during her days as a police officer, but now she, Krista, and Dave are unexpectedly part of the throng. They inquire about Andrew Papke at the receptionist's window. The receptionist looks up at them abruptly and points them to the door of the security office. After handing over identification to hospital police and stating their relationships to Andrew, they wait in the office for clearance to see him.

The hospital police escort them into the section of the emergency room where Andrew lies. He immediately recognizes the three of them and bursts into tears.

"I'm so sorry. I'm so sorry." Andrew sees the horrified look on his mom's face, and a new reality hits him cold and hard. *What have I done?*

Long after midnight, the house of the barefoot man is still and quiet. The man does not go to bed. Instead, he sits in his living room recliner with his swollen feet propped up all through the night, rarely shutting his eyes. When he does close them, all he sees is the wreck scene with its demolition and gore.

The next morning his wife and daughter, using tweezers and needles, will extract multiple glass shards from his feet.

State trooper Chris Brannen, his notebook considerably more inked since writing down Andrew's belligerent response to his initial question, has worked with other cops through the night and early morning to reconstruct the crash scene. A little after 2:00 a.m., he runs a routine check on the driver's licenses of the two occupants of the Acura. Discovering a warrant issued for Andrew Papke for a previous charge of vehicle vandalism, he tells the other officers that he's going to Brackenridge Hospital to arrest the perpetrator of the wreck.

Brannen finds Andrew in a wheelchair in the security office with one of the hospital police officers.

"Are you Andrew Papke?" Brannen questions him.

"I'm here."

Brannen tells Andrew he is under arrest for a vandalism warrant and also for two counts of intoxication manslaughter* and one count of intoxication assault. The trooper reads Andrew his Miranda rights, while handing him a card printed with the same.

---

* *Most states use the phrase "vehicular manslaughter" or "vehicular homicide." Texas specifically uses "intoxication manslaughter."*

After Andrew puts the card aside, Brannen tells him he is investigating the accident and wants to know more details about it.

"You're aware that two people died and it's your fault?"

"That's what I heard."

Brannen cuffs him and takes him to the Travis County Jail's booking unit.

Chapter 6

Cops and those who have stayed at the county jail's booking unit refer to it as the "drunk tank." Dank like a cave, the holding area is messy and ingrained with faint odors of vomit and urine. Some of the arrested brought to this processing area will eventually be released. Others will be moved to the county jail. Brannen shackles Andrew to a bench alongside other suspects and releases Andrew to the custody of another officer. After taking Andrew's fingerprints and mug shot, the new charge officer grasps Andrew by the arm and walks him to a holding cell. He tells Andrew to sleep it off. The new detainee crumbles into a bunk.

Pastor David Sweet, his wife Melissa, their children, and others in their extended family are packed to go on a family vacation to New Mexico—a two-car caravan of six adults and four kids escaping the hot Texas summer to enjoy the cool Rocky Mountain altitude for a week. The previous night, the Sweets pushed and squeezed camping gear, along with snacks for the kids, into their car. After finishing their packing, sleep was fitful for the pastor and his wife who were excited by this long-awaited trip. Typically, on a Sunday morning, Pastor Sweet is leading worship and preaching. This beautiful dawn morning promises to be different: The open road will be his congregation, with the boundless, white-dolloped blue Texas sky westward a blissful choir joining heaven to earth. The pastor lifts up a prayer with his family in the driveway, and they take off at 8:00 a.m.

Five miles from their home, the two-car caravan stops at a McDonald's for breakfast. As the pastor leads the group into the restaurant, his pager lights up. He's not surprised to see that it's a call from the church. It's probably someone needing to find the key to the coffee cabinet. He goes to the pay phone and calls the church. His shoulders slump as he listens to the news from a church elder. A deeply committed family in their congregation, the Earlys, has lost Beth to a drunk driver.

Pastor Sweet goes to the table where his wife and their family are sitting and tells them what he just heard. Melissa, each word punctuated by a sob, tells them that Bethany has babysat their children. The pastor quietly says to his wife that he'll have to stay back. The travelers gather hands around the table and pray for the Earlys. Melissa offers to stay home with her husband, but he insists that she go with the kids as they had planned.

Pastor Sweet hugs his wife, kisses his children, and tells them he'll try to join them as soon as he can. The caravan will go on without him. He calls the Earlys, expresses his grief for their horrific loss, and tells them he'll be over as soon as he can get there.

Andrew wakes up in his cell groggy, sweaty, and sore. He secures permission to use the phone and calls Robbyne, telling her that the accident wasn't his fault, and requests that she relay the same message to D.R. She doesn't respond to Andrew's request, but simply says that D.R. is still in the hospital and that he'll be there for a while.

As Andrew hangs up the phone, he hears his name being called. An officer approaches him and tells him he's being transferred to the fourth floor of the Travis County Jail.

Pastor Sweet arrives at the Early house and hugs Adrian and Martha. The grief and agony on the Earlys' faces confirm that neither has slept since hearing the gut-wrenching news. The pastor extends his sympathy to Beth's teary-eyed younger brothers, placing his hands on their shoulders. He sits and listens to Adrian and Martha—they're unsure how to proceed, never having been through something like this. All five join hands and ask for God's strength.

They make plans for a church funeral service, and Pastor Sweet recommends that they call Harrell Funeral Home in South Austin to take care of accommodations for visitation and burial. Adrian Early makes the call and sets up an appointment that afternoon to go to the funeral home. The Hollands will do the same. None of these parents—with their children teenaged and younger—is prepared for the dreadfully surreal experience of planning a funeral and purchasing a cemetery plot for one of their children.

The Travis County Jail is on the fourth floor of a newer building adjacent to the old county courthouse. Andrew ends up in a cell on the building's north side. The monotony of the cell's walls, grime-coated cinderblocks that were once painted beige, are offset only by a small rectangular slit of a window six feet high.

After spending most of the afternoon alone, he feels nausea rising from his gut. He leaves his cell and the nausea subsides. Approaching the common area, he sees and hears a television that sits high in a metal cage. Other jailed men, most of them young, mill about. Andrew notices sparse interaction between the men. None wants to be here, and none wants to talk about it.

A weekend news report blares from the television. "Drinking and driving. It's a deadly combination that claims lives every holiday. But the Fourth of July is the worst of all. The holiday isn't even here yet, and problems are already starting. Police say that this man—nineteen-year-old Andrew Papke—caused an accident last night that killed two people. Papke is in jail for drinking and driving that led to two deaths. Here's where it happened near the intersection of Brodie and FM 1626. We're told the two cars were headed in opposite directions when one crossed over the yellow line and onto the wrong side of the road ... The two people killed in the crash were also teenagers, seventeen-year-old Bethany Early of Buda and nineteen-year-old David Holland of Austin."

Andrew hears the television news report that permanently links his name with the deaths of Bethany and David. In pain, and dazed from the events of the past two days, Andrew doesn't care if anyone around him matches his face with the accused in the news report.

On Monday, July 1, a judge sets Andrew's bail at $300,000. He will remain in jail because no one in his family has immediate access to the required amount—$30,000—to gain his temporary release.

Andrew's father, Howard Papke, hasn't been able to sleep since receiving a call from Jan, his ex-wife, at 3:00 a.m. Sunday morning, informing him of the wreck. Jan's words, "Andrew was involved in a head-on accident, and there were two fatalities," bounce around in his head like pinballs cursed with perpetual motion.

He tells his wife Cathy that he's numb and doesn't know what to say to his son. He hires a gutsy lawyer named Jamie Balagia who specializes in drunk-driving cases. Balagia, a former police officer turned lawyer, knows most of the people—cops, judges, prosecutors, expert witnesses—who will determine Andrew's future. Balagia's starting point is simple: Andrew has to plead not guilty. Balagia tells Howard that the legal system produces its verdict—guilty or not guilty—based upon a structured dance of compromise between two adversaries, state and defendant. The lawyer says that he will need his client to stand firm. Balagia explains to the elder Papke that the Texas legislature recently classified drunk-driving death offenses punishable to twenty years, up from the previous maximum sentence of ten years. Pleading not guilty is the best way to avoid a long sentence in the Huntsville penitentiary.

That same morning the phone rings at the Early house. Adrian answers the call. A friend of Beth's says that he wants to speak to her.

"Well ... you can't do that."

The caller wants to know why. Adrian tells him plainly that Beth was killed in a wreck.

The caller says he heard some of his friends say something about a wreck, but he didn't believe it. He wanted to prove them wrong, he says, because Beth was the nicest and most beautiful person he ever met.

A young funeral director prepares Beth's body for viewing. The Early family told him that they would like to have an open casket for the viewing and the funeral. Jason Harrell, a recently licensed mortician, rallies all of his artistry to try and make the Beth in the casket look like the Beth in the pictures provided by her parents.

Monday evening, the funeral home in South Austin overflows with mourners—many of them high schoolers—honoring Beth, praying the rosary for David, and offering comfort to both families.

The next morning, Tuesday, July 2, at Hays Hills Baptist Church near the Early house, Bethany's family and friends come to say goodbye to the vivacious girl who loved animals.

The chapel holds up to 200 people comfortably. Almost double that amount show up. The service starts at 10:00 a.m., and multiple musicians offer their talents to help comfort those who have gathered. Martha, who sings in the church's choir, and Adrian have picked the songs by which to remember their daughter. "It Is Well with My Soul," an enduring, nineteenth-century hymn written by a Chicago lawyer after the maritime deaths of his four daughters, is sung immediately before Pastor Sweet addresses the congregation.

The youthful pastor steps up to the pulpit. In a calm but bold voice, he tells the crowd about the young woman he remembers: "Beth was industrious and confident. And she loved her family. She always sat with them during Sunday services, not something most of our teenagers do. Not only that, she sat beside her two younger brothers and actually enjoyed them!"

The mourners listen as Pastor Sweet shares his belief that God is able to bring about good even from the direst circumstances. If people are open and willing, he says, God can use even the worst tragedies for good. Perhaps, he says, the wreck can serve as a wake-up call for people to examine their purposes in life. He recalls Thornton Wilder's play *Our Town*, highlighting the hard-luck character Emily Gibbs, who wonders if any human beings truly understand the value of life while they live it.

Pastor Sweet refers to the ups and downs experienced by Job in the Hebrew Bible and quotes ancient wisdom. "Life is a gift and there are no guarantees. The moment we are born, we're old enough to die."

The same mortician works to prepare for David's funeral mass scheduled for the following day, twenty-four hours after Beth's. David's family has decided that his casket will be closed during his funeral service. More mourners come to pray the rosary for David that evening at the funeral home.

The next morning, July 3, many of the same people, and others, gather at a Catholic church on Austin's west side to say goodbye to the free-spirited young man with the mischievous smile. Just as it was at Bethany's funeral the day before, there aren't enough seats for the overflow mourners at St. John Neumann Catholic Church. Father Thomas Zarbist, proficient in five languages, leads a bilingual mass. During his opening remarks, the priest instructs those wanting to make memorial donations to do so, in David's name, to Mothers Against Drunk Driving. Later in the service, a passage from the Book of Wisdom is read: "The just man, though he die early, shall be at rest."

The service concludes with a slow and soothing Spanish hymn, "Pues Si Vivimos," based on a message to the Romans in the Christian Testament: "Whether we live or die, we belong to the Lord."

This afternoon, David Sweet flies to New Mexico to rejoin his family. The change in place, with its fresh pine-scented mountain air, allows his mind to focus on something other than the horrors and consequences of drunk driving. After settling in with family and briefly recounting for them the events from Austin, he sleeps straight through the night. He only wakens when pounced upon in bed by two kids screaming, "Daddy, Daddy!" the next morning.

On the evening of July 4, he and his wife spread multiple blankets on the ground so their family can relax and watch a fireworks display. The pastor sits with his two young children, their early morning energy long since spent, one on each side of him. He clutches them extra tightly as electric reds, blues, and greens burst and flood the skies above them.

Chapter 7

Lawyer Jamie Balagia responds to an interview request from the *Austin American-Statesman*. He says that he will conduct his own field investigation of the collision. "I went out and drove along that road, and it has a very dangerous slope that makes you overcorrect, and I think that contributed to this terrible accident."

He also tells the reporter that he's known Andrew's mother since both of them worked as Austin police officers in the early 1980s. "When you're an officer and see the harm that drinking does, and then someone you love is involved in something like this—it cuts deep."

David Holland's stepmom, Helen, also responds to the same reporter's request for an interview. The subsequent newspaper article explains that lawyer Helen Holland worked with MADD for five years, helping victims recover compensation. In the back of her mind, her work served as a type of insurance policy. "I think I hoped that by working for MADD my own children would somehow be protected from tragedy.

"It can happen to you," she says. "Don't drink and drive, and drive defensively, because even if you are doing right—somebody out there may not be. I don't want any family to have to go through what we are going through."

The article further documents that a number of her former clients from MADD have been in touch with her since David's death. "It is an incredible comfort when they call and console me. Now I know exactly how they felt when they had to rebuild their lives."

Later in the year, Helen Holland's law firm will forego alcohol at its well-attended annual holiday party. Instead of serving alcohol, the firm will donate its allotted party budget for alcohol—$5,000—to MADD as a tribute to David.

Howard Papke, after meeting and exchanging multiple phone calls with attorney Balagia, now has quite a bit to say to his son. During Andrew's first week of confinement, Howard spoke briefly with his son on the phone, but only to inquire about his well-being and emotional state.

On Friday, July 5, the elder Papke drives downtown from his South Austin auto shop to visit with his son at the jail. He clears security and is told he'll have a visit allotment of fifteen minutes. Howard greets Andrew and says he has a lot to tell him about the legal process.

Andrew tells his dad he needs to say something to him first.

"Dad, I'm so sorry," he says, shaking his head back and forth. "I never meant to bring this on the other families or you."

After a few weeks, Andrew adopts the habit of standing on his tiptoes and looking out his rectangular slit of a cell window. He especially likes looking out toward the courthouse parking lot when visiting hours approach to see if his dad's truck or another family member's car appears.

One Saturday morning, he spies his dad's red truck pull into the lot. When Andrew sees his dad some twenty minutes later in the visiting area, he thanks him for coming and tells him that he's able to see to the parking lot through the small window in his cell.

Howard asks him if he's being treated decently. Andrew shrugs his shoulders and nods his head. The father reminds his son not to talk to anyone about the wreck and to be patient the best he can. They shake hands, and Howard tells his son he'll see him next week.

Andrew returns to his cell and takes his perch at his window, gazing out on the parking lot. He eventually sees his dad cross the lot and walk toward his red truck. Suddenly, Howard stops and looks up at the bank of rectangular windows dotting the building's upper exterior. He then walks over to a sign in the northeast corner of the lot where the building's employee parking area is marked off from the larger lot. Andrew has noticed the sign before and is able to read its large-blocked lettering: NO PARKING — ALL VIOLATORS WILL BE TOWED AT OWNER'S EXPENSE.

Andrew sees his dad stop near the sign and look back up to the jailhouse windows. Howard extends his right arm, pointing to the sign. Reaching farther, he points his index finger toward the word ALL, and holds his pose for a moment. He then points to the words WILL and BE. He then backtracks and points his finger to the letter O in the word

NO, and then to the K in the word PARKING. Just as Andrew finishes mouthing the last letter quietly to himself, he falls back and crashes onto his bunk, his eyes filled with tears and his entire body trembling with chills: **All will be O.K.**

Chapter 8

After three weeks and a few days in the downtown jail, Andrew is transferred to a larger county jail east of Austin. This recently constructed jail has air conditioning, and it blows cold day and night. After logging one week in the facility, Andrew comments to a jail mate in the lunch line that he's continually freezing in the place. His counterpart responds that the jail is kept cold to keep tempers cool. Andrew shakes his head, not exactly sure if the other guy is joking with him or not. Despondent and depressed, Andrew doesn't continue the conversation.

The following week, the first week of August, a chaplain under contract with the county contacts him. Ivan Jameson is a retired public high school teacher who became involved in prison ministry through his church. Jameson is so soft-spoken and gentle that people are surprised when they hear about his commitment to minister to inmates. He's spent countless hours visiting with numerous detainees over the past few decades. While teaching Sunday school to his adult class at his church in Austin, he often shares his experiences and talks about a movement in the prison ministry community called "Restorative Justice." Repairing the harm done by crime, beyond what happens in the courtroom, is how Jameson explains the concept in his class.

Jameson comes to see Andrew in the visitation area and tells him he remembers hearing about the wreck on the news just before July 4. Despite what happened, the chaplain tells Andrew, God still loves him. Andrew hangs his head.

After a pause, Jameson asks Andrew about his family. The two discover that Jameson used to teach high school with Andrew's grandfather—his mom's father, William Dunlap. Jameson asks Andrew how he's doing with everything that has happened and how he's feeling. Andrew says that a lot of the time he doesn't care if he lives or dies.

The chaplain tells him that God will forgive him and help him stitch his life back together. Andrew says he went to church when he was growing up but got away from it when he became a teenager—and that he's been running from everything ever since. Jameson reminds Andrew of the prodigal son in the Bible who wasted his father's inheritance, hit bottom, and decided to go home, where his forgiving father took him back into the family. Andrew looks at the floor and says, "Yes, sir, but the son didn't kill two people like I did."

"Correct," Jameson responds, "but at least the prodigal had the courage to admit his mistakes and ask for forgiveness."

After a long silence, Andrew clears his throat. "I really don't have anywhere else to turn," he says. "God, if you're real, I need to know you now more than ever."

The chaplain stands up, places his hands on Andrew's shoulders, and starts to pray for him. Andrew's shoulders heave and his tears fall on the visiting area's cement floor.

I n the middle of September, a Travis County grand jury considers evidence against Andrew as presented by Howard "Buddy" Meyer, Travis County Assistant District Attorney. Robbyne, Krista, Kim Thonhoff, and D.R.—from a wheelchair—testify and answer questions. D.R. doesn't remember the wreck itself, although he does give the jury an account of the events leading up to it.

Afterwards, Krista tells a friend that she felt pushed around by the prosecutor's team and that they took words out of her mouth and twisted them. Andrew did commit a horrible crime, she says, but he's not the type of devil the prosecutors made him out to be at the hearing.

T he last week of September, Andrew receives official notice of the indictment issued by the Travis County DA's office on behalf of the State of Texas. As he reads it, two words stand out as if printed in red ink. *Intoxication manslaughter.*

Andrew, dressed in prison whites, thinks about the unwanted identity the phrase gives him. The gravity of the legal phrase and the memory of the night it happened hound him—even while he sleeps. The collision frequently fills his dreams, never deviating from the brutal reality of the actual event. In his nightmares he knows to avoid the oncoming car, but every time he slams head-on into the little red Volkswagen. Many of these nights, drenched in sweat and waking as if coming up for air from deep water, he can't go back to sleep.

Each of the two counts of the indictment levied against him by the State of Texas carries a prison sentence of two to twenty years. Some mornings he wakes up and, for the slightest moment, forgets where he is and what he's done. The cruel innocence vaporizes as soon as he tries to grasp it, and reality hits his consciousness like a runaway truck. In other waking moments, he does the disheartening math: In forty years he'll be closer in age to his grandfathers than to his father.

Chaplain Jameson comes to visit Andrew again. Andrew smiles when he sees the older man and thanks him for praying for him during the previous visit.

"When we prayed, I kind of got a peaceful feeling. All of a sudden after that I started thinking about all the things I had done wrong in my life—the people I had hurt—and it's like I never felt sorry for anything my whole life before, and then all of a sudden, this one time in my life I felt sorry for everything I had ever done all at once."

Andrew also tells Jameson that the tide is turning—he's starting to have more moments of wanting to live again than not. Every day, though, he says his mind wanders back to the shoulder of Brodie Lane where he sat immediately after the wreck, holding his head in his hands, unable to believe what he had just done.

Jameson invites Andrew to a group session with other inmates where they'll talk more about forgiveness and coping with prison life. He adds that they'll also work on accepting what has happened.

Andrew tells Jameson he'll come to the group session.

Chapter 9

With Andrew's indictment made public, attorney Balagia busies himself at the Travis County Courthouse filing multiple motions: discoveries for the state's list of witnesses and mitigating evidence, suppression of physical evidence and photos, and other requests. He's told Andrew's father that these motions are all a part of the process. He also makes a request for pre-trial reset—delaying the start of the trial.

Balagia's interest in representing Andrew, and others in similar situations, comes from his embrace of life's hard knocks—some by his own causing.

In 1988, federal drug enforcement officials disclosed that Balagia, an Austin police officer, had visited a known drug house off-duty. With a promise from the force not to fire him if he cooperated with the related investigation, he admitted to police department internal affairs investigators that he was dealing with drug addiction. The force reneged on its side of the bargain and fired him anyway. He appealed the dismissal and won reinstatement. Sobered up, he then quit the force and went to law school. He passed the bar and went to work representing those he felt needed a second chance, just like he did.

Andrew meets with Chaplain Jameson and other inmates for the group session. Jameson suggests that the group talk about whether or not any past events in their lives contributed toward their criminal acts. Jameson is careful to explain that such events don't excuse the criminal acts but might shed some light on why they occurred.

When it's his turn to speak, Andrew tells the group that he has a problem with alcohol. He also says that what happened wasn't the fault of anyone in his family. He says no more.

On November 7, attorney Balagia stands before a judge and successfully arranges for Andrew's release on bail. Andrew's father, Howard, has leveraged a few bank accounts and a property holding to meet Andrew's bail requirement.

Andrew's release the next day comes with specific orders: an electronic monitoring device braced to his ankle, no consumption of alcohol or drugs and weekly urine testing, no driving of any vehicles and surrender of his Texas driver's license, drug and alcohol counseling as approved by the court, and no contact with Robbyne or D.R. Initially, the order strictly confines him to stay inside his mom's house and not to venture even to the backyard or the garage.

Andrew is also required to report weekly to a pre-trial representative of the court and to request permission for any activity away from his mom's house. His requests for the first few weeks are limited to visits with his lawyer and counseling appointments.

After the wreck, Krista's insurance company declined to provide any coverage reimbursements toward her mutilated car. Then, when the manager of the apartment complex where she and Andrew lived found out about his indictment, he invoked its felony rule. Showing Krista the small print of the rental agreement that stated no felons could live at the complex, the manager told Krista she had to go. At Jan's invitation, Krista moved in with her and Dave with the plan that when Andrew made bail, he'd also join them at Jan's place.

Jan and Krista, the day after Andrew's bond hearing, drive to the county jail to pick him up. All three are happy to leave together. Andrew asks his mom if she'll have the heat on at the house. They all laugh, as Jan and Krista know all about Andrew's reports of the cold county jail.

As they drive home, Andrew cautiously smiles as he sits in the car, passing by familiar places he hasn't seen in four months. They pull into the driveway of his mother's home. Andrew walks in through the garage and sees the washing machine. His stomach knots and his feet stop their progress. He sees, as if it were a frozen frame from an old movie reel, his whole life distilled into one moment: his decision not to wash clothes here that last Saturday in June. His momentary immobilization lasts only until he summons up a curse at the machine.

Later, as he sorts through new clothes that his mom and Krista purchased for him, he remembers a line he heard from a fellow jail mate in one of Chaplain Jameson's group sessions: *Being out of jail doesn't necessarily free you from what put you in jail in the first place.*

The calendar hits November 18. At the breakfast table, Jan wishes her older son a happy birthday. Now twenty years old, Andrew quietly thanks his mom.

A few days earlier was his brother Dave's eighteenth birthday. Like she did with her older son, Jan wished her younger son a happy birthday at the breakfast table. She then apologized to him, explaining that with Andrew now at home, it wasn't the right time for Dave to have his friends over for a party in the evening.

Andrew's old bedroom, which he hasn't lived in for almost two years, has been taken over by Dave and his extensive collection of small and medium-sized reptiles. Andrew and Krista have made a makeshift bedroom for themselves on the first floor, content to stay as far away as possible from Andrew's old bedroom upstairs.

The thoughts of what his future holds hover over Andrew like a dark cloud. The newest piece of his wardrobe, a small black box attached to a plastic-coated metal strip that rides his right ankle, has merged onto his person like a large insect that he can't swat off or kill. In bed at night, in the shower each morning, or while he's wearing his boots during the day, the ankle monitor shouts out to him, as if it were a bullhorn, his new identity: *Andrew Papke, felon-in-waiting.* A couple of times a week, he has to connect a specialized phone receiver to the black box to transmit the monitor's data to the court.

Lawyer Balagia's meetings with Andrew focus on the same things Balagia told Andrew's father: the trial strategy starts, plain and simple, with a not guilty plea. The lawyer tells Andrew that he messed up by drinking and driving, but he deserves a second chance. It's a fine line, the lawyer says, between one drunk driver who runs into a telephone pole and the other one who kills someone in a wreck. For now, Balagia tells him, don't admit to anything.

And who knows? Maybe Andrew wasn't completely at fault in the wreck. Did his car really cross over all the way to the other lane? What about the victims in the other car—perhaps there is some evidence showing negligence on their part. Even if the accident report comes out solely blaming Andrew, there still might be basis upon which to challenge it. The gouge marks in the pavement at the scene of the wreck might reveal fault by the other driver.

Balagia tells Andrew he's seen the courtroom drama up close and personal many times. State versus defendant plays out on the main stage with twelve jurors attentive in the front row. Victim family members, with little say in the drama, watch and wait. Everyone expects, the lawyer says, for him to plead not guilty. He's stupid if he doesn't.

Chapter 10

For the approaching Thanksgiving holiday, Jan has invited the whole family to her house for dinner. It's a calculated risk—the entire family has not gathered in the fifteen years since Jan's and Howard's antagonistic divorce. Andrew's four grandparents, his dad and stepmom Cathy, his brother Dave and stepsister Luci, and Krista respond to Jan's invitation to support Andrew. If collective nervousness could be revealed by the amount of food the family members carry into the house, it's an apprehensive group that is coming to gather around Jan's table.

Jan calls everyone into the dining area. She motions to her guests where she wants them to sit and asks them to first stand behind their chairs while they say grace. The table is nearly overflowing with turkey, ham, mashed potatoes, green beans, cornbread dressing, gravy, and pumpkin and pecan pies.

Looking over to Andrew, Jan asks him to say grace. He looks back at her with raised eyebrows and takes a deep breath. He looks at the empty chairs surrounding the bountiful table and can only think of two other empty chairs, one each at the Early and Holland households. *This is their first*

Thanksgiving without their kids. His closing eyes tear up, and he begins to mouth a humble prayer. While trying to give God thanks for his family, internally he questions his own stupidity and lack of judgment. His throat tightens, and his words vanish. Krista puts her arm around him. Jan finishes the prayer and then asks everyone to sit down.

Andrew dries his eyes and sits. He passes the food and fills his plate. After a few bites, he feels the ankle monitor burrow into his leg like an oversized tick. He asks to be excused and goes to the makeshift bedroom. He slumps onto the bed, his gut a pit filled with guilt and grief. *It's just not right. My whole life and everything I've done up to now is worthless. I should have been the one who died in the wreck.* He tries to stifle his sobs as Krista knocks on the door frame.

Krista sits beside him and gently puts her arm around his shoulders. Andrew can't lift his head as tears drop onto his jeans. He whispers, "I feel guilty to be alive."

The Monday following Thanksgiving, the court supervisor grants him permission to leave his mom's house for three other activities besides lawyer visits and counseling: work at his father's auto shop, church, and A.A. meetings. If he goes to church or an A.A. meeting in the evening, he must return home no later than 10:00 p.m. Any violation could land him back in jail.

Chaplain Jameson belongs to a large Baptist church in southwest Austin. By Jameson's invitation, Andrew has started to attend worship services there with his dad and stepmom. Jameson tells Ken Baldwin, one of the pastors at the church, that a detainee he's been working with from the jail is ready for baptism. Baldwin knows all about Andrew Papke and the wreck and smiles upon hearing the news from Jameson.

It's been five months since the wreck, Jameson continues, and Andrew seems to be advancing forward on the long road of accepting responsibility for what he's done. Baldwin is glad to hear that and says there's no reason not to have the baptism on the coming Sunday. Jameson says that Andrew will be ready and knows to bring an extra change of clothes for the baptism.

On Sunday morning, December 1, the 10:00 a.m. service at Bannockburn Baptist Church starts with the singing of "I Have Decided to Follow Jesus." Standing next to Pastor Baldwin, Andrew is barefooted and dressed in a white robe that covers white gym shorts and a T-shirt. As the congregation concludes the opening hymn, the pastor and Andrew step down into the baptismal pool.

"Andrew Papke, I ask you to take God as your Father, Jesus as your Savior, and the Holy Spirit as your guide—freely, completely, and forever."

"I will."

With that, Andrew immerses himself in the water. He comes up a second later and takes in a fresh breath. Through wet eyes he can detect his dad wearing a faint smile, looking at him from the front pew.

After the service, Chaplain Jameson converses with Baldwin in the pastor's office. Jameson says that he noticed the pastor seemed to lose his place during the first stanza of the well-known opening hymn. With a cramped smile, Baldwin responds to his colleague: "I looked down and saw Andrew's ankle monitor. And I realized I had never baptized anyone before with an ankle monitor."

The next day at 8:00 a.m., Andrew arrives at his dad's auto shop for work. Andrew remembers one of the workers from five years earlier when he hung out there as a young adolescent. The man greets Andrew and tells him that he's sorry to hear about what's happened. The man also tells him that he's glad to have worked the past number of years at the shop, and that Andrew's dad is a good man. Andrew nods his head in response. The day passes slowly until his mom picks him up at 6:15 p.m.

While the next number of weeks in the auto shop keep Andrew's hands busy, his mind covers old territory in a new way. In the shop with its odors of oil and exhaust, and the tat-tat-tat of its air compressors driving wrenches and jacks, a lesson his dad taught him when he was younger comes back to him and takes on fuller meaning. His dad always told him to put tools back where they belong—"that way you, or someone else, can find them the next time they're needed." Life, Andrew realizes for the first time, is about fixing things that are broken—or better, taking care of things well enough so that they don't get broken in the first place. But, he asks himself, *How can I ever fix what's happened?*

Seeing each other five times a week at the auto shop, Andrew and his dad start a new custom. They go out to lunch once or twice a week, grabbing hamburgers or tacos.

One December day right before New Year's, Howard and Andrew drive to Dan's Hamburgers in South Austin. Seated in a booth waiting for their food, Andrew again tells his dad that he's so sorry for what he's done. Their last name isn't Smith or Jones, he says, and it's now been dragged through the mud.

His dad looks at him and uses a fatherly tone. It's a tone of voice that Andrew couldn't stand to listen to when he was fifteen years old. But things have changed. "Son," Howard says, "it's not our name you need to worry about—it's the two other families and what's happened to them."

On a cold afternoon in early January, Andrew pages D.R. and convinces him to come by the auto shop, telling him he has new information about the wreck. Andrew instructs his friend to drive around to the back of the shop.

Thirty minutes later, in a low voice, Andrew tells his confidant that maybe the wreck wasn't his fault. Perhaps it was really an accident, a fluke of timing and bad luck. Brodie Lane, he says, doesn't have reflective markers in the center stripes, and there is no sign indicating a curve. Neither, Andrew says, is the curve properly sloped—it banks to the outside lane.

Andrew asks him to think about these things and tells him that the trial might start in April.

Chapter 11

Aweek later, a man named Ron Prince stops by the auto shop to pick up Andrew for an evening A.A. meeting. Shortly after his release on bond, Andrew met Prince at the alcoholics' support group. When Andrew found out that Prince had been sober ten years, he asked him to be his sponsor. Prince nodded but told Andrew his one condition: Andrew would have to work through the twelve steps of the program, no exceptions or excuses. Andrew agreed.

Andrew likes Prince for his no-nonsense approach and listens to him more than he's ever listened to another adult. That evening the leader announces that the focus of the meeting will be on step five. He reads it aloud: "We admitted to God, to ourselves, and to another human being the exact nature of our wrongs."

As they drive home from the meeting, Prince tells Andrew to read the fifth chapter in a book he's given him, *Twelve Steps and Twelve Traditions*. This fifth step, Prince tells him, is perhaps the most important step of all—he needs to admit, like a confession in church, to another human being face to face the wrongs he's committed and take responsibility for them. Prince asks him if he can do that and if Andrew has a specific person he can talk to.

Andrew says he can talk to Chaplain Jameson.

J ameson drives an old Buick that reflects his frugal yet generous nature. The chaplain has told Andrew he'd rather give money to church ministries than to car companies. He has two sandwiches that he picked up on the way to the auto shop. For this lunch hour, Andrew has a special request for the chaplain. He wants to drive down to Brodie Lane to the site of the wreck. It will be Andrew's first return there, almost seven months to the day since he and D.R. were evacuated on a helicopter and David's and Beth's bodies were covered by a white blanket.

Upon arrival, the men see flowers and mementos placed in memory of David and Beth on the east side of the road. As they sit in the car, pulled off on the other side of the road, Andrew talks slowly and pauses often as he recalls the fateful day and evening. It's as if a veil has been lifted, and Andrew is seeing what happened in a fresh way. Jameson listens and doesn't interrupt the recounting. So much pain, Andrew says, he has caused the two victim families and his own. His words this afternoon at the site of the wreck are starkly different from the ones he used on June 29, and even a few weeks ago while meeting on the sly with D.R. The words take on a new common denominator: the wreck is his fault and no one else's.

The old Buick ambles back to the auto shop parking lot two and a half hours after it left.

That night, Andrew visits the wreck scene again while he sleeps. He finds himself driving the Acura on far South Brodie Lane, just like before, with the Volkswagen approaching. He smells burning plastic and tries to turn the steering wheel. The red car comes closer, but his steering wheel jams stuck. A bottle of transmission fluid falls from a shelf in his dad's auto shop. Andrew fumbles for it but can't impede the bottle's plunge. It bursts open on the floor—and he slams, once again, head-on into the Volkswagen. The floor of the auto shop is covered in blood and it's his fault. He bolts awake in bed, sweat-drenched with his heart racing.

His mother Jan picks him up at the shop at the end of a work day in the early February spring. On their drive home, they pass by fields starting to green up with the promise of spring wildflowers—bluebonnets and Indian paintbrush. Their talk turns to the upcoming trial that attorney Balagia says will start in April. Andrew hints at having second thoughts about pleading not guilty.

"Look, Mama, it's not your fault or anyone else's. How many times did you tell me not to drink and drive?"

"About a thousand."

Inside the Travis County Courthouse in downtown Austin at a pre-trial hearing, Andrew sits at the defense table in a courtroom and watches his attorney do his work. Jamie Balagia's long black hair, combed straight back and shading gray at the temples, covers his neck and softly curls upon a black leather jacket framed by his wide shoulders. He sports a full goatee that tints gray below the chin, matching the silver-plated pendant of his bolo tie. Wheeling around the courtroom in pointed-toe, black cowboy boots, Balagia plays the part of criminal defense attorney with bravado.

The pre-trial hearing consists of three sets of motions: for discovery on behalf of the defense, for defects in the State's charge, and for admission or suppression of evidence. There will be no entry of a plea by Andrew until his arraignment at the start of the full trial two months away.

Balagia is in battle mode with the two attorneys representing the Travis County DA's office. The State's attorneys and Balagia are trying to convince Judge Bob Perkins of the merits of each of their arguments concerning crash photos to be admitted as evidence in the trial. Balagia is protesting the admittance of multiple crash scene photos. Seven photos, not twenty or more, are sufficient, according to the defense lawyer.

Leaving the judge's bench, Balagia walks over to the table where Assistant DA Buddy Meyer and his colleague sit. With his back to the judge, Balagia bends at the waist to meet his opponent's eyes and begins to pound close-fisted on the table, slow and steady. "My client is getting a raw deal," Balagia says quietly but emphatically. Buddy Meyer stares at Balagia for a few seconds, rubs his mustache, and looks away from his legal opponent without saying a word.

As Judge Perkins sips a diet soda and studies the photos, Balagia's objection rings off-key in Andrew's ears. *Raw deal? Me? I don't think so.* Andrew bites hard on his lip, nods his head, and makes a critical decision affecting his life and the others drawn into this tragedy.

Guilty. He sees the faces of David's and Bethany's parents. They seal Andrew's decision. How can he utter *Not guilty*, two words of self-defense, reasonable doubt, and denial in the faces of these five persons and those of their family members, whom he has pained beyond imagination? He can't do anything but plead guilty. The consequences of this decision, no matter how severe, will be part of the reality of what happened that summer night eight months earlier.

When they walk out of the courtroom this late February afternoon, Andrew cordially lets Balagia know that his services are no longer needed because he's decided that he can't plead innocent to the charges. Balagia rarely hears such talk. Stupefied, he stops and grabs Andrew by the shoulder and tries to convince him otherwise.

"Andrew, this thing is not entirely your fault."

Andrew, running his hand over his thick and recently trimmed brown hair, takes a deep breath and stretches to his full six feet two inches. He stands taller than Balagia and bends his head slightly to meet the attorney's eyes.

"Yes, it is, sir. Thank you all the same, but I will plead guilty," he says. Balagia looks at Andrew and starts to speak, then stops. He cocks his head to the side and rubs his goatee. He shakes Andrew's hand and walks away.

Andrew turns around and looks back at the courtroom entrance. He sees his father walking toward him. Andrew says to his dad that he just told Jamie Balagia they didn't need him anymore and that he'll plead guilty. Nodding his head, Howard tells his son that he agrees.

Andrew strides tall with his dad and feels the fresh breeze upon his face. For the first time in a long while, he's made a decision he won't have to apologize for: *Thank you, Lord*.

Chapter 12

Jan, Krista, Howard and Cathy, the Earlys and Hollands are among those seated in the gallery of the 331st District Court at the Travis County Courthouse for Andrew's arraignment. It's Monday, April 14, 1997. His dark slacks and cowboy boots concealing an ankle monitor, Andrew sits erect and attentive at the side of his new lawyer, Sam Ireland. Andrew and his dad told Ireland that he was hired on the non-negotiable condition that Andrew would plead guilty.

Ireland is a highly regarded defense lawyer in Austin. He and Andrew figure pleading guilty and trusting the jury to give a fair sentence is a viable, although risky, strategy. Pleading guilty, Ireland has told him, severely limits their options.

Judge Bob Perkins reads the State of Texas's charge of double intoxication manslaughter and asks Andrew how he wishes to plead. All eyes in the courtroom gaze at Andrew, who stands tall in a white shirt collared by a dark blue tie. True to his word and in the presence of those he wronged, Andrew formally answers the judge and enters a one-word plea: "Guilty."

Ireland has requested a jury trial and a consolidation of the two separate charges for the purpose of having one trial. The prosecutors, Travis County Assistant DAs Buddy Meyer and Gail Van Winkle, formally agree to the motion, and Judge Perkins declares its entry into the trial record. There is no plea bargain agreement—for two separate reasons. The prosecution wants to have a trial in order to send a message to the perpetrator and the community. Andrew wants to have a trial, hoping that it and its resolution somehow help the Earlys and Hollands through their grief.

Judge Perkins reminds Andrew of his right to remain silent and of the punishment range of two to twenty years for each charge. The judge pauses and seeks Andrew's eyes. "Mr. Papke, knowing everything which I have told you in terms of your constitutional rights and in terms of the other admonishments that the Court has just given you, is it still your desire to plead guilty to both charges of intoxication manslaughter as you have stated to me on the record?'

"Yes, sir, it is."

"Mr. Papke, do you wish to have a jury trial in terms of the issue of punishment in both these charges? Is that correct?"

"That's correct."

Judge Perkins closes the hearing and states that the trial will continue in one week's time, with the additional presence of twelve jurors.

The 331st District Court occupies space on the third and top floor of the Travis County Courthouse. Bob Perkins has occupied the judge's bench in this courtroom since 1982. Raised by educator parents, Perkins grew up speaking Spanish and English in Eagle Pass, Texas, on the other side of the Rio Grande from Piedras Negras, Mexico. A graduate of the University of Texas and its law school, Perkins has always gravitated toward Austin's southeast side where he sings Mexican mariachi songs by heart, and where his career in public service started when he won election for justice of the peace, Travis County Precinct 4.

Judge Perkins garnered national attention in 1991 when five-time Speaker of the Texas House Gib Lewis was indicted on misdemeanor ethics charges. When Lewis failed to show for arraignment in Perkins's courtroom, the judge ordered the high-profile politician jailed. Lewis eventually pleaded no contest to accepting improper financial gifts and, as part of a plea deal, didn't seek reelection. Perkins would later say of the confrontation with Lewis, "Was I going to run my court? Or was he going to run it? It didn't matter who you were, you were going to have to follow the law."

Ireland and a handful of Austinites have told Andrew and his dad that Perkins is a fair judge, but father and son worry about the Texas legislature's recent classification of intoxication manslaughter punishable to twenty years. Andrew's is the second intoxication manslaughter case, and the first with multiple fatalities, to be tried in Travis County since the classification, and neither DA Ronnie Earle nor Judge Perkins, both elected officials, wants to be labeled weak on crime by potential opponents in the next election cycle.

Chapter 13

The next Monday afternoon at 2:20 p.m., Judge Perkins formally asks the defense and the prosecution if they are ready to proceed with the case. All lawyers answer affirmatively. "The State of Texas versus Andrew Papke" officially begins with the selection of the jury. The candidates, forty-one in all, are seated in the gallery of the 331st District Court.

Buddy Meyer stands up from the prosecution table, nods to Judge Perkins, and then turns to face the jury candidates. Taking the lead in the state's *voir dire*, Meyer explains the Old French term that means "to say the truth." In Texas, the *voir dire* process produces an empaneled jury. Meyer tells the pool of candidates that, because of Andrew's guilty plea, the sole job of the jury will be to decide the punishment in this case. Even so, he says, they have to be open to a sentence range from the minimum punishment of two years to the maximum of twenty years.

Meyer fits a stereotypical definition of a Texan. His handlebar mustache, slightly bow-legged walk, verbal accent and cadence give the impression that he would be perfectly comfortable seated on a horse and wearing a wide-brimmed hat in the middle of a mesquite-covered ranch in West Texas. Travis County DA Ronnie Earle hired him as an Assistant DA in 1982.

Seated at the prosecution table is Gail Van Winkle, Meyer's co-lead partner, an attorney who has a reputation of superior intellect and calm efficiency. The legal profession is in her blood and her brains, thanks to her law-professor father, an instructor at the University of Houston law school from which she and Meyer graduated.

Meyer walks toward the gallery as he addresses potential jurors: "There are generally three objectives for punishment. You may be able to think of more, but generally these are the three: retribution, deterrence, and rehabilitation. As for deterrence, we're talking about two different kinds—specific deterrence in terms of the particular individual, and general deterrence in terms of the message the verdict sends to the community."

Meyer explains that even though the consolidation of charges results in one trial, there will still be two sentences for the defendant. Judge Perkins will decide—in the case of prison time determined by the jury—whether the sentences will run concurrently or consecutively. Meyer tells the potential jurors to make their sentencing decision without any burden as to what Judge Perkins might do with the sentences, either stacking them or letting them be served simultaneously.

Prior to 1994, convictions for deaths caused by driving while intoxicated or under the influence in Texas were categorized under the penal code for involuntary manslaughter with a punishment range of two to ten years. When Governor Ann Richards, a recovering alcoholic, signed Senate Bill 1067 into law in the summer of 1993, a new classification entered the Texas penal code: intoxication manslaughter, a second-degree felony, punishable up to twenty years. Texas, with its tradition of drive-thru ice houses where thirsty drivers purchased cold longnecks, popped them open, and drove away, still allowed passengers to have open containers of alcohol in moving vehicles after the signing of SB 1067. The political landscape, however, was changing in Texas. Elected politicians, district attorneys, and judges were starting to crack down on drunk-driving crime.

Meyer questions the potential jurors, asking if they are ready and fit to serve. One man responds that he lives in the neighborhood where the wreck occurred and drives by the crosses erected in David's and Beth's memories every day. "I'd really like to serve on this jury, but I need to be fair to both sides. I don't think there's any way that I can do that."

The man further explains that his emotions about the case wouldn't allow him to be very logical. He says the only punishment he'd consider would be the max sentence. Judge Perkins thanks him and dismisses him.

Another potential juror says he has no tolerance for DUIs and that he wouldn't consider anything but a max sentence. Judge Perkins tells the man he is free to go.

Sam Ireland addresses the group for the defendant's portion of the *voir dire*. He makes the case that Andrew, because he is pleading guilty, is taking responsibility for his actions. "I suggest you come down to this courthouse any day of the week and look at the cases that come into this courtroom and look for the individuals, regardless of the status of the evidence, regardless of the situation they're in, who are unwilling to take responsibility for their conduct." Andrew, by contrast, he says, has pleaded guilty and will take the stand in this case and face cross-examination from the prosecutors.

Ireland once more references the word "responsibility" and says of his client, "It's what this man has determined to do."

After Ireland closes his address to the pool, two more people admit they couldn't consider a light sentence. Judge Perkins dismisses them. A third man approaches the bench and confesses that when he was Andrew's age, he caused a similar wreck that nearly killed his best friend. He also says he's known the Holland family for a long time and that his sympathies lie in two directions. The three lawyers and Judge Perkins agree to dismiss the potential juror.

After a brief recess, Judge Perkins calls twelve names to serve on the jury and dismisses the rest of the pool. No alternates will be needed. He thanks those leaving for their participation in the process. Perkins asks the twelve who've been chosen to stand, and he swears them in. Their instructions follow: Consider only the evidence that comes from the witness stand, and do not talk to any fellow members of the jury or other persons about the case until it is concluded. He then recesses the court for the day and instructs all to be back at 11:00 a.m. the next day.

Chapter 14

"All rise!" The bailiff's command reaches to the back wall of the courtroom where overflow watchers already stand.

Judge Bob Perkins, his black robe swishing in his wake, strides to his bench. Simultaneously taking his seat and bidding "Good Morning" to the jury, he calls the trial to order for its second day. Gail Van Winkle, on cue from the judge, follows by reading the grand jury indictment of Andrew Papke in the double cause of intoxication manslaughter. Andrew, standing in a blue shirt and red tie, in turn repeats his plea of guilty to both charges at the request of the judge.

It's 11:23 a.m. on Tuesday, April 22. Plaintiff and defendant supporters have filled the gallery. Andrew's supporters consist only of a dozen family members and Krista. The remainder present in the courtroom, besides a handful of media, has come to support the Hollands and Earlys.

Representing the State of Texas, Buddy Meyer stands to give the jury his opening statement. Summarizing the evidence that the state will present, he claims that the wreck was no accident because Andrew had been going down the wrong road for some time.

Meyer challenges the idea, brought up by Sam Ireland the previous day, that Andrew is taking responsibility for what he has done. "When you listen to this evidence at its conclusion, I want you to tell us whether the defendant has accepted responsibility for his actions that killed two people. I believe the defense is going to call witnesses who will tell you some things that the defendant has done since the wreck—counseling and maybe some other things. But is that accepting responsibility? Has he learned his lesson? Maybe. Or is it a strategy? Is it a plea for mercy? Ladies and gentlemen of the jury, we're in a court of law, not a court of mercy."

Meyer nods at Judge Perkins and sits down. The judge calls Sam Ireland to address the jury with his opening statement. Ireland admits that Andrew has made a number of bad decisions in the past three years, all of them, especially the offense that took the lives of David and Beth, involving the use of alcohol. "There are reasons for Andrew's excessive alcohol consumption on the date of the offense. What I want to make clear is that there are reasons. They are not justifications."

While his client made some bad choices, Ireland concedes, he is not evil—he's no saint, but he's no devil, either. Perhaps a few months ago, Ireland continues, he was still trying to paint himself as not entirely at fault. "The fact is, that now, Andrew Papke admits to being the sole cause of the wreck. He came here to plead guilty to this and to be punished for this. And I submit to you, when you hear all the evidence—from bad comments at the scene, to bad and good conduct here and there—you'll be able to make a determination of who this young man is. The determination has already been made about what he did."

Ireland sits down. Judge Perkins instructs Meyer and Van Winkle to call their first witness.

A high school girl named Vanessa comes forward. She states that she is fifteen years old.

She was in the back seat of the Acura the afternoon of the wreck, traveling into Austin with her friend to spend the night. She testifies that she hadn't met Andrew prior to that day and that she was "kind of scared" when Andrew was tailgating other cars east of Austin on Highway 71. "I could see the speedometer and stuff, and it said 110 mph."

After she shares details about Andrew almost hitting a tree when he swerved off a dirt road, Meyer asks, "Did you learn any lessons from the time you spent with Mr. Papke?"

"I learned not to get in a car with people who are drunk, because it could have been me instead of the two other people who died."

Robbyne is called to the witness stand. Meyer asks her about the night in question, specifically the last time she saw Andrew and D.R. just before the wreck when they dropped her off at her mom's house.

"I said to D.R., 'Can you please try to get the keys from Andy?' D.R. said he'd try his best."

Meyer asks her about Andrew's drinking habits.

"I could basically say that he was an alcoholic. He drank all the time."

Van Winkle calls D.R. to the stand. After he answers a few questions about the evening of the crash, he confesses that he doesn't have any memory about what happened after he and Andrew had their last beers in the parking lot of Railroad Barbeque, just before the wreck.

"The next thing I remember is that everything was black, and I was sitting in the passenger seat, and I didn't really know what was going on, and then someone came up and started asking me my mom's name and phone number."

"Do you know how long you were pinned in the vehicle?"

"From what I've been told, twenty to thirty minutes."

"Do you even remember being taken out of it?"

"I remember bits and pieces. I remember hearing firefighters talking about, 'Well, we're going to have to cut this, we're going to have to cut that.'"

"Do you remember how you got to the hospital that night?"

"No, but I've been told I was taken by helicopter."

"Do you recall any police officer or trooper coming to talk to you briefly at the hospital?"

"Detective Brannen came and talked to me after I was in a hospital room, but I don't really remember what we talked about."

D.R. then tells Van Winkle that he was confined to a wheelchair for three and a half months after the wreck. She asks him if he knew David or Bethany.

"I worked with David at Little Caesar's over in Westlake, and I spent a few nights hanging out with him because my brother also worked there."

"Did you know Bethany, his girlfriend?"

"I met her through David, but I really didn't know her."

"Did you know they had been killed that night?"

"That night, no, I didn't know. But the next day, when my brother told me it was David and Beth, I passed out."

"When was the last time you saw the defendant, Andrew Papke?"

"He had been paging me quite a bit after the wreck, and I went and talked to him at his dad's shop."

"Any idea about when that was?"

"About a month and a half, two months ago."

"And he talked to you about the collision at that time?"

"A little bit. He told me what some investigator showed him—the skid marks on the road looked like he hadn't been the one who caused the accident or anything like that. Basically, he was saying that it wasn't his fault; it looked like it was really no one's fault."

D.R. steps down.

Seated outside the courtroom after having been instructed to talk to no one about the trial, Kim Thonhoff hears her named called by the bailiff, who peeks his head outside the courtroom entry door. Her husband Bob and son Travis, who is prepped to testify, are with her. Kim squeezes her husband's hand as she gets up to enter the courtroom. After a nervous walk to the judge's bench, she swears the oath and takes her seat in the witness stand.

She states her name for the jury and responds to Van Winkle's opening question about her employment.

"I work for the Austin public school district as a kindergarten teacher. I've taught kindergarten and the second grade for eighteen years."

Van Winkle asks her about the wreck. Kim details what she saw, emphasizing that the Acura never wavered or weaved, and explains that she was completely overwhelmed by what she witnessed. She wasn't able to sleep after getting home—her mind was so agitated. She and her son sat side by side and recorded what they saw. Kim typed her account on a computer and Travis wrote his by hand.

"The collision was just like a pop-bang sound. And then it was totally silent. I initially thought everyone was dead because it was so quiet."

Van Winkle passes the witness to Ireland. He declines, saying that he has no questions.

Kim walks out of the courtroom to where her husband and son wait for her. Relieved but emotionally drained, she tells Bob that she became extremely nervous when she walked in the courtroom and saw all the faces—the perpetrator, the victim family members, the lawyers, and the judge. Her husband says he's relieved that their young son didn't have to testify. The prosecution team told the Thonhoffs when they arrived that morning that if Andrew Papke maintained his guilty plea, Travis would not be called to the witness stand.

A parade of paramedics, cops, and firefighters who were on the scene that night is called forward by Van Winkle and Meyer to testify. Mike McKenzie, a licensed emergency medical technician, takes the stand to testify late in the afternoon. Van Winkle asks the four-year volunteer with the Manchaca EMS team if he remembers the night of June 29, 1996.

"Yes, I do." He explains that he tended to Andrew in the ditch.

"Did you ask him what he had been doing that evening?"

"He said he came up from Railroad Barbeque, and he indicated that he had two beers that night."

"Based on your experience, did you have an opinion about whether or not he was intoxicated?"

"In my opinion, he was intoxicated. He smelled of alcohol. He had urinated and defecated on himself. And his pupils were sluggish to react to light."

"Did you personally know how many beers he had that night?"

"No, but he told me two beers. Everybody tells me two beers."

Chapter 15

The state's evidence on the third day of the trial reveals that immediately prior to the wreck, both David and Beth were wearing seat belts, and neither had drugs nor alcohol in their systems.

Additional evidence shows that Andrew's blood alcohol content, seventy-five minutes after the wreck, was .23, significantly higher than the legal limit of .10 for intoxication. Other witnesses testify that Andrew has led a troubled past five years: underage driving, speeding, vandalism, fights, shoplifting, failure to appear in court.

An Austin police officer also testifies that Andrew tried to sell him marijuana while the officer was working undercover. The officer further testifies that Andrew tried to bargain with him during the arrest, saying an arrest would blow his chances of becoming a firefighter. Cross-examination by Ireland, however, reveals that the marijuana—a half-pound bag that Andrew bought for $40—was no more than stems and seeds, essentially dirt weed. Andrew was trying to sell it for $50.

Andrew's arraignment for that charge, ironically, was scheduled for July 1, the Monday after the wreck. The arraignment was postponed.

Maria Soriano Holland, Richard Holland, and Adrian Early will testify on the fourth day of the trial as witnesses for the state.

Before their testimonies, expert forensic witness Herb Treat testifies and explains his animated reconstruction of the collision.

Van Winkle asks about his computations and conclusions. He explains that a major part of the calculations was based upon study of the gouge marks—made by the front tires of the vehicles at impact—left in Brodie Lane. He emphasizes that there were no skid marks on the asphalt from either vehicle.

The prosecutor asks him the estimated speeds of both vehicles.

"The black car was going 59 miles per hour and the Volkswagen 43 miles per hour."

"Based on your calculations, would the driver of the red Volkswagen have been able to react in time to avoid this collision?"

"The other vehicle, according to the witness, wasn't weaving or anything. There was nothing to warn him at all. So suddenly the black vehicle is on top of him. In my opinion there simply was no time to react."

Ireland declines the opportunity to cross-examine the witness.

Buddy Meyer calls Richard Holland, David's father, to the witness stand. Holland, a courtroom lawyer, appears comfortable despite the circumstances of the trial.

"Mr. Holland, I want you to identify a photograph. Would you explain to the jury what this is a photograph of?"

"Yes. David and Beth in their prom clothes. It's a picture I took to show them, and it's a picture I took to show their kids many years from now. It's like when our folks took pictures of us when we went to prom."

"What prom were they going to?"

"Beth's—she was a junior then. This was to be her senior year at Hays High School. David was already out of high school."

"Thank you."

Richard Holland steps down from the stand.

Van Winkle calls David's mother, Maria Soriano Holland, to the witness stand. Born in Guadalajara, Mexico, she explains that she's lived in Texas for the past twenty-three years. She was married to Richard for fourteen years; David was the oldest of their three boys. For the last couple of years, she says, David lived with her while her other two sons lived with Richard and Helen and the boys' half-sister. She hasn't touched anything in David's bedroom in the nine and a half months since he perished. A pendant gracing Maria's neck shows the smiling face of her first-born son.

"Were you and David very close?"

"Yes, very close."

"Would you tell the jury what you miss about David? Can you do that?"

"It's just so hard. Everything has changed. Nothing is the same. The house looks like it's going to fall apart. There's no life in anything. The grass is very tall. Everything is ..." Her voice trails off and she dabs a tissue to her eyes.

Van Winkle waits for her to continue.

"I don't know, ma'am, it's so hard because I feel like my life went with him, too."

Ireland passes on the witness and Van Winkle calls Adrian Early, Bethany's father, to the stand. He explains that Bethany, like David, was the older sibling of two brothers.

"Is there anything in particular that you miss about Beth that you can tell this jury?"

"I miss Beth being there. I miss her love of animals. We taught her to care about people, everybody, no matter who they were, no matter what."

Judge Perkins thanks Mr. Early and recalls Richard Holland, the state's final witness.

"Mr. Holland," Buddy Meyer asks, "will you please tell this jury how David's death has affected you and your family?"

"I will do my best. You have to know who David's family was to begin with. He had two families—a family of choice and a family of blood. His mother, Benjamin, Lucas, myself, Mindy, his half-sister, Helen, his stepmother ... that's his close family."

Holland points toward the back of the gallery where some of David's friends are standing. "That row of teenagers back there. David went camping with them, and they panned for gold. That's his family of choice. And both of these families make one whole. We reach out and hug each other, and David was a part of that hug.

"I can tell you about the family of choice that came to his funeral. If they had walked in late and not known what it was, they'd have thought it was David's and Beth's wedding because we were there with Adrian and Martha and their children, all our children at the front of the church. Father Zarbist was there. The families of choice were there, backed out into the street. It was like all of those kids were there to be the best man or woman and fill out the rest of the wedding party. But, unfortunately, the kids we call friends had to serve as pallbearers."

Many in the courtroom openly weep.

Holland gets up from the witness stand, picks up a wooden chair, and places it between the lawyers' tables and the witness stand.

"When we wake up in the morning and go to the table, there's an empty chair there. When Benjamin buys a ticket to *Star Wars,* he buys one for David and sits next to an empty seat. When the holidays come we look like Miss Havisham's house. You remember Miss Havisham? If you take high school English, you may have to read Charles Dickens' *Great Expectations.* It's the sorriest book you'll ever read because Miss Havisham was a woman who sat in her wedding dress for twenty years in a roomful of covered furniture with the slips left on, waiting for someone who never came. We keep waiting for David to burst in the door and say 'I'm here.'

"He was my buddy. He was my friend. There's a hole at our home that was his." He points to the wooden chair: "And now there's an empty chair there, too."

Chapter 16

August Swain, the first witness for the defense, steps up to the witness stand. A clinical social worker, Swain testifies that he counseled young Andrew for about two years after Howard and Jan divorced. Andrew was no more than six or seven years of age at the time.

"He was a super kid who had come through quite a bit in terms of the back and forth movement between his parents.

"He and his brother belonged to Little League. I'd get reports about baseball and other exploits as they got older. Reports about how they were doing in school and periodic checks on their welfare."

"Was there a point when you basically lost touch with Andrew?"

"Yes, when he was approximately fifteen or sixteen."

"When is the next time you had contact with Andrew?"

"When he was incarcerated. The circumstances were terrible. He was behind bars and depressed."

Chaplain Jameson comes forward to the witness stand. He explains that he responded to a request at the Travis County Jail that he talk to Andrew.

"I called Andy out and had a session of an hour, an hour and fifteen minutes with him. I introduced myself and listened to him."

"How much contact would you say that you've had with Mr. Papke since and under what circumstances?"

"I met with him generally once a week while he was in jail. Sometimes twice a week. He was not only in one-on-one meetings with me, but he came to one of the groups that I conduct. I call it a cross between Bible study and group therapy. We talk a lot about the forgiveness that the prisoner needs to develop about things in his earlier history, and about coping with jail and prison and making it a useful time.

"When he got out of jail, I went to see him at his father's auto shop. He told me he had a problem with alcohol. I was surprised at his openness, his candidness, in accepting what he had done and his concern for what he had done to the families involved and for what he had done to his own family. He said he wanted to take full responsibility for the wreck."

After Jameson steps down from the witness stand, Ron Prince is called forward.

Prince says he met Andrew in A.A. meetings after his release from jail. Prince credits his ten years of sobriety to the support group.

"Typically, most people come to A.A. through events in their lives that create circumstances that bring them to a decision that they have a drinking problem. That happened with me. I went to meetings. I got a sponsor and I worked the steps. And I have been active ever since and haven't found it necessary to drink.

"I met Andy right after his time in the county jail. He came to meetings every week, sometimes twice a week."

"On how many occasions would you say that you have been with Mr. Papke at a meeting?" Ireland asks.

"More than thirty. Andy asked me to help him with the steps, so I've been his sponsor. This is for my benefit as much as his. It's very difficult for me to teach somebody how to stay sober if I end up getting drunk before our next meeting. So it's the way I stay sober also.

"I'm not a doctor. I'm just a drunk that doesn't drink anymore. I'm very grateful for that. And I've had a gift from God. I have two kids. So I understand the families and the things that are going on in this courtroom. I also understand that I could be in any seat here. I can be in his, and I can be in the parents' seats. So with Andrew's and my activity, it's very serious. There's been no joking. No kidding around. Andrew's worked very hard. He's done everything I've asked him to do. And he's helped me a great deal to get through a lot of things that I need to deal with, too."

Ireland inquires further: "I have to ask you this, Mr. Prince. Do you find that people sometimes come to meetings and are not genuine in their attitudes?"

"Yes, sir."

"What has been the case with Andrew?"

"We have a book called Alcoholics Anonymous. When someone asks me to sponsor them I say, 'Okay, read the first two chapters and call me.' If they do that, then we proceed and go to the next chapter and they call me. Typically, people who are being dishonest can't stand it. I'll get the first phone call or the second, but that's it. Andrew has never stopped. He's done everything I asked him to do when I asked him to do it, and it's from sincerity and honesty. It's his desire to help out and quit drinking."

Van Winkle cross-examines Prince, asking if he knows that a condition of Andrew's bond release is that he attend alcohol counseling. Prince says he wasn't aware of it but emphasizes that A.A. meetings and alcohol counseling aren't the same thing. He also says he hasn't signed any papers for Andrew from a judge or a court officer.

"No further questions," Van Winkle states.

Andrew's mother, Jan Dunlap, comes forward to the witness stand. Earlier, the jury heard that she served as an Austin police officer for six years when Andrew and his brother were much younger.

Ireland asks her about raising the two boys after she and Howard divorced. She tells the jury brief details about two custody lawsuits and the boys going back and forth to live between her house and their father's and stepmom's. There were many crises, she admits, between her and the boys' father.

Jan discloses that she began to worry more than usual about Andrew when, halfway through his freshman year of high school, he lost interest in the marching band. "The band director was extremely impressed with his ability to play the trombone. But a couple of months into the semester, I could tell Andrew was starting to lose interest."

She pauses in her testimony in tears. "It's very upsetting."

Andrew wasn't living with her then. "I would receive calls from the high school principal saying that Andrew had not gone to classes. I was really concerned." She explains that Andrew moved back in with her when he was fifteen or sixteen. But after that, trouble with police and alcohol escalated. It was, she says, difficult for her to predict or control his behavior.

Judge Perkins recesses the court for lunch until 2:00 p.m. After the recess, Sam Ireland will call his final two witnesses, Howard Papke and his son, Andrew.

Chapter 17

"Andrew was, in my opinion, normal like any other kid—curious, caring, loving. He wanted our approval for just about anything." Howard Papke, a tall man with an enduring will, speaks plainly without haste.

"He used to wash cars for me when he was little. I'd give him two dollars to wash a car when he was ten or eleven. Later, he worked at my shop. At first, he would just sweep and clean up around the place. As he got older he became interested in the business. He wanted to fix cars. Through the natural course of things, I taught him some mechanical skills. He eventually became a mechanic in the shop and worked on commission one summer."

Howard explains that things started to change toward the end of that summer. Andrew got arrested for shoplifting and started to challenge his father's authority.

"When he was about fifteen it got to the point," Howard Papke pauses and raises his brown eyebrows, "that he was beginning to act like he was smarter than me. We pretty much just broke communication, and he moved out.

"We alienated each other pretty much totally. I think we were both afraid that if we tried to talk or see each other at that point, we would have ended up in conflict or some sort of argument."

Howard explains that he's had Andrew working at the shop since December, after his release on bond.

Ireland asks: "Your relationship with your son, you described it in terms of good points and low points. How would you describe your relationship since the time that he was released from custody?"

"We're very close. He's a changed person. He's very responsible. He's loving. He takes care of business. He does what he's told. And," he pauses for a moment, "he's someone who could live in my house again."

Ireland nods his head at Judge Perkins. Meyer declines to ask Howard Papke any questions.

Andrew takes the stand and swears to tell the truth.

Ireland instructs him, "State your name for the record, please, sir."

"Andrew Gene Papke."

"Are you the same Andrew Papke who stands charged of two causes of intoxication manslaughter in this courtroom?"

"Yes, sir, I am."

"Do you have a memory of what you were doing the day of the wreck?"

"Some."

"Was this a period of time in your life, Mr. Papke, when you were drinking alcohol excessively?"

"Yes, sir, excessively."

"Is there any question that on the day of June 29, 1996, that through much of the day you were drunk?"

"No, sir, there's no question."

"You heard testimony about driving, details about driving too fast. Did you drive too fast that day?"

"Yes, sir."

"I want you to tell me what you recall as you were driving down Brodie Lane immediately prior to the collision. What happened?"

"I recall turning onto Brodie. I recall driving along for a short period of time, and I recall seeing the headlights of the car I hit."

"Andrew, you heard testimony about your conduct out there at the scene. Do you recall running around and using obscenities?"

"Yes, I recall."

"For the jury, who was on your mind at that time, Mr. Papke? Were you thinking about the people in the other car?"

"No, sir."

"Who were you thinking about?"

"I was thinking about myself. I was scared."

"Did you tell people the truth out there about what you had to drink?"

"No, sir."

"Did you tell the officers the truth?"

"No, sir. I didn't want to get in trouble."

"When was the first time that you were told that some people died in the wreck?"

"I believe it was in the hospital. I remember a nurse coming in and asking if I was okay. Then she asked if I knew that two people died in the accident. I believe I said yes. She showed me a couple of pictures of the cars."

"What concern, if any, did you express, Andrew, at the time about the two people in the other car?"

"I didn't express any concern."

"Is there anything at this time that you would like to say to the people in this courtroom, the families involved here, and to the jury?"

"Yes, there is. I would like to say that I am sorry to the people that had to witness this. I'm sorry for the two families of Beth and David, and the Roberts family. This isn't the time or place right now, but I'm ready to talk in any and every way."

Ireland passes the witness to Buddy Meyer.

Meyer presses Andrew about what happened after his bond release when he contacted D.R., which was not permissible according to the conditions of the bond.

Andrew counters that he was interested in seeing how D.R. was doing. They were friends, he says. "At one point he came by my father's shop and we talked about the wreck. I was under the impression from other people I had representing me that it was nobody's fault or that it was their fault. I was told not to admit anything. After that I stopped paging him. But about two months ago he came by my house out of the clear blue. I hadn't instigated that."

"You were trying to convince your friend that the wreck wasn't your fault?"

"The time he came to my house I told him that I was sorry for what I had done to him. I didn't try to persuade him in any way to believe that I wasn't at fault."

Meyer changes topics: "How many times did your mother tell you to not drink and drive?"

"Countless."

"Your dad?"

"Many times."

"How many times did other people on June 29, 1996, try to prevent you from operating a motor vehicle?"

"A couple of times."

"And now you're going to counseling ... I want the jury to be real clear that the reason you're going to counseling is that you were ordered to do that as a condition of your bond release. Is that correct?"

"All I know," Andrew says in a quiet voice, "is that I'm clean and sober since the accident, and I've tried to get the help I've needed, not just for substance abuse, but for emotional counseling as well."

"And it took killing two people for you to realize that?"

"Sadly, yes."

"No further questions."

Judge Perkins invites the lawyers to give their closing statements. Gail Van Winkle reminds the jury about its duty to send a firm message to the community about drinking and driving. A light sentence, she says, won't accomplish that task.

"The defendant would like you to think that he is rehabilitated. But how can you rehabilitate him? Just because the defendant tells you that he's not going to drink and drive anymore, does that mean he's rehabilitated? Is he still going to lie and cheat and steal and blame other people for his actions and try to talk his way out of taking responsibility?

"I can only hope that twenty years in the penitentiary on each of these causes may give the Hollands and the Earlys some peace. Thank you."

Sam Ireland follows and similarly addresses the jury on the question of the trial's message to the community. He argues that maybe Andrew should have kept his previous lawyer and pleaded not guilty, not taken the stand, and kept his mouth shut—but he didn't do that. Ireland says that giving the maximum sentence to someone who has pleaded guilty sends the wrong message. "You've got to start somewhere when you've committed the crime Andrew has. You have to start to make good choices. He's done that, and it's got to make a difference."

Buddy Meyer also asks the jury to give the maximum sentence. "Andrew Papke has earned it. Not because he's evil, but because we as a community need to hold people accountable for this type of offense and say to them that this is the appropriate punishment."

Judge Perkins instructs the jury and asks them to deliberate their verdicts. It's 6:50 p.m. on the trial's fourth day, Thursday, April 24.

Andrew, Krista, his parents, siblings, and grandparents go to a nearby Kentucky Fried Chicken for dinner. They order the food to go and retreat to Sam Ireland's office two blocks from the courthouse, congregating in its small reception area. Doom dampens what feels like a last dinner for Andrew. No one says much of anything nor eats much of what was ordered. The office's entry door squeaks and creaks as, one by one, most of the family members step outside. Krista, however, stays seated at Andrew's side.

A few minutes after 9:00 p.m., Sam Ireland emerges from his office and says the jury has made a decision.

The jury files back into the courtroom at 9:30 p.m. Judge Perkins tells Andrew to stand and asks the jury foreperson to read the verdict to the defendant for the first cause in the death of David Holland.

"Yes, your honor. We, the jury, find the defendant, Andrew Papke, guilty of intoxication manslaughter as alleged in the indictment. We, the jury, assess the defendant's punishment at twenty years in the Institutional Division of the Texas Department of Criminal Justice."

The jury finds similarly in the second cause for the death of Bethany Early, assessing the same twenty-year sentence.

Andrew shows no reaction.

Judge Perkins asks the lawyers for additional comment before he issues a determination on how the sentences will be served. Meyer asks for the sentences to be stacked. Ireland demurs, saying that he's already made his comments in the Court's presence.

Without delay, Perkins confirms the sentences, upholding the jury's decision of maximum sentencing and the accompanying fines totaling $10,000. "Mr. Papke, the Court did have a conversation with the jurors following their decision on the verdict to try and get some idea what their thinking was. In terms of the decision about whether to run these sentences concurrently or consecutively, the Court is aware of the fact that despite your efforts to change yourself following this accident, in terms of what happened prior to that accident, in terms of the numerous times you were driving in a reckless fashion—at high speeds, cutting curves, cutting off other drivers—I am convinced that you're one of the people that scares us most about driving, because we simply don't know who's coming around the next curve. When we come to a hill where we can't see the other side, we don't know when we crest that hill if there's going to be someone like you in our lane.

"The two lives snuffed out by you at nineteen and seventeen years of age, basically with their whole lives in front of them, coupled with your refusal to let anyone else drive on the night in question, cries out for consecutive sentences.

"And so in both cases, this Court orders that the sentences run consecutively. The second sentence will not begin until you have served the first sentence of twenty years."

The courtroom is still.

Andrew, having previously received permission from Judge Perkins, says, "Your honor, I would like to make a statement."

Perkins tells Andrew to proceed.

"Your honor, I would like to say that I hope this sends a message to those people out there tonight who are doing the same thing I was doing. I hope that this message keeps people from situations like mine. I hope this makes a statement to people that drinking and driving is not right. Engaging in the activities that I did is not right. What I've come here to do is to own up to what I've done, to be honest about the way I was, to see what the public wants to do, and to get an honest verdict. I feel that this verdict sends a strong message. I leave it in God's hands. Thank you."

Judge Perkins tells him to be seated and announces that the trial will conclude with victim statements. The judge instructs the court reporter to cease recording. Adrian Early and Maria Soriano Holland address Andrew.

Richard Holland then comes forward. He speaks of his family's pain and grief, all at the hands of a young man who knew better. Looking directly at Andrew, he wonders how and why Andrew—having been to the anti-drinking and driving assemblies at school, and having been warned by his parents numerous times not to drink and drive—did it anyway.

Richard pauses, and then his measured words buttonhole Andrew, giving the guilty young man a purpose which he will find hard to reject. He says Andrew has a chance to turn his life around. If he's able to, perhaps he can communicate with people just like him so these tragedies don't happen anymore. The words sear themselves into Andrew's psyche, as though becoming part of his DNA. Staring straight ahead as if in a trance, Andrew doesn't noticeably respond to Richard Holland's final statement.

Hearing the judge call his name, he snaps out of his mini-daydream. "Mr. Papke," Judge Perkins says, "at this time I'll remand you to the custody of the Travis County Sheriff's office." Andrew looks over at Sam Ireland, and the two men shake hands.

Adrian Early approaches and puts his hand on Andrew's shoulder as he starts to stand up. He tells Andrew that he's sorry the sentences are stacked and walks away. Andrew quickly hugs Krista before she runs sobbing toward the courtroom door. Outside the courtroom Andrew sees his mom and her dad consoling each other. This grandfather of his, a retired army major, is the strongest man Andrew has ever known. He sees his grandfather's shoulders shake. It's the first time he's seen the man cry.

A sheriff's deputy brusquely grabs Andrew by the arm, cuffs him, and leads him through a side door of the courtroom.

Forty years at the state penitentiary in Huntsville await the just-sentenced felon.

PART II

AN OPEN LETTER

Chapter 18

Andrew spends his first night as a convicted felon in the new county jail east of Austin, where he was previously held. Storms rage through the night, but somehow the drum rolls of thunder don't disturb him, and his slumber is free of the wreck nightmare he's known so well the past ten months.

He wakens in the morning and can't remember the last time he's slept so well.

Within a week, a prison transport bus will take Andrew and other prisoners, handcuffed and shackled one to another, 160 miles east of Austin to Huntsville. He'll land at the Holliday Transfer Unit, an immense structure of cement and metal with no air conditioning, seventy miles directly north of Houston.

The good sleep Andrew experienced at the county jail doesn't travel with him to Huntsville. As with most rookie prisoners, fear fills his soul. Steady illumination at night, a metal rack for a bed, strange and disturbing noises, barbed wire, dogs, guards, heat due to lack of air conditioning, and menacing glances from other inmates strip him of any sense of calm. He knew a similar fear in the county jails, but the fear that he carries in this penitentiary is heavier, more threatening, and permanent. During the day, he goes where he's told and keeps his head down, attracting as little attention as possible. During the night, the images of his head-on wreck resurface. This nightmare, constantly invading his sleep, is the same one from which two young people, David and Beth, will never wake.

The Holliday Unit, recently constructed and able to house 2,100 inmates, is the first stop for almost all new Texas prisoners. They are sorted here and wait for permanent assignment according to their criminal status, age, and work abilities. The housing is dormitory style, with fifty men, two to a bunk, sharing a partitioned common living space.

All prisoners—save those on death row or in solitary confinement—are required to work. Andrew is assigned to a manual labor crew. On his first day on the job, he falls in line and follows other inmates as they approach the prison unit entrance gate. Their destination is a ditch adjacent to but outside of prison property, where they will tear out overgrown weeds with their flat hoes. He's not shackled to another prisoner but able to walk free. Immediately upon exiting the gate, he sees a prison guard riding high on a horse, a rifle in his hands and a pistol holstered to his side. The rookie prisoner hears the measured tone of an inmate behind him: "Don't even think about running, new boot. There are plenty more high riders waiting where we're going."

Mother's Day 1997 dawns bright in Austin. Maria Soriano Holland, accompanied by her sons Benjamin and Lucas, arrives at the site of the wreck on Brodie Lane. A dozen other friends and supporters—including Trooper Chris Brannen and Assistant DA Gail Van Winkle—join to erect a memorial cross for David and Beth. Seventeen days have passed since Andrew Papke was sentenced to forty years at the state penitentiary.

Maria has brought the cross from her home state of Jalisco, Mexico. "David" and "Beth" are beautifully welded onto the horizontal bar, the names separated at the cross's intersection by a budding, five-petal Mexican violet etched into the metal. As the cross is placed in fresh concrete, Trooper Brannen says a prayer for David and Beth. At the prayer's conclusion, all say "Amen," and Maria lays fresh flowers at the base of the cross. "David used to bring me flowers or breakfast on this day," she says, as a newspaper reporter writes in his notepad. "Now I'm bringing him flowers."

It's Benjamin Holland's first visit to the site of the wreck. About to graduate from the same high school that David did, he says the cross will serve as a sign of remembrance and guidance. "Now it's just time to live. Not to forget, but to keep on living and learning from this lesson."

Later that day, Maria returns alone to her empty house. An artist, she stopped working after David's death, her soul-energy exhausted by the wreck. Her friends, however, encouraged her to take up her brushes again as a way to express her grief. She eventually agreed.

Weary but determined, she sits down at the dining room table where countless photos of David and Beth surround her like autumn leaves about a mother tree. She picks up a brush and continues her work on two paintings—one of David and one of David and Beth together.

When Andrew wakens on the last Sunday in June, he remembers the moonlit night exactly one year before. He won't think of anything else this day. He lets the deep anguish about what he did flood his consciousness without trying to fight it off, as a form of self-punishment. He tells himself that he deserves all of it—the horrible memories, the suffering, the confinement.

He relives how he floored the Acura's engine while making a beer run with D.R., just an hour before the wreck. Driving to a nearby quick mart store, Andrew parked the car toward the street, away from the store's lights, and let the engine idle. He grabbed a baseball cap from the back seat, pulled the brim down to eye level, and winked at D.R. He slowly exited the car, looked around, and walked across the lot into the store. Moments later, lugging a twelve-pack of beer in his right arm, Andrew punched the store's door open with his left hand, awkwardly catching its metal edge. He jumped in the car and D.R. pumped the accelerator. A block away, D.R. pulled to the side of the road to let Andrew take the wheel. They gunned it back to Robbyne's dad's place, giddy about their ability to steal beer. Glancing down, Andrew noticed blood on the steering wheel and instinctively wondered whose blood it was. Realizing it was his, he cursed in anger.

Lying in his metal bed this morning, he recalls this event along with the other ones of that day and evening in vivid detail. The same question rises in his mind, as it has for the past 365 days and nights: *Why?*

He imagines that in Austin, family and friends of his two victims will gather on this first anniversary of the wreck at gravesites in two cemeteries.

His dad has been to the graves of David and Beth and has described to his son what he saw. Where Beth has been laid to rest, Texas live oak trees spread wide and offer respite and shade to visitors. Beth, the strawberry-blonde lover of animals, is remembered with a pink granite marker with etchings of a dog's head and praying hands showcasing the biblical words: "Absent from the body, present with the Lord."

Toward the far southwest section of Austin, David's grave is marked with a bronze overlay depicting a skateboarder parting the clouds, with words from Psalm 18: "He brought me into a spacious place; he rescued me because he delighted in me."

Andrew imagines that all those gathering to remember David and Beth detest him and will talk about how he needs to rot in prison for years to come. He tells himself that he doesn't blame them—he'd feel the exact same way if the situation was reversed.

Andrew meets with a psychotherapist contracted by the Texas Department of Criminal Justice, the TDCJ. Asked how he feels about himself, Andrew says that most days he feels like he has dirt and poison coursing through his veins.

He remembers feeling this way some before the wreck, but now because of what he has done, he feels it almost every day. When the counselor asks him if he feels depressed, Andrew clamps his mouth and stares past his questioner to the wall behind him. *Really?! Who wouldn't be depressed living in prison?*

The visitor list for Andrew Papke, offender #791425, consists of his mom, his dad and stepmom, his brother and stepsister, and Krista. Krista is not categorized as a family member but comes up with Howard and Cathy or Jan to see Andrew. The parents typically cut their visits short so Andrew and Krista can visit by themselves. Offenders are allowed three contact visits per month from immediate family members, children, and spouses.

Inmates meet their visitors in a room under strict supervision. All visitors sit in folding chairs on the entry door side of long tables, and inmates sit on the far side, no exceptions. All inmates are duly warned that visiting privileges can be withheld for any violation of the code—including any attempt at sexual behavior. When an inmate uses up the allotted three contact visits prior to the end of the month, additional visits occur in a different area of the prison where a glass barrier separates them and their visitors.

Jan comes alone to Huntsville to visit her son toward the end of August. It's a non-contact visit, and the barrier glass separates. They talk to each other on an intercom telephone.

Jan begins to cry.

"Mama, what's wrong?" Andrew asks.

"This glass wall between us," she says, "makes it like we're in two different worlds."

Andrew puts his right hand up on the glass at eye level, off to the side. He looks at his mom and asks her to place her hand on the glass opposite his. She does, and their hands mirror one another, separated only by the glass. Andrew continues to look at his mom and says to her, "The Earlys and Hollands can't do this with Beth or David. Think about that."

Jan nods her head and continues to cry.

Krista has started a new job at a large medical clinic. She wants to go back to school but will have to wait until her financial situation improves. Not only did she have to buy a car, but also new clothes. Almost everything she had to wear was in the hatchback of the Acura, rocketing up in the air at the wreck's impact, and falling haphazardly onto the asphalt of Brodie Lane.

Through everything that has happened, Krista and Jan maintain their close relationship. Living in the same house, they talk together more now than ever. They discuss how Andrew grew up during his time out on bond and during the trial—showing remorse, offering apologies, assuming responsibility. They talk about how Andrew needs all of them so much now—and how hard it is to drive the three plus hours from Huntsville back to Austin after a visit. They also wonder about how things must be beyond difficult for the Earlys and Hollands.

At the very beginning of his imprisonment, Andrew tried to convince Krista to move on with her life without him. He told her it just wasn't fair for her to stay with him and that she should leave him. By the third visit, Krista had heard enough. She told Andrew to shut up and listen to her. Krista told Jan about it as they drove home to Austin after that visit. The younger woman said she looked at Andrew and asked him who did he think he was, and that she was going to be there with him whether he liked it or not. Krista laughed and told Jan that Andrew put on a sheepish grin after he heard her out.

Krista tells Jan that she's never been able to walk away from anyone who needs help and that she'd always felt that she and Andrew were meant to be together. "We've shared so much by now. Leaving him would be like cutting off one of my own legs, and I'd forever limp through the rest of my life without that limb to support me." She tells Jan that she and Andrew are going to marry—not sometime in the future, but now, by proxy. Krista explains that Andrew needs her support and that the certificate of marriage will facilitate contact visits when she goes to see him by herself.

It's 11:55 a.m. on Tuesday, October 7, 1997. Krista is on her lunch break. Howard Papke, in jeans and a T-shirt, meets her at the office of the justice of the peace in Austin's third precinct. Krista looks splendid in a long red and white skirt with a red short-sleeved suit jacket. Howard has brought her a single white rose—he will stand in for his son, marriage by proxy, legal in the state of Texas. The judge talks them through the brief ceremony, signs the marriage certificate, and banters that both Papkes, father and son, are lucky men.

Howard gives Krista a peck on her cheek and says he'll see her soon.

Krista hustles back to work as a newly married woman— to a man sentenced to serve the next thirty-nine years in Huntsville.

Three days after the ceremony, Jan puts on a dinner party at the house to celebrate Krista and Andrew's marriage. Homemade cream gravy covers chicken-fried steaks for Krista, Jan, and Dave. Jan will later tell a friend about the great happiness she felt during the party, but also about the fear that welled up in her as the evening went on—not only for her son and his future, but also for this beautiful young woman, hitched to her imprisoned son. What in the world awaited her?

Cut off and isolated, Andrew discovers that he has an artistic touch. He draws pictures of childhood memories: his grandparents' houses, the tree forts at his dad's place, and the dirt bikes he raced around with his dad and brother. It helps him momentarily escape the depression that dogs him on a daily basis.

He also remembers that Chaplain Jameson, from group therapy sessions in the Travis County Jail east of Austin, encouraged purposeful activity as a way to combat prison depression. He contacts the prison chaplain in his unit. She tells Andrew that she's offering an overview of a book called

The Seven Habits of Highly Effective People, and that he's welcome to sign up for the class. He says, "Yes, ma'am, count me in, please."

The explanation of the second habit hits Andrew because he's rarely considered it: Envision what you want your future to be and have a personal mission statement to guide your decision-making to get there. *Personal mission statement?* The phrase initially strikes Andrew as egotistical and selfish. But then he thinks back to when he wanted to be a firefighter. His decisions and actions at that time didn't help him reach the goal and landed him in prison instead.

Chapter 19

Acalendar on Andrew's dorm partition shows a date which neither inmates nor guards at the Holliday Unit want to celebrate. Today, November 27, 1997, is Thanksgiving Day. Turkey, or some derivative of it, is being served in the prison chow hall. It mostly reminds inmates they'd rather be somewhere else. A few of the guards are glad for the holiday overtime pay, but other ones look forward to punching the clock at the end of their shift more than usual.

Lying on his bunk later this night, Andrew remembers last Thanksgiving and how the empty chairs at his mother's house made him think about David and Beth. He recalls how Richard Holland used the same image during his testimony at the trial.

The other words Andrew heard during the victim impact statements of his trial are permanently seared onto his soul and have become his own: *You have a chance to turn your life around. If you're able to, you can communicate with people like yourself so these types of tragedies don't happen anymore.* Andrew sits up with a start and walks over to a table, grabbing a pen and yellow legal pad on his way. He starts to write. He's never written anything in his life other than assignments for English class, but now he feels compelled to write.

Two weeks later, during a visit with his dad and stepmom, he tells them he's written fourteen pages of an "open letter." He says he's sent it to them; they should get it early in the coming week. "Would you," he asks his stepmom Cathy, "please type it up on your computer?" He asks his dad to send it to schools and anyone else who might be interested in it.

Cathy and Howard both say that they'll do as Andrew asks.

*T*he purpose of this letter is intended in the nature of giving. My story is all that I have. I want to share a part of me; something personal that would perhaps give something back to society, even if it means helping just one person from making a tragic mistake. The following is a mere glimpse of the event that changed my life ...

Andrew details the day of the wreck, his arrest and initial imprisonment, the trial and subsequent incarceration. Imprisonment, he writes, made him begin the painful process of self-examination.

I grew up in a Christian home and I knew that it was possible that "a" God could exist, maybe. But as I entered the high school scene, I began to drink and go to parties. I quit going to church with my family. Alcohol became something of a deity for me. I loved it, and from the beginning I knew that I liked to drink. I liked to be drunk. It seemed to make it easier for me to talk to people and make friends ... I just figured that this is what all teenagers did. But then it seemed like almost overnight I was deep into a downward spiral, making poor judgments with no regard or responsibility for my own success.

Andrew says that depression nearly consumes him because of what he did to David and Beth and their families, to his family, and to his own life.

The weight of my crime was choking me. Desperate and lonely, scared and confused, I did a lot of thinking: "Why? Why? Why?" The nightmares and continued bouts of severe depression were like a roller-coaster ride of plummeting emotions.

I spent a lot of time in my cell, and it dawned on me that maybe God has his own agenda for me. I was still alive after all that happened. There must be a reason, and I was going to seek out that reason.

Andrew credits his prison chaplain Ivan Jameson and the A.A. community for helping him find a purpose in his broken life.

I now know that it is only by God's will that I live. He has given a sinner like me another chance to do good and help others. This is not something I take lightly. I often feel that I do not deserve God's grace, but like my earthly father, he still loves me.

The burden I carry is enormous, but the Lord guides me. I pray constantly for grace and direction. However hard times may be, I still try to make each day count. For me, the only resolution is to share my experience and try to help people, especially younger ones, to stop making foolish decisions. We never see the full impact of what stupid choices can lead to until it is far too late. I sincerely believe this is my calling and I plan to continue this work whether I am incarcerated or free. No matter what!

He concludes the letter by returning to David and Beth.

It hurts me deeply that all the plans and dreams David and Beth had were thwarted by me. I took those dreams away from them and now I live with this monster inside of me.

I often think of the "What ifs," and wish that I had stayed home that day. I never meant to hurt anyone, and I relive that crash with every breath. I know that my words probably would not help the victims, but I truly am so very sorry. And to write these words down severely minimizes, almost insults, how badly I feel inside. I know that I can't trade places with them, though I wish I could. And I know I can't bring them back no matter how hard I pray.

I will never be able to restore their places in the hearts of their loved ones. I have the guilt and knowledge of those families' grief resting heavily on my soul. Not a day goes by that I don't think about them. I have to trust, though, that all of our frightened, confused, and angry feelings are in the hands of God. I pray that He is holding the relatives and friends of the deceased in his loving arms. Only He can soothe their sorrow. I hope that maybe one day I will be able to go to them and express how sorry I am. I also hope that time will begin to heal the wounds and call us together, giving all sides of this tragedy a chance to be heard and understood.

I am paying a very high price for my mistake, and however much I want to lay down and give up, I know I must not forget that I do have a purpose, a mission to witness to others, even though I am in prison. And with each morning prayer comes the hope of a possibility that the Lord may have a use for me in the free world once again.

I say all of this so that these two innocent kids may not be forgotten, and that their memory may serve as a reminder to make right decisions, to do the next right thing, and uphold life's most important teaching as we hear in the words of Jesus, "I tell you to love each other, just as I have loved you."

PART III

FACE TO FACE IN TEXAS

Chapter 20

As a young boy, Adrian Early listened to and obeyed his mother. When camping, hiking, or strolling together in their neighborhood, she taught him to observe nature, its plants and animals and insects. Young Adrian was fascinated by nature, and he wanted to know how the world was held together and how its working parts meshed. Years later, he was awarded his Ph.D. in chemical engineering. His proud mother clapped and beamed at his doctoral hooding ceremony. Adrian's unquenchable yearning to understand how things worked energized his scholastic journey and helped guide his navigation through the world of good and evil.

When his daughter Beth perished, it was Adrian's desire that her casket be open for the visitation and the funeral service. It was no easy decision, but it fit with how he looked at the world. Difficult problems whether of a scientific or personal nature, he told his wife and two sons, had to be faced head-on.

Two years and a few months after the wreck, in September 1998, Adrian contacts the TDCJ's Victim Services office and requests an opportunity to participate in their Victim-Offender Dialogue program with inmate Andrew Papke.

The Texas criminal justice system offers surviving victims and family members of violent crimes a structured opportunity to sit across the table face to face from their case's particular offender. In 1994, Texas became the first state in the nation to offer such a program to victims of violent crime. David Doerfler, who designed the TDCJ's program, instituted two strict mandates:

- Only crime *victims* can initiate the process, and
- *Offenders* must admit complete fault and guilt for their crime in order to participate in the program.

Doerfler responds to Adrian's request by letting him know that he'll be placed on the program's waiting list. And he tells Adrian that he'll talk to Andrew Papke to see if he'll agree to the mandate required for his participation.

For his part, Andrew doesn't know David Doerfler or anything about the program Doerfler directs. Neither is the young offender aware of the set of improbable circumstances that made Texas the nation's leader in offering a Victim-Offender Dialogue program in cases of violent crime through its criminal justice system.

Doerfler is state coordinator for the program but brushes off credit for its development. The program, as he tells all who ask, belongs to crime victims because they are the ones who willed it into being.

Doerfler played high school football in Corpus Christi, where his skills as a shifty yet powerful running back blossomed. His success continued at Texas Lutheran College, where he captained the football team. Upon graduating in 1971, he moved to Iowa for seminary studies to become a pastor.

During his second year in Iowa, he traveled home to Texas for Christmas break. Just days later, a terrible car wreck completely sabotaged the family's holiday. One of his sisters, her husband, and their young son were blindsided by a drunk driver whose car crossed over the highway median before slamming into theirs. Doerfler's sister Christine survived to bury her husband, Jerry, and their only child of seven months, Jeffrey, the day after Christmas.

When Doerfler returned to Iowa, he projected an air of normalcy, thinking it befitting of a pastor-to-be. A seminary professor noticed the guise and offered his guidance. "David, don't move so fast. Hold on to this pain." Doerfler had no idea that he would never forget the older man's words.

A few years later, Doerfler was pastoring a church fifty miles northwest of San Antonio. On a sunny fall day, his wife was driving a rural Texas road with their seven-month-old daughter Meredith strapped into a child's car seat next to her. Out of nowhere they were struck head-on by a drunk driver. The straps of Meredith's car seat slackened on impact, and she flew into the dashboard and windshield. Doerfler's wife was bruised and battered but had no major injuries, protected by her seatbelt. Meredith, however, suffered extreme trauma to the right side of her brain. Meredith would recover, but the wreck would inflict her for life.

The young man who plowed into the Doerflers' car was apprehended at the scene. A number of months after the crash, Doerfler and his wife stood twenty feet from the man before a judge in a rural Texas county courtroom. The perpetrator, who spent no time in jail, admitted to guilt for causing the wreck, but he was not charged with any crime. He had no vehicle insurance. He made no apology to Doerfler or his wife.

The judge, exhibiting a permissive attitude toward drinking and driving common in Texas at that time, told him not to do it again and dismissed him with a wave of his hand. Expecting some type of restitution from the man or the legal process, the Doerflers walked out of the courtroom flabbergasted. They received a $5,000 settlement from their insurance company for coverage of uninsured motorists. Nothing more.

Following the tragedy, the Doerfler family received much love, support, and attention from their small congregation. So much so, that Pastor Doerfler began a secret affair with a woman in the church. The affair continued on and off but unexposed for three years as the adulterous pastor did his best to rationalize his behavior to himself. His leadership suffered, and he spiraled downward into self-loathing.

By the end of 1983, the affair was exposed and he was forced to resign as pastor of the small congregation. His wife divorced him.

He and the woman with whom he had the affair decided to marry. A small church opportunity opened up elsewhere, and he was back in a pulpit preaching on a part-time basis. He also found full-time work coordinating Parents Anonymous support groups—for parents who have abused their own children—for a forty-county area in Central Texas. Two jobs, one requiring extensive travel by car, kept him busy. Just when it looked as though his life was coming back together, he suspected that his new wife was seeing another man.

Doerfler broke down emotionally. In fact, he lost his voice. He could speak only in whispers. With nothing left to lose, he ended up at an out-of-state treatment center. For the first time in his life, the twelve-step program of Alcoholics Anonymous made sense to him. He began to speak about past events in his life with fresh honesty.

Back in Texas with a renewed sense of self, Doerfler left his part-time preaching post and committed himself fully to the twelve-step work of the Parents Anonymous groups. The bond between him and his second wife, meanwhile, disintegrated. He understood the end of the relationship in a new light and didn't let it devastate him. Rather than seeing himself as a twice-divorced preacher, he told others that he was a human being in need of healing.

A TDCJ social worker invited Doerfler to begin a P.A. group at the women's prison in Gatesville, Texas. Sixteen women were in the first group that he worked with. He was floored—twice—by what he heard from the women.

Nine of the women had killed either a child of their own or a child in their care. That was a shock. In talking with the women, Doerfler encountered what seemed an unassailable wall of shame. The shame, Doerfler discovered, wasn't borne only from the taking of innocent life. He also learned that the women shared another story of shame—the second shock—each of the sixteen claimed to be a childhood victim of sexual abuse.

Doerfler in turn formulated a sex-offender treatment program for P.A. prison populations, in which paroled sex offenders were required to listen to victims of sexual abuse tell their stories. "Mixed groups," Doerfler called them, consisting of offenders and actual sex abuse victims—not victimized by any of the offenders in the group—powerfully impacted parolees. And many victims, initially reluctant to participate in the program, experienced unexpected healing by sharing their stories of pain in the presence of those who had caused similar pain to others.

These mixed groups—surrogate victims and offenders—meeting face to face, later served as a template for another kind of mixed group. Doerfler instituted a Victim-Offender Dialogue process for the Department of Victim Services of the TDCJ. It was through this department that Adrian Early requested a meeting with Andrew Papke.

Doerfler's program didn't debut, however, until five women—a gritty state governor, three undaunted crime victims, and a risk-taking TDCJ employee—set the stage for its entrance.

Chapter 21

Ann Richards was elected Texas governor on November 6, 1990, the second woman to govern the state. An experienced politician, she narrowly defeated Republican nominee and political novice Clayton Williams, a wealthy business tycoon from Midland and self-described good ol' boy. While he enjoyed a comfortable lead in the polls, Williams made a reckless quip during the campaign that linked bad weather and rape: "If it's inevitable, just relax and enjoy it." The remark doomed his chances to win the election. At her inauguration, Richards vowed to open government to all Texans.

One of her initial acts was to appoint a crime victim, Ellen Halbert, to the Texas Board of Criminal Justice. The board overseeing the prison system was typically comprised of lawyers, businessmen, and politicos.

In 1986, Halbert was brutally attacked and left for dead in her home by a drifter who, the night prior to the attack, hid in her attic. Halbert required more than 600 stitches for her wounds and was hospitalized for two weeks. Initially, she couldn't imagine recovering from such sheer and uncontrollable violence. But recover she did, with lots of help from doctors and nurses, individual and group therapy, and loving support from family and friends.

Her physical rehabilitation, including plastic surgeries, went on for six months after the brutal violation. Her attacker, nineteen years old and mentally disturbed, was arrested, prosecuted by Travis County DA Ronnie Earle, sentenced twenty years to life, and imprisoned.

Two years later, Ellen spoke publicly for the first time about her experience at a crime victims' event at the steps of the Texas capitol in Austin. She confidently signed up to speak, encouraged by her friend and fellow crime victim Nell Myers, a few weeks prior to the event. Halbert expected a small gathering and anticipated making a few brief remarks and answering a question or two. Upon arriving, she saw TV cameras and lights, banners, microphones and amplified speakers, and lots of people. Terrified, her mind raced through possibilities for ducking out. She desperately wanted to leave but knew she couldn't. Standing behind the podium at the south steps of the capitol, she began to speak to the large gathering. She told her story with stark honesty—it was all she had—and as she did, a sense of power and control came over her like never before. Unexpectedly empowered, she found a voice she didn't know she had and continued to speak at more events.

Friends and victim rights' advocates, led by Nell Myers, flooded Ann Richard's office with letters in support of Ellen Halbert's appointment to the Texas Board of Criminal Justice. The new governor was swayed and appointed Halbert, early in 1991, as the first crime victim and second woman to serve on the board.

Nell Myers's twenty-year-old daughter Cydney was raped and murdered in 1979. Initially immobilized by her death, Nell sat in her Austin house day after day, staring at pictures of her beautiful blonde daughter. In the evenings, she sat in her backyard garden alone and in silence, until the darkness that surrounded her matched the gloom in her soul. This went on for almost one year.

She then read a newspaper account of a murder of a sixteen-year-old girl, a crime very similar to the one that snuffed out her daughter's life. Anger and rage at both murders combusted deeply inside her, and she decided to raise a vicious storm. "This is what you got to do," she said to herself. "You go fight."

Doggedly and with full-on determination, Nell forced the Texas criminal justice system to wake up to the needs of crime victims. She founded PAVC—People Against Violent Crime—in 1982 and advocated relentlessly for crime victims' rights. With the help of DA Ronnie Earle—who would later introduce Nell to Ellen Halbert—she authored a bill of rights for Texas crime victims and successfully championed its adoption into the state constitution in 1989.

With the adoption of the Crime Victims' Bill of Rights, a toll-free number was established for crime victims to access information about parole hearings, inmate release dates, victim compensation pools, and where to send victim impact statements. The toll-free phone calls were funneled to the TDCJ's headquarters in Austin, to the parole division's office of public information, led by a woman named Raven Kazen.

C athy Phillips of Abilene, Texas, wanted to meet with the imprisoned killer of her daughter. Except for seeing his picture in the local newspaper, she didn't know the man. She harbored, however, an unquenchable need to tell him face to face what her daughter meant to her and what his actions did to her family. Anthony Yanez was sentenced to four life sentences for the brutal 1990 kidnapping, rape, and murder of nineteen-year-old Brenda Phillips. Most of Cathy Phillips's friends told her she was crazy, but she was undeterred. As there was no official means by which to pursue her desire, Phillips appealed directly to new Texas governor Ann Richards.

The governor's staff responded to Phillips by instructing her to call Raven Kazen at the public information office of the parole division. Phillips called the office and told the secretary that she would speak only with the director, Raven Kazen. When Kazen spoke with Phillips on the phone the next day, the grieving mother wasted no time in making her request known, in a voice slow and unwavering: "I want to meet Anthony Yanez face to face. I need to know how long it took Brenda to die."

Upon hearing the bold request of the crime victim, the wind in Kazen's voice box vaporized. Kazen couldn't breathe nor even move her suddenly dry mouth—she was sick to her stomach and her heart thumped double-time. After time seemed to stop, she recovered her composure and told Cathy Phillips she'd have to see what she could do, promising to call her back soon. Kazen knew prison officials and the warden at Yanez's unit would be extremely wary about any type of meeting between an offender and a crime victim family member. It would be a huge security risk, and the potential for re-victimization and disaster was off the charts. Crime victims simply didn't go into prisons and talk to the perps who had brutalized them. It just didn't happen—ever. Prison walls, razor wire, and the rifles held by guards in watchtowers served one overriding purpose: separation of inmates and civilians.

Chapter 22

There was only one person Raven Kazen thought to contact after hearing Cathy Phillips's request—Ellen Halbert, recently appointed by Ann Richards to the Texas Board of Criminal Justice. Since hearing Halbert's story at a PAVC conference two years previous, Kazen had kept up a steady conversation with Halbert on the subject of crime victims' rights. Kazen reached out to Halbert as she tried to figure out what to do with Cathy Phillips and her uncompromising request.

Ellen Halbert had taken on her appointment to the criminal justice board with the fervor of a new convert. She visited the Walls Unit in Huntsville and toured other prisons throughout Texas. She was overwhelmed by the heat, the smell of sweat, the cramped conditions, and the noise in the state pens. She spoke with and listened to fellow crime victims. As she studied and evaluated the extensive prison system, she perceived early on what many criminal justice researchers already professed: Punishment, part and parcel of the retributive justice system, did little to change inmate behavior.

Halbert responded to Kazen's phone call with a simple question: Why not allow Cathy Phillips her request?

Understanding perfectly Phillips's crime victim mentality, Halbert responded that she would certainly like to confront her own attacker in order to know why in the world he assaulted her the way he did.

Raven Kazen returned Cathy Phillips's call with the news that her unvarnished plea for justice had started to penetrate the seemingly unassailable wall of Texas's mammoth criminal justice system. Kazen asked her to be patient and promised to call her again soon.

Ellen Halbert urged her fellow board members to allow Phillips to have her day across the table from Yanez. Phone calls went back and forth between the board's director and the governor's office, and then between Raven Kazen's office in Austin and the Ellis Unit in Huntsville. An agreement was reached. Ann Richards's overarching promise to open state government to all Texans extended to a grieving mother in Abilene. Raven Kazen called Cathy Phillips with a guaranteed assurance: She would have her day at a table across from her daughter's murderer, and soon.

Kazen, charged with the responsibility to make the meeting happen, hired a professional mediator from Oklahoma. The mediator arrived in Huntsville the night before the encounter and met individually with Phillips and Yanez, spending an hour with each. The face-to-face meeting the next day at the Ellis Unit allowed Phillips to unburden a part of her soul. It wasn't about forgiveness or reconciliation—it was about honesty and disclosure. She told Yanez how she saw the dirt underneath her dead daughter's fingernails, the blood-encrusted scrapes on her knuckles, and his handprints on her swollen neck. Face to face, she posed to him the question that had been tearing the fabric of her soul since the first days of the awful reality: "Why did my nineteen-year-old have to die?" Yanez countered that he honestly didn't know. He said he was married at the time and was always arguing with his wife. His abuse of drugs and alcohol caused frequent blackouts, he confessed, and diminished his memories of what happened.

The meeting occurred late in 1991, toward the end of Ann Richards's first year in the Texas capitol. Yanez, despite his poor memories of his deadly actions, offered an apology to the grieving mother. Cathy Phillips said she felt better after the encounter, with some of her questions answered. She no longer had to play the "What you don't know will drive you crazy" game.

Ellen Halbert met with Kazen in her parole division office to debrief the mediated dialogue between Cathy Phillips and Anthony Yanez. Kazen reported that Cathy Phillips wasn't fully satisfied with the work of the mediator—he could have pressed Yanez to answer more precisely. Somehow, Kazen said, the approach needed to be victim-oriented. Halbert agreed without hesitation.

"If," Kazen continued, "we have another victim who has a request like Cathy Phillips, we need to hire somebody to be in charge of it."

Raven asked Ellen Halbert to help formulate a job description and search for a mediator. They needed someone who could work both sides of the table—someone who was honest and courageous with victims, and trustworthy yet challenging with offenders. It was a tall order.

David Doerfler, working with prison populations through Parents Anonymous, emerged as the right person. Ellen knew that Doerfler, like herself, was a crime victim who was connected with the national Restorative Justice movement. Most importantly, she said, he was committed to a radical idea: seeing how victims could be compensated—not just financially, but emotionally and spiritually—by offenders. He was the perfect combination of practitioner and student of the movement.

Victim Services was born within the TDCJ. Five women—a governor named Ann, three crime victims named Ellen, Nell, and Cathy, and a risk-taking TDCJ employee named Raven—gave it birth.

Chapter 23

At the end of 1994, Kazen and Doerfler debuted the Texas Department of Criminal Justice's Victim-Offender Dialogue, the nation's first victim-initiated, mediated dialogue program, bringing offenders and the victims of their violent crimes together face to face. Doerfler compiled a program manual to prep participants for dialogues. Kazen and Doerfler wholeheartedly agreed on the guiding principle of the manual: The victim is always right.

Keeping criminals and civilians separated was still the main mission of prison wardens throughout Texas, but now they also had to provide an opportunity, in the very bowels of their concrete and cyclone razor-wired fortresses, for victims and offenders to safely encounter one another in the presence of a mediator. It was a new day.

Doerfler and Kazen structured the program to be victim-centered. Requests for face-to-face meetings would only be considered when victim-initiated, and offenders had to admit to complete fault and guilt in their crimes. Participation in the program would not lead to sentence reduction or parole board favor for the offender.

Doerfler insisted that the preparation process for both participants be in-depth and thorough and not tethered to a timeline. The director and coordinator stipulated that a face-to-face encounter would happen only when the mediator in charge, working with both victim and offender, gave approval for their readiness and felt confident about the meeting's success.

Kazen hired a woman named Lisa Looger to work as Doerfler's assistant.

The national Restorative Justice community started to take notice of what was happening in Texas. Practitioners and scholars came to Texas, as did media outlets, to see what Kazen, Doerfler, and Looger were doing for crime victims. Face-to-face encounters between violent crime victims and offenders had only been attempted by criminal justice systems in two states other than Texas—New York and Ohio. Texas, however, took the lead by insisting that the dialogue process be initiated by crime victims and serve, first and foremost, their needs.

Chapter 24

Four days have passed since Andrew received the news that Adrian Early wants to meet with him in the Victim-Offender Dialogue program, sponsored by the state's prison system. The request and its implications have been forming new pathways in Andrew's brain. It's all he's thought about since. He welcomes this new mental activity, but the thought of saying yes to the request frightens him.

His conviction and sentencing in Austin seem a world away. Fifteen months as a felon inside the Holliday Unit at Huntsville have schooled him. He's seen violent encounters between men he couldn't have imagined before coming to the pen. He thought he had an anger issue. He's perceived a type of anger, from some of his fellow inmates, as if it was a hovering evil spirit waiting to pounce and devour its next victim. Through smarts and luck, he's learning how to survive in this new environment. Meeting Mr. Early, however, could completely change everything.

Andrew is ashamed of what he's done—there are no regret-free days for him. He never meant to take David's and Beth's lives, but he did choose to drink and drive that fateful day. The wreck on Brodie Lane could have been avoided, and he is fully responsible. It was his horrific mistake and his alone. Shame, though, isn't a topic of conversation among prison inmates. He's learned to keep it to himself. To survive in this dungeon, he needs to hide his shame and put on a bad-boy mask. It's the code followed by almost all of his fellow inmates. Any type of vulnerability—physical or emotional—gets exposed and exploited in this lockup environment.

Deep down, he's beginning to learn a grave irony about prison life: What helps him survive today will harden or kill him in the long run. Meeting with Mr. Early will require him to take off the bad-boy mask and let out the vulnerability that hides inside. He's not sure he can do it. He's afraid to do it. Confidentiality doesn't exist inside prison walls. If he participates in this program, word will spread.

He struggles with knowing who he really is and sometimes doesn't recognize the face looking back at him in the mirror. *Who am I? A future hardened felon, or just some kid who really messed up?*

With the backdrop of his forty-year sentence, Andrew experiences days as both long and short. Long, because of emotional turbulence. It's a lot of work to keep everything bottled up inside while continually having to watch your back. Short, because each day is exactly the same, especially when you're under someone's thumb from sunup to sundown—every single day. And all the days blend back into one regrettable day and night of drinking: June 29, 1996. He gave no thought to an act that resulted in so great a consequence.

On this late night, sweaty and agitated, he slaps his face with lukewarm water at the dorm lavatory. He looks in the plastic mirror bolted to the wall above the sink and remembers pieces of his trial: pleading guilty, saying he was sorry, not contesting anything, not groveling for leniency—especially in the presence of the Earlys and Hollands. And then the state-ment he spoke toward the end of his trial testimony to the two families he victimized: *This isn't the time or place right now, but I'm ready to talk in any and every way.*

He decides that he needs to follow through on his prom-ise, even if it goes against what he's learned about prison culture and the potentially dangerous exposure it carries. Remembering how Adrian Early reached out to him at the end of his trial to say he regretted that the sentences were stacked, Andrew looks back into the mirror: *I wonder what Mr. Early might say to me now.*

Chapter 25

Andrew finishes his breakfast in the Holliday Unit chow hall. He drops off his plastic tray and dishware and walks outside to join the inmates who stand in line at the dispensary window for medications. Even though the end of September approaches, the south wind offers no hint of fall's arrival. It gusts hot and kicks up dust as Andrew walks with his mouth closed and his arm covering his eyes.

Diagnosed as bipolar shortly after he became a ward of the state, Andrew has been taking heavy doses of anti-depressants for over a year. His turn at the window finally comes. He displays his identification card to the pharmacist, takes the paper cup of pills offered him, swallows them down, and then shows the prison guard tending the line that the cup, his hands, and his mouth are empty. With a bored expression and sleepy eyes, the guard nods him along.

Andrew has a pass from the field labor crew this day. Because of his positive response to Adrian Early's request, he has an appointment to meet a prison system representative about the Victim-Offender Dialogue program.

A guard escorts Andrew to the chaplain's office to meet Lisa Looger, who has driven up from Austin.

Looger greets Andrew enthusiastically. She tells the inmate that she and David Doerfler will work with him and Adrian Early in the preparation process for their meeting. She says to Andrew that he's going to have to put in a good amount of work for the meeting to happen.

It's impossible for Lisa Looger, tall, loud, and the bearer of a colorful wardrobe, to sneak into a room. Her personality and experiences make her a singular fit as Doerfler's assistant coordinator in the Victim-Offender Dialogue program. Looger previously worked as a parole officer. She's a fierce advocate for crime victims. Twenty years in the recovery movement has also made Looger accepting of others. She realizes that offenders need an opportunity for a second chance. She tells all offenders, including Andrew today, that a second chance often comes through honest confession and self-scrutiny.

She carries herself with a moxie that is bold, compassionate, and wise. There aren't many people who, seated between a victim and an offender at a dialogue table, are as comfortable with the moment or as effective at diffusing tension as Looger. She simply has a way with people—whether in the bowels of the Walls Unit in Huntsville or, on occasion during a free weekend, doing stand-up at a leading comedy club in Austin.

Looger tells Andrew to start by reading the material in the packet and writing responses to the accompanying questions. Either she or Doerfler will be back to Huntsville in a month to meet with him and process his initial work.

"Okay, ma'am. I'll take a look at it," Andrew says as he offers his hand.

Returning to his dorm partition, he places the packet in his footlocker, out of view from his bunkmates. He intends to look at it after dinner. Later that evening, reclining on his bunk, he thinks about retrieving the packet that he stashed away. It remains untouched, however, as late evening morphs into deep night.

Five days pass, and Andrew's reading material and worksheets to prepare for the Victim-Offender Dialogue haven't moved. This evening, from the same metal bunk perch as before, Andrew thinks about the packet in his footlocker and tells himself that he needs to start in on his homework. Why does telling the truth, he wonders, take so much work and commitment? His wondering lapses into gentle snoring, and he maintains his prone position until morning.

When he wakes up, he decides to visit the chaplain in order to convey a message to Austin. He's simply not ready to do what's needed—this much he knows. It won't be the first time he's dropped out of a class or gone back on a promise.

Andrew writes a letter to his A.A. sponsor from Austin, Ron Prince. Thanking him again for his attention and mentoring while he was out on bail, Andrew lets him know that he's still working the twelve steps behind prison walls.

Almost all prisoners, Andrew writes, seem to be on meds. Maybe they're all depressed, or maybe it's a way to keep the prison population sedated. He writes that some of the guys in his A.A. group have encouraged him to stop taking his meds.

As late October gives way to November, a fall chill finally descends on Huntsville. The Holliday Unit is heated, but the cavernous metal building conserves little of the heating system's output. Andrew doesn't mind.

For two hot summers he's labored in the farm fields of the TDCJ and in the various bar ditches that border Huntsville's main highways. Tending fields and cutting weeds in the brutal Texas sun has blistered his hands and burned the back of his neck. Verbal insults hurled from passersby on the roadways have made his hair stand on end but have also thickened his skin. He's seen heatstrokes fell some of the older prisoners, while guards on horseback, trained for their own safety not to be sympathetic, yell at the fallen to get up.

These fresh summer memories latch onto the fateful summer memory ever-present in his mind, from the night of June 29, 1996. Because of what happened and what he's forced to do now, the scar on his soul seems not to be fading with time, but still developing in breadth and depth.

The cooler air at least tells him that summer is over. The anniversary of the wreck has passed and won't come again for a number of months. Additionally, his birthday is approaching. When he turned twenty-one last year as a relatively new boot in the Holliday Unit, no one greeted him with the two words he'd heard from his parents and grand-parents every year on the date. He remembers how sorry he felt for himself.

This year he decides to give himself a present for his twenty-second birthday. Swayed by some of the guys in his A.A. group, he'll adopt a new post-breakfast routine. He will stop going to the pharmacy dispensary window where he consumed the contents of the little white cup. The guard positioned there will have one fewer open mouth, tongue wagging, to inspect.

Chapter 26

t's a special evening in Andrew's partition of the unit. The guards have granted permission to watch a live event on television. Andrew won't join his block mates gathered around the big TV—by his own choice. The materials that Lisa Looger gave him still lie in his footlocker where he put them four months ago. On this last evening in January 1999, Andrew fishes the papers out of his locker and, with a firm two-hand grip, walks them to a nearby table. Laying the packet down squarely, he gets ready to work. While a number of his fellow prisoners watch the Super Bowl in the common area, Andrew begins to read through the manual that David Doerfler compiled for participants in the Victim-Offender Dialogue process.

"You have agreed to a process that is difficult, even painful, but it can be healing. No matter what the initial or subsequent responses of the victim, your preparation for a possible face-to-face meeting will prove to be the most helpful. The preparation process which you have already begun will allow you to stay with your feelings, take responsibility for your offense, and be accountable.

"You are to be commended for the courage it takes to risk participation in this process. There are no guarantees; nevertheless, there is hope and promise for you.

"To facilitate this process, you are encouraged to feel, reflect, and work through the following questions alone, as well as with family members, friends, and counselors. You might find group therapy especially valuable to receive others' personal perspectives, caring confrontation, feedback, and support. Write down as much as you are able. Many have found daily journaling of feelings during this process time very helpful.

"Throughout the process, be challenging and open with yourself. Remember:

- Until you are honest with yourself and face your past, the past continues.
- Until you admit your guilt and take responsibility for your offense, the offense continues.
- Until you become accountable beyond yourself, to your victim and your community, there can be no healing."

Andrew pushes the materials aside, goes to the lavatory sink, and looks in the plastic mirror. The face that looks back at him in the warped, scratched mirror is funhouse-shaped and momentarily reminds him of his drinking days. Even so, he tells himself plainly: *Mr. Early has waited long enough. It's time to do this.*

The next day Andrew reaches out to Victim Services in Austin. More than four months have passed since he backed out of the commitment to meet with Adrian Early. He tells the office that he's changed his mind and that he'll restart the preparation process in the Victim-Offender Dialogue program.

Lisa Looger contacts Adrian Early to let him know of offender Papke's change of mind. Adrian, undeterred by Andrew's previous reluctance, tells Looger that he is still fully committed to participating in the process.

A week and a half later, Andrew is summoned to the prison doctor's office. Recently, a nurse in this same office drew two vials of his blood according to routine practice. The doctor enters the small room where Andrew has been waiting and says the lab results reveal that he's not taking his meds. This is not allowed, the doctor tells him. The doctor inquires if Andrew is going through a manic phase or if he's experiencing heightened hostility.

Andrew tells the doctor that it's nothing like he's implied, but that he doesn't want to continue what he was doing when he was drinking—numbing his pain and anger. "Listen, doctor, I'm a normal human being and I did something terrible which I feel horrible about ... it kills me inside. And I don't know how I'm going to deal with it. But I don't want to take these meds anymore, and I don't want to get in trouble for not taking them."

The doctor, with Andrew's file before him, looks over his reading glasses at Andrew with a raised eyebrow. After a moment of silence, he responds by saying that Andrew doesn't have the meds in his system and that there aren't any recent disciplinary reports on his file.

Okay, he says—he'll put an order into the prison psychiatrist requesting that he stop Andrew's drug therapy.

Chapter 27

David Doerfler drives up from Austin to the Holliday Unit to check in with Andrew about his initial progress in the preparation process.

Dressed in jeans and boots, Doerfler greets Andrew with a smile in the chaplain's office. After sitting down at a small table and dabbling in some conversation about Andrew's formative years in Austin, Doerfler asks him what changed his mind about restarting the Victim-Offender Dialogue program.

Andrew responds that he just wasn't ready before, and that surviving in the prison environment was simply all he could handle. Now, however, he's committed to doing whatever it takes to make things better for the families he victimized. He wants them to know that he's sorry, and he wants them to feel that justice is being served.

Doerfler tells Andrew that he understands he pleaded guilty at his trial.

"Yes, sir, it was the right thing to do," Andrew offers.

Doerfler reconfirms that Andrew accepts complete fault and responsibility for the deaths of David Holland and Bethany Early—and that he has no expectation of a sentence reduction due to his participation in this program.

"Yes, sir," Andrew states plainly.

The Victim Services representative explains to Andrew that the program will give him the opportunity to process on a deeper level his ways of thinking that led up to the wreck and his emotions and feelings since the accident. What Doerfler says, Andrew realizes, is strikingly similar to what Chaplain Jameson said to him in the Travis County Jail.

"Crime creates relationships," Doerfler says to Andrew as he gives him a folder with additional reading material and worksheets. One of the first exercises to complete, he says, will have him consider the impact of his crime on his victims. Also, the exercise will ask him to put himself in his victims' shoes. Empathy—the ability to emotionally identify with his victims—decreases the likelihood that he will re-offend.

Whether he likes it or not, Doerfler tells him, Andrew Papke has a relationship with the Earlys and Hollands. A criminal trial, Doerfler continues, can end up being a contest between attorneys, with the main players—victims and offenders—becoming disposable commodities. Ultimately Andrew has wronged these two families, and he needs to answer to them.

Doerfler stands and places a hand on Andrew's shoulder, saying that he's made a good decision but that it's going to take a lot of work to get to the meeting table with Mr. Early. "Andrew, this is a process, and it's not going to happen in one or two or three steps. Healing is sloppy work. But this program is the closest thing we have to pure accountability." Depending on how the preparation process goes, Doerfler says, it might be six months or a year until Andrew sits down with this particular victim of his crime, Adrian Early, face to face.

Andrew stands to meet Doerfler's eyes and tells him he's ready to give it a try, however long it takes.

t's 2:00 a.m. on Friday, May 7, 1999. A guard approaches Andrew's bunk and kicks it forcibly. Andrew, sound asleep, startles. The guard kicks Andrew's footlocker. The loud clanging tells Andrew that his time has come.

"Papke, what's your number?"

"791425."

"Get up! Pack your stuff. You're on the chain bus."

Per prison custom, transport happens in the dead of night. Andrew's first stop in the system, at Huntsville's Holliday Unit, has ended. He scurries to round up his meager possessions from his footlocker and bunk. He has fifteen minutes to fit them into a metal container, 1' x 1' x 2,' slightly larger than his footlocker. He'll place the metal container into a commissary sack that will be thrown in the back of the transport bus along with the sacks of other prisoners. Each sack and metal box will be thoroughly inspected when the prisoners arrive at their new destination.

At the bottom of his commissary sack, safely protected inside the metal box and couched between the pages of his preparation materials packet, are sacred pictures held together by a rubber band: Andrew standing proud in front of his Camaro from high school days, he and Krista riding horses on a beach, Andrew sitting in Grandfather Dunlap's lap as a boy in front of a Christmas tree, and individual photos of family members. He's carefully fit everything he has, from treasured photos and letters to personal hygiene items and a second pair of shoes, into the box.

He steps onto the chain bus with other inmates, each one handcuffed to another, and hears that they'll be going to the Ferguson Unit, twenty miles northwest of Huntsville. Ferguson, just outside of Midway, Texas, is a medium security unit that exclusively houses younger inmates. Their crimes include aggravated robbery, burglary, murder, and manufacturing or possession of drugs.

Because of its younger population—only a minority of inmates are older than twenty-five—Ferguson is noisy, raucous, and more dangerous for inmates and prison personnel than other units, unlike the penitentiary system's main unit in Huntsville, called The Walls, which is generally populated by older inmates.

Like the Holliday Unit, the Ferguson Unit doesn't have air conditioning for its prisoners. Neither does it have heat. Even though it houses up to 2,100 inmates like the Holliday Unit, it has tighter quarters and employs more security personnel. Ferguson is riddled with racial tensions and gangs. The prison is nicknamed "Gladiator Farm" for the reputation of its inmates who like to fight—as if they were long-lost descendants of Roman gladiators who fought wild animals and condemned criminals to death in front of violence-loving fans in the Roman Colosseum.

Andrew is put into a cell at Ferguson. He doesn't know a single person—not an inmate, guard, or prison employee. He feels like he's starting over. The fear that's lodged in his psyche has him constantly watching his back as he scopes out his new surroundings.

Two weeks after his meeting with Doerfler, Andrew, now in his cell at Ferguson, reads about the 1974 criminal case that started the modern Restorative Justice movement. In Elmira, Ontario, two drunken teenagers vandalized twenty-two properties during a two-hour crime spree. They were arrested the next day. Frustrated by the recycling of offenders through the criminal justice system, a probation officer suggested to the presiding judge that the two offenders meet their victims face to face. Surprisingly, the judge concurred.

A few days later, the offenders walked up to their victims' front doors, accompanied by two probation officers. From one house to another, the two offenders apologized to their victims, heard them out, asked for forgiveness, and agreed on monetary restitution. They assured the victims that the occurrence was a random act of violence. Some of the victims offered forgiveness, whereas other victims wanted the offenders duly punished. One of the offenders, a man named Russ Kelly, would later say that meeting the victims face to face was the hardest thing he had done to that point in his life.

Nervous energy jolts through Andrew's body as he personalizes what he reads about the offenders encountering their victims in person.

Andrew reads on about the differences between two types of justice—retributive and restorative. The often-heard phrases, "If you do the crime, you do the time," and "Pay your debt to society," make sense to him as descriptions of retributive justice. Police, courts of law, judges, jails, and prisons—entities that he knows intimately—constitute retributive justice. But, the material asks, where do crime victims fit in, and how are their needs addressed?

Restorative Justice, Andrew reads, focuses on giving crime victims a chance to be heard and to dictate what really matters for the resolution of their issues. He thinks of Richard Holland and Adrian Early giving their victim impact statements, neither speaking more than ten minutes on the last day of his trial. He remembers Maria Soriano's impact statement, and how she could hardly read what she had written, bits of it emotionally discharged in Spanish through tears and sobbing. Difficult as it was for Andrew to hear what they had to say, he knew he needed to hear it. What if any of them—or other victim family members—had more to say to Andrew on a different day?

Some victims, the reading material states, are stuck with unspeakable pain and unresolved issues from the crime event—even after the legal resolution of the trial and a guilty verdict. A face-to-face encounter in a safe environment with the particular offender who has torn apart their life can help a victim find hope and resolution. This is the main goal, the reading says, of Restorative Justice. Paradoxically, the material continues, offenders are sometimes able to discover a self-awareness and an empathy that helps them embrace deeper accountability and, consequently, experience rehabilitation.

Taking out a pen, Andrew prepares to respond to the first written assignment in the packet. It challenges him to consider—at a level he's never approached before—the impact of his crime on his victims. He sees the first page of questions and digs in. *Give me the courage, Lord, to tell the truth the best I can.*

It's late in May 1999, and Andrew has plenty of homework—a new type of truth-telling—to keep him busy for a number of months. He works in the evenings in the privacy of his cell, slightly removed from the tension and turmoil lurking just outside of it.

During the day, the suffocating laundry room at Ferguson exhausts him. Along with his workmates, he washes and dries bedsheets, towels, T-shirts, boxers, socks, and the dull white prison-issued tops and bottoms that he and all other inmates wear. The washers and dryers are industrial grade. The dryers could pass for human-sized hamster wheels. Heat surrounds Andrew and his co-workers: the torrid sun radiating down on Ferguson, the blue flames hissing from the dryer motors powered by natural gas, and the hot air that expels from the inmates' lungs as they lug around hundreds of pounds of laundry every shift.

Andrew doesn't mind the work because it tends to distract him from the stark, day-to-day monotony of prison existence. Labor is a way for him to keep his head down and spend less time in prison. Hard workers not only merit respect from prison guards and fellow prisoners but gain half-days of credit against their sentences. At slow moments during his shift in the laundry room, however, he wishes he was back outside working in the fields at the Holliday Unit. The sun was scorching and the work rigorous, but the distraction was greater.

During their meeting in the chaplain's office back at the Holliday Unit, David Doerfler told Andrew that he had an alternative name for the initial assignment in the packet: "the empathy development program." For two and a half weeks now at the Ferguson Unit, Andrew has wrestled with this first chunk of homework. From the open-ended questions about perceiving his victims' feelings about his crime and its effects on them, Andrew has formulated a "crime impact statement." He's built it upon the things Richard Holland, Adrian Early, Maria Soriano, and others said during his trial, but he's stretched his awareness to new places. It's not just the chair at the family table left empty by David or Beth during holidays, but the little things that remind their family members of their absence: hearing a favorite song of theirs on the radio, noticing a young woman with flowing hair like Beth's, seeing a young man who drives by in a car customized like David's VW Beetle.

As Andrew looks at his responses to the assignment's questions, he notices a twist: Even as he comes to know more about what his crime did to the Earlys and Hollands, he'll never fully understand the pain and difficulty experienced by these two families he's victimized—ever.

Lisa Looger has driven up to the Ferguson Unit to work with Andrew in the preparation process. Seated together in the chapel, she commends Andrew for his initial work on the crime impact statement, telling him that he's making progress.

But, she says, he needs to step it up. The open letter that he wrote—Andrew asked his dad, the previous month, to send Lisa a copy of it—helps drive home her point. Yes, she says, it is about what he's lost, but the two families have lost so much more. "Less 'me,'" she says, "and more 'them.'" She suggests that he revise his letter now that he's completed the crime impact statement.

Healing is painful, she tells him, and most people—whether prisoners or civilians running free—don't want to go through the necessary steps. The discomfort these exercises bring, she says, will tell him he's growing, even in this prison environment. She tells him to keep at it, even though the required work might bruise a few spots in his heart.

The following week Andrew tackles the next assignment in the preparation packet. What he reads stuns him like a bucket of cold water thrown in his face. He purposely doesn't imagine leaving prison because of his forty-year sentence—he knows such a fantasy would only make his present reality worse. If he were, however, to achieve freedom from confinement, the second assignment asks, how much worse would it be to re-offend and have to come back?

The reading challenges him to examine his feelings and how they relate to his actions: "Usually, people don't get into trouble when they feel competent, loved, or important. People who feel they have their lives under control don't do things that cause arrest and imprisonment. But when they feel that their lives are not under control, that they are alone and others don't care about them, there is danger.

"How you feel influences how you behave. If you don't pay attention to your feelings, if you stuff them, ignore them, and don't address the needs that your feelings are pointing to, you can get in serious trouble. There are typical patterns which lead people into trouble. You should learn about these patterns and how they apply to you. After you learn about the problems connected with these patterns, you need to learn what you can do to help keep you out of trouble."

The assignment asks Andrew to consider a scenario where he could re-offend. He imagines himself out of prison, but alone and feeling lonely on Christmas Eve. Lighting up a cigarette, he remembers a gift bottle of champagne in a holiday fruit basket. Not wanting to be rude to the giver of the basket, he decides to pop the cork. He tells himself he'll just have one glass of cheer. Feeling better after one glass, he pours another and watches the little bubbles dance. He dulls his guilt about drinking with the rationalization that Christmas comes only once a year. As he finishes his last cigarette, he decides to drive to a quick mart store right around the corner to get more smokes. On his way there, he remembers he forgot his wallet and skids out a quick U-turn. In the process, he crashes into another car and commits the same offense that killed two people and put him in the slammer for forty years in the first place.

In his packet he writes the following conclusion: "I know it's not safe for me to ever have a drink of alcohol again. Not a hard decision—alcohol makes me smell blood and burning oil."

PART IV

MORE LETTERS

Chapter 28

very evening at the Ferguson Unit, guards change shift at 6:00 p.m. Weekdays, the new guard on duty carries a mail bag over his shoulder from the prison post office. All of the mail in his bag—minus confidential mail from lawyers representing prisoners—has been checked and read through, passing inspection. After taking the shift-change prisoner count, the guard calls out the names of the lucky ones who have received mail. The mail bag doesn't contain junk mail—when a prisoner's name is called by the guard, it's usually a good thing.

Like a drill sergeant, the guard yells out, "Papke." Andrew takes a letter from him and reads the name and return address on the envelope. Seeing "Martha Early" makes his heart clench. Andrew had written a long letter of apology to the Earlys the previous year. Martha's letter is dated June 3,

1999. Her flowing handwriting appears gentle and neat on six pages of notebook paper.

"Dear Andrew—I am sure you have been anxiously waiting to see if you would hear from me. I have not had the chance to write back to you because of how busy I am. I suppose Adrian has told you he and I are divorced ..."

A cold chill pulses through his body as he immediately wonders how the wreck impacted the Earlys' marriage. He reads on as Martha explains that she's had to go back to work to support her two sons and that she comes home exhausted every day, but thankful for church friends and relatives that help her make ends meet.

"Now," she continues, "let me focus on the real intent of this letter. Andrew, I <u>forgave you</u> soon after the wreck." Tears well up in Andrew's eyes as he reads the two words that Martha underlined. He continues reading.

"I am a Christian, saved at age twenty-five. I had gone to church all my life, but never knew Christ personally— never had a true relationship with him as a teen. I strayed and drank and went to bars. I felt I was no better than you, then, because I could have caused a wreck and killed someone too ...

"Besides all that, as a Christian, God's spirit dwells within me. He commands us to forgive all who hurt us. When Bethany was taken so violently and suddenly from me, it was such a shock—I felt no emotions for days. God's word seemed empty when I read it, but God was there to carry me. I turned to Him and knew I had to forgive you.

"I pictured Bethany's spirit at the scene of the wreck being taken by an angel of the Lord to be with Christ. I had sickening butterflies in my stomach, though, for weeks every time I thought of how horrible she must have looked—crushed, mangled, and bloody. I read the autopsy and tried to picture it in my mind. That's when the tears came.

"I heard that you went forward for baptism at Bannockburn Baptist Church several months after the wreck and accepted Christ. I do hope this was genuine. The deaths of David and Beth were not good, but through it, God can bring good from it. So, I hope the work you are doing will have positive results.

"Life is hard for me now, but the joy of the Lord is my strength (Psalm 16:11; Psalm 43:4–5). I cannot waste my energy and time being angry, bitter, or resentful. I turn that sort of stuff over to the Lord. The anger, bitterness, and resentment would only hurt me.

"It was a struggle within me to know you had to be punished in some way, and I know prison was a bad place to be, but I also felt you had to pay for the bad choices you had made or else you would never learn. God forgives you, but you still have to live with your choices and the bad ones are hard to live with, but God's grace is sufficient."

She closes the letter by telling Andrew that she will pray for him and that he may write back to her.

Maria Soriano, doing her best to reconstruct her life without her oldest son, receives some bad news. Someone has vandalized the memorial she and others dedicated to David and Beth on Brodie Lane more than two years earlier on Mother's Day. The cross that she personally brought from her native Mexico and placed in the wet cement with her own hands has been yanked from the ground and stolen. "It was like someone had slapped me in the face," she tells a newspaper reporter. She says that she'll go back and place a new cross at the wreck site. "That place is meaningful to me because David didn't die in a hospital or in a house or in my arms. He died there."

A few weeks later, a friend helps her place a new, metal cross, painted white, at the memorial site. The names "David" and "Beth," lettered in black on the horizontal bar, flank a centered image of a butterfly. Despite the early summer heat, Maria wears black. When the original cross was placed in the wet cement more than two years before, she was accompanied by close to twenty people, with a newspaper reporter jotting notes. Today she's practically alone in her labor and her remembering.

A hot, mid-day, August sun beats down on Kim Thonhoff's car as she drives home from setting up her kindergarten classroom. In less than two weeks, excited five-year-olds and their nervous parents will energize her classroom with zest and commotion. Today, though, she enjoyed the classroom's stillness and friendly conversations in the hallway with other teachers making their own preparations.

Her trip home on FM 1626 to Brodie Lane this day traces the exact path she traversed with her son Travis a little more than three years ago on the last Saturday night in June. Approaching the wreck scene, she slows her car as the road bends right. Kim sees a woman tending to the memorial for David and Beth. Her conscience tells her to stop, but she reasons that she doesn't want to invade the person's privacy. She proceeds to her home.

Later that night, Kim tells her husband what she saw when she passed by the wreck site and how sadness and heartbreak dominated the rest of her afternoon. She regrets not stopping to say hello and pay her respects. The woman at the site, she guesses, had to be either Beth's or David's mother.

Before turning out her bedside lamp that night, Kim vows that every time she passes by the site, she will say a prayer of healing for David's mom, the Hollands, the Earlys, and the Papkes. The cross placed there, Kim will write in her journal the next morning, will remind her to pray for them.

Chapter 29

Adrian Early and his fiancée, Kathy, head from Austin toward Midway, Texas, on Thursday, October 14, 1999. Lisa Looger has asked Adrian to come to the Ferguson Unit a day ahead of time to get ready for his face-to-face dialogue with Andrew.

Looger gives Adrian a late afternoon tour of the Ferguson Unit. It's standard procedure for participants in the Victim-Offender Dialogue program to briefly tour the prison where their offender dialogue partner resides. Adrian has been to jails as a visitor before, but it's his first time inside a penitentiary. The last place Lisa shows Adrian is the contact visitation room where the dialogue will take place.

The next morning, just before 9:00 a.m., Adrian and Lisa walk into the visitation room together and take their seats at the table. Another Victim Services employee, who drove up with Lisa from Austin the previous day, makes last minute adjustments to a videotape camera anchored to a tripod. A few moments later, Andrew arrives accompanied by a prison guard. Lisa thanks the guard and lets him know she doesn't need him to stay in the room. Lisa's co-worker presses the camera's record button as Andrew approaches Adrian to shake his hand.

"It's good to see you, Mr. Early," Andrew offers. Adrian, in his mid-forties, returns the greeting in a manner cordial and respectful.

As Andrew takes his seat at the table, he recalls the pictures he's viewed of Bethany and realizes that she inherited her blonde hair and high forehead from her father, and her sweet smile and curly hair from her mother.

Andrew does his best to mask his intense nervousness. Although he's been in this room a handful of times visiting with family, this meeting is completely unlike visiting with his dad or Krista. He considers the possibility that Mr. Early might explode and let him have it. If he does, Andrew tells himself, it would be completely understandable. Yesterday Lisa told him that Adrian had the best intentions coming into their meeting. Still, Andrew can't be sure.

Adrian Early, much shorter than Andrew, wears large, wire-rimmed, rectangular glasses that contrast yet harmonize with his round bearded face and balding head.

Andrew apologizes for having halted the dialogue preparation process earlier, explaining that he just wasn't ready. Adrian responds with an inviting and kind smile and says he's glad that Andrew is ready now.

Lisa Looger tells both men that she's encouraged by the work they've done to prepare for the dialogue. She asks Adrian to start.

The main reason he wanted to participate in this process, he says, is in response to Andrew's decision to take complete responsibility for Beth's and David's deaths. He's here today to validate Andrew's decision to fire his original lawyer and plead guilty at the trial. He's grateful for Andrew's cooperation with the prosecution.

Clearly articulate and intelligent, Adrian speaks in a measured way that contrasts with the reactive and confrontational language that Andrew has heard repeatedly from fellow inmates during his two and a half years in prison.

"It makes a big difference to me that you care, that you're really sorry," Adrian continues. "The legal system and justice are approximations of what should happen. I'm not sure that your stance has been taken into account in the punishment that was meted out."

Listening and nodding his head, Andrew wants Adrian to know he's doing his best to take in his every word. The prisoner's nervousness eases slightly as he realizes Adrian did not come to this meeting to yell at him or berate him.

Adrian tells Andrew that he would like to understand better what was going on in Andrew's head on the day of the wreck. Over the next ninety minutes, the engineer asks Andrew various questions to help piece together how one thing led to another, resulting in the deaths of two young people with extremely bright futures.

Andrew goes into greater detail about circumstances which Adrian knows about only generally: Andrew's frustration with the lack of direction in his life, the abortion, the all-day drinking, and the fateful flooring of the Acura's gas pedal on Brodie Lane just before 10:41 p.m. on the night of June 29, 1996. The details Andrew shares with Adrian are couched within a humble double offering: repentance for the act, and the promise to do anything that would ease the suffering of the two families he victimized.

After thanking Andrew for rehashing the details of the wreck, Adrian tells him that he survives by understanding how things work and why things happen the way they do. He says he has a deep need to learn from events, not only for his own benefit, but so that he might potentially be of benefit to others in the future by sharing what he's learned.

Lisa Looger has hardly spoken since the beginning of the mediation when she asked Adrian to start the dialogue. No prodding or guidance has been necessary from the mediator. She asks the two men if they'd like to take a brief break. Both decline.

Adrian says he'd like to continue the conversation in a chronological manner and tell Andrew of two experiences he had shortly after Beth's death, that gave him significant insight into the grieving process.

The first occurred at a grocery store a few months after Beth's passing. Adrian says that after his daughter's death he tried not to focus on the fact that a drunk driver had killed his daughter. He wanted to postpone his anger if he could, in an effort to control it. He wanted to concentrate on the loss of Beth free of indignation and rage.

"One evening in the grocery store checkout line with my sons, while I was buying some potato salad for a potluck meeting of 'For the Love of Christi,' a support group for families of drunk-driving victims, my 'managing anger' charade was broken. A man in front of me had stepped away to pick up something additional to buy. He came back in line with a twelve-pack of beer. I got very angry. It was all I could do to refrain myself from grabbing the carton of beer, smashing it on the floor, and screaming at him that a drunk driver had killed my daughter. The man paid for his items and went on, totally oblivious to my turmoil inside. I drove the boys to the meeting, working hard to keep my anger under control but driving at a higher rate of speed than I should have.

"I was never some anti-drinking extremist, either before or after Beth's death. But I was filled with rage at that time because of what had happened. The grocery store customer's actions were just a trigger for releasing my anger.

"Once the dam of anger was broken, it came out fairly regularly." Adrian clears his throat and tells Andrew that he's discovered that emotions serve as a bridge between life events. Losing Bethany, he says, was an immense tragedy, but the anger he felt over her loss became linked to an earlier event when a supervisor lied to him about a business matter as Adrian was leaving his position with the company. The two events were completely unrelated, but anger fused them together.

"Fortunately, I was allowed to take walks at my new job when I needed a moment away. While taking a walk one day, I was thinking about the fact that my previous supervisor had lied to me. I thought I was sufficiently over the anger that I experienced during the walk, and I was returning to work. I didn't realize I was totally unprepared to control my actions.

"For some reason, as I was taking the elevator to my office, I became totally consumed with rage. I was yelling and swearing and smashed several glass mirror panes in the elevator with my fists before the door opened and someone called, 'Hey, what's going on?' Andrew, I now understand the term 'fit of rage.' I had absolutely no control over myself until that other voice brought me back to reality. I had to have the blood washed from my hands and went to the emergency room for stitches."

Adrian tells Andrew that this fit of rage occurred shortly before the beginning of the trial in April of 1997. Trying to be strong for his wife and his kids, even as his marriage was teetering, Adrian was carrying more of a burden than he realized. If Andrew had pleaded not guilty, Adrian says, he's not sure how he would have handled it.

Adrian takes off his glasses and rubs his eyes. After a pause, he tells Andrew that his honesty at the time of the trial was a gift. He looks directly into Andrew's brown eyes and says that his honesty now is also a great gift. Andrew has never heard anyone say such a thing to him before.

The two men heed Lisa's suggestion to take a break. Andrew and Adrian have talked for more than three hours.

The conversation resumes and the two men talk about marriage. Adrian assures Andrew that the wreck was not the cause of his and Martha's divorce. Perhaps, he says, the wreck sped up the process of the marriage's inevitable dissolution. Andrew shares the news of his and Krista's proxy marriage. Adrian smiles and congratulates him.

Adrian asks Andrew about prison life and what he's doing specifically to improve himself. Andrew tells him that he's studying for a paralegal degree and continues to be involved in A.A. and various correspondence courses with Bible schools.

Encouraging Andrew to continue his studies and self-improvement pursuits, Adrian says that Andrew can add value not only to his own life but to the lives of others. This, he says, is of utmost importance—it's what we've been put on earth to do.

Andrew says he feels compelled to speak to youth. He tells Adrian about the open letter he wrote and says that through his dad's efforts, an insurance company contacted Andrew and received permission from the warden to do a video with him, intended for teenage drivers. The video portrays what can happen from bad choices and shows the reality of life in prison. If he can reach one kid, then it's worth it.

Adrian says he completely agrees.

Forgiveness, Adrian tells Andrew after another break, was not his original purpose when he asked to meet with Andrew. He tells Andrew that even though he is a deeply committed Christian, that's not why he wants to forgive him. Andrew's guilty plea at the trial was the starting point. And now, two and a half years later, Adrian says, he can tell that Andrew is working hard on changing his lifestyle. It only makes sense to forgive him.

"I forgive you, Andrew," Adrian says, looking directly at the inmate whose actions permanently altered his and his family's life. In response, Andrew whispers, "Thank you," while hanging his head and muttering that he doesn't deserve any forgiveness.

Adrian reassures the younger man of his forgiveness and asks Andrew to look at him.

Adrian waits until their eyes lock. "I've forgiven you, Andrew." He pauses before upping the ante. "Now, I want you to forgive yourself."

Andrew stammers to respond. He looks down again and bites his lip.

The father, who's carried so much sadness, persists and repeats his bewildering demand. The criminal, burdened with the feeling that he owes an unpayable debt to his counterpart, listens but can't respond.

A deep silence settles on the room.

At 4:00 p.m., Lisa suggests that the two men work on a requirement of the dialogue, the "affirmation agreement." David Doerfler included the affirmation agreement in the preparation manual as a way to extend accountability beyond the face-to-face encounter between two adversaries.

Andrew insists that Adrian, when anger resurfaces about the wreck and Beth's death, should get angry at him and not at God. Andrew emphasizes that it wasn't God who caused the wreck, and it wasn't the devil either—it was fully his responsibility.

Adrian, for his part of the agreement, insists that Andrew continue his education while in prison, that he love himself as he loves his neighbor, and that he should genuinely be himself. Andrew told Adrian that prison culture requires an inmate to keep his head down or wear a tough-guy mask in order to survive. All the same, Adrian says, he wants Andrew to take a few moments each day to recall who he really is.

Lisa Looger has both men sign the agreement that she wrote as they spoke. She compliments both of them for their attentiveness to each other and their conversation. Then she asks both men if they'd like to pray together. Both nod their heads. After the long prayer, which mirrors the territory that the men have covered—understanding, self-improvement, forgiveness, faith—Adrian and Andrew stand to shake hands. The handshake turns into a long embrace. The men thank each other and then thank Lisa. Tears blot and redden all of their eyes. Lisa's co-worker hits the off button one last time on the video recorder. It's 6:00 p.m.

Later in the evening, Adrian drives home to Austin with his fiancée, as do Lisa and her co-worker. A crescent moon looks down on their paths. Andrew goes back to his cell, so drained that his shoulders slump and his feet drag as he walks. Even so, his sleep this night is not restful. He dreams again of Brodie Lane and of the demolition, by his hands, that the Acura brings upon the VW Beetle, and upon all those who love its two unfortunate passengers.

Chapter 30

Kim Thonhoff sits under the same crescent moon in the bleachers at Burger Stadium in South Austin on this October evening. She and her husband Bob watch a Bowie Bulldogs football game. They support the team, but they're much more interested in the upcoming halftime show. Their son Travis, now a fourteen-year-old freshman, marches in the band with a trombone as did his older brother, who graduated from Bowie the previous spring.

Earlier that afternoon on her way home from teaching her kindergartners, she passed by David's and Beth's memorial site and said a prayer for healing, comfort, and strength for all the families involved—the Earlys, Hollands, and Papkes. Today she also included D.R. and his mom in her hushed petitions.

The football game ends and the band members load all their equipment onto the band program's semi-truck trailer. Kim, Bob, and Travis finally arrive home just before midnight. Kim is spent and quickly falls asleep.

As she's done many times, she dreams about the wreck, especially the figure of the woman running, stride by desperate stride, past parked-car headlights that illuminate her adrenaline-fused sprint to the crumpled Acura. Kim sees her face close up, filled with horror and shock, revealing its deepest fear: What if the boy in the passenger seat of the Acura is dead?

In the morning, Kim tells her husband that the nightmare happened again, that she immediately awoke with a start and couldn't go back to sleep for the longest time. Bob gives her a hug just as he did more than three years ago in the ditch a mile from their home, when Kim was unable to drive the van after what she saw.

At Bowie High School, where Andrew, Krista, D.R., and Robbyne attended, cheers spill out from the second-story room where the journalism class gathers to study and work. Their teacher has just fist-pumped while holding up a copy of the student newspaper's second edition for the new school year and tells the class they've done great work. The cover of the *Lone Star Dispatch,* dated October 22, 1999, invites readers to look at a story on page thirteen, "A former student's letter from prison." Andrew's open letter is reproduced as an in-depth feature, the first of three parts. The subsequent parts will be reproduced in the following two editions later that fall.

When the school year started, Andrew asked his stepmom to send a revised version of his open letter to Bowie High School, written specifically for its students. Andrew tells them that he was in their shoes from 1990–1994, and that they have an opportunity to learn from his mistakes. He signs the open letter, after thanking them for reading the letter all the way through, "Pleadingly."

Almost two years after handwriting his open letter intended for students like him, it goes public. Bowie is the
biggest high school in the Austin area. The print order for
the *Lone Star Dispatch* numbers more than 3,000, enough so
that a copy of the newspaper ends up in the hands of each
student.

Chapter 31

Karen Gonsoulin, a teacher at a correctional high school north of Austin, walks out onto the driveway of the house where she lives with her husband and two college-aged kids. She won't see her students today. It's New Year's Eve morning, December 31, 1999, and she reaches down to pick up her copy of the *Austin American-Statesman,* chucked onto her drive before dawn.

At the breakfast table with her husband, she throws aside the front section. She tells him she'd rather sit on a tack than have to read another article about the potential Y2K—Year 2000—catastrophe. They've already decided to spend a quiet evening at the home of good friends and to take a long walk in the morning. They're confident the world will still be spinning in the new year and will simply wait to see if their home computer boots up like normal, averting the rumored disaster.

An article on the front page of the Life and Arts section, titled "Letter from prison: A night of drinking, a life of regret," draws her attention. She sees the double-image of a young man's mug shot, straight on and profile—it could easily be one of her students—accompanying the article. Underneath the image, the caption reads: "Andrew Papke, the writer of this open letter, will be in prison until 2036." She begins to plow through the article, subtitled "Drunken driver says: If you party hearty tonight, don't drive."

The article's words spill onto the second page of the section, and she turns to where it continues under the subtitle, "Drunken driver finds reason for living." Silently, her eyes race as she reads to the closing paragraphs:

As I sit here in my cell, I wonder if you are listening enough to think about this the next time you drink. Ask yourself: "Is it worth it?" "Do I want to wake up tomorrow a murderer?" "Do I want to wake up tomorrow at all?" If you do cause a tragedy like this, you will be lucky if it only kills you.

Do yourself a favor and listen. If not, well, from all of us here in Huntsville, we'll leave the light on for ya'.

Karen tells her husband to read the article. She says she's going to take the piece to school and use it with her students.

Like he did with his letter to Bowie High School, Andrew reworked his original open letter, and then tailored the ending to directly question youth who are doing the same types of things that he was doing when he was their age. He asked his stepmom to send this latest version of the open letter to the Austin newspaper after the Bowie High School newspaper printed its version. An *Austin American-Statesman* staffer edited it down to one thousand words. A special New Year's Eve run of 175,000 newspapers was printed, with one of the copies landing on Karen Gonsoulin's driveway and another on Howard and Cathy Papke's driveway.

Later that week, Howard Papke pens a letter to his imprisoned son. "Hey," the father writes, "you made the paper again." This time, however, he notes that it's for a much more positive reason than when Andrew's crimes and felony trial were detailed by the same newspaper.

Gonsoulin, a thirty-year veteran teacher, is in her fourth year of teaching at the correctional school north of Austin where she receives students, in various forms of trouble, for six-week cycles from the school district's regular high school and middle schools. To teach both English and social skills, she regularly assigns her students a letter-writing project. She tells her students to write a teacher, a family member, a friend, a military service person, a business, or a public entity. Her goal with the assignment is to help her students develop social skills, and she figures it will enhance their job prospects in the future.

The first week of January 2000, after having read Andrew's open letter in the Austin newspaper, she gives her students one additional letter option for the assignment. She tells them they can write a letter to a prisoner named Andrew Papke and say how alcohol has affected them personally or someone in their family. She passes out a copy of Andrew's article from the newspaper and develops the topic further, telling them about her dad and her first husband and the difficulties alcohol created for them, and how she has never tasted alcohol in her life.

"As far as I'm concerned, if this young man had killed one of my kids, he could rot in prison." Indirect but blunt, she's telling her students not to drink and drive.

Letters from Austinites and other Central Texans who saw Andrew's article in the newspaper arrive for him in Huntsville. One Austinite writes that he's new in the recovery community after his recent arrest for drunk driving. Reading Andrew's moving story has left him feeling sad and lucky at the same time. One's life can suddenly change forever—the two of them did a similar thing, and he's sitting at a Starbucks drinking coffee while Andrew does time in Huntsville. The writer of the letter tells Andrew that he used to work at the Walls Unit and hopes that Andrew is safe and not being bullied. Reading Andrew's letter, he writes, reminds him not to take for granted being clean, sober, and free from incarceration. He tells Andrew to keep his chin up and that he'll keep him in his prayers.

Another Austinite writes to Andrew and commends him for the tremendous courage and honesty it took to share his feelings so openly. She says that she was in the courtroom during his trial, supporting her good friend Maria Soriano. She says that she identifies with the pain that all the moms—not only Maria, but Helen, Martha, and Andrew's mom, Jan—have suffered because of the wreck.

The woman continues, however, that she most identifies with Andrew. An A.A. member with twelve years of sobriety, she admits to the past Christmas and New Year's holidays being hard—the first time in years she's felt left out and wishing she could drink. She started to think, "Oh, what's the use?" but then happened to read Andrew's letter in the newspaper. The article was for her an "epiphany, the showing forth of God working," reminding her how treasured a gift sobriety is in her life. Thanking Andrew again for his letter's sincerity, she tells him that she's shared his letter with her sponsor and other friends in A.A. She closes with a blessing and a wish for good luck, and reminds Andrew, using A.A. lingo, to look not for differences with other human beings, but similarities.

By the end of the second week in January, Karen Gonsoulin's students start to turn in their letter-writing assignments. She is shocked by what the kids put on her desk. There's no deviation. Every student's first letter is written to Andrew Papke. The students relate to him and tell him so by what they write to him. Many claim to have made poor and regrettable decisions while drunk. Some have driven drunk, and many have parents that drive drunk. They like Andrew's honesty. Most of the letters, while not approving of his behavior, strike appreciative and sympathetic tones. A few, however, tell Andrew he deserves the consequences he's suffering.

Usually, Karen sees basic, one-paragraph letters, written to a family member or teacher, churned out for the assignment. Numerous multiple-page letters to Andrew Papke are now piling up on her desk. Later that night she tells her husband that she had no idea this new assignment would take off. He tells her she's hit on something and she best run with it.

The next morning the teacher fires off a letter to the *Austin American-Statesman*. She wants to know how she can send her students' letters to Papke in Huntsville.

A few days later, she gets a phone call from a columnist at the newspaper, telling Karen that her letter will be published and asking if the paper may include her name with it. "Yes," Karen says. On Monday, February 14, the newspaper runs Karen's letter:

"The *Austin American-Statesman* printed a letter from Andrew Papke titled 'Letter from prison: a night of drinking, a life of regret.' I teach English at the alternative school in Leander and used his letter for an assignment. The students wrote Andrew a letter describing its impact on them. I would like to mail him the letters. Can I mail them to the *Statesman* to be forwarded, or mail them directly to Andrew at Huntsville?"

The columnist answers in print: "The *Austin American-Statesman* does not forward letters. Unless written by attorneys or the press, mail to inmates is opened before the inmate sees it. You may send the missives to Papke (No. 791425) at Huntsville Unit, P.O. Box 99, Huntsville 77342. Letters should not contain personal information or addresses."

That morning Howard Papke happens to read the column in his office at his auto shop. He's stunned by it and calls out to his wife who's crunching numbers in the back part of the office to tell her about the article.

Later that night, Karen Gonsoulin's phone rings. The man calling says, kindly and matter-of-factly, that he is Howard Papke, the father of Andrew. He tells Karen he's pleased that she's using his son's letter for her students. It's exactly what Andrew wanted, he explains, when he wrote the first version of his open letter over two years ago and asked that it be sent out to schools and churches.

"It's the first good thing that has come from him being in prison," Howard tells her. He says that while he feels complete compassion for the Early and Holland families, it's as if he's lost his son as well because of the long sentence he received. He'll do everything he can, he promises, to help facilitate the contact between her students and his son.

Karen hangs up the receiver. She briefly tells her husband about the call and what Howard told her. She then sits down, quieted, next to her husband on the living room sofa. After a while she tells him that there's another side to this story which she hadn't considered until now.

The teacher writes her own letter to the prisoner, dated February 17, 2000.

"I'm an English teacher at the alternative high school in Leander. Students who have been in serious trouble with alcohol, drugs, behavior, etc. are sent to our school for six weeks or longer. They're not allowed to talk, look around, or get up without permission. If they have a question, they must raise their hand. It is a very structured environment. We have boys and girls, sixth through twelfth grades, with different learning abilities, including a large number of special education students, all in the same room."

She explains the letter-writing assignment to Andrew and tells him that all the students have agreed to have their letters sent to him. She says she plans to use his letter in the future and will forward all the letters to him, good or bad, that the students write.

"I have talked to your father on two occasions. He told me some of what both of you have gone through. I shared this with my class. I also shared with the class how my daughter was out drinking one night when she was a junior in high school and agreed to take some boy home that she had never met before. She totaled her car, and luckily neither one was killed. My daughter could have killed someone because of drinking. I don't know what I would have done if my daughter had been sent to prison. I know what a good person she is and how people can make stupid decisions in relation to alcohol. I can tell how much your dad loves you and also how proud of you he is. I hope that there will be a time for you to be together again. May God bless you and keep you safe while you are in prison.

"Thank you again for taking the time to write your letter and share your experience in the hopes of preventing others from making the same mistake."

After Andrew receives the letter, he places it with his collection of treasured pictures and letters at the protected back of his footlocker.

Chapter 32

Post-midnight orders—this time a rattling of his cell bars—tell Andrew to gather his things so he can board a prison transport bus. He leaves the Gladiator Farm at Ferguson, chained to another prisoner, on a brilliantly clear and cold winter night. His next residence will be at the main unit of the expansive Texas penitentiary system called "The Walls." The name derives from the imposing red brick walls that encompass the structure in downtown Huntsville. Andrew has read about the unit's storied history—it was the only state penitentiary of the old Confederacy to survive the Civil War, and it served as the headquarters of the Texas prison system until the establishment of the Texas Board of Criminal Justice in 1989. Ominously, it houses Texas's notorious death row chamber, the most active in the United States since the reestablishment of capital punishment nationally in 1977, and in Texas in 1982.

Andrew's stay at the Ferguson Unit is cut short because he has applied to pursue a college degree. At The Walls he can take classes that are taught by local professors from Lee College, a junior college that began its prison extension program in the mid-1960s.

His first job assignment at The Walls is in the auto shop as support staff. Prison vehicles are maintained and serviced there, including some of the chain buses that transport prisoners in the dead of night. Plenty of inmates are experienced as mechanics. Andrew, on a waiting list to work in the garage, works in an adjacent office, logging maintenance information about prison vehicles into the computer system. He's happy to be away from the Gladiator Farm but would much rather turn wrenches and screwdrivers than punch a keyboard.

On his first Sunday at The Walls, he decides to attend worship at the chapel. Three plus years behind prison bars has accustomed him to his surroundings: endless razor wire and fencing, armed guards in watchtowers, bare white walls decorated only by warning signs, uncomfortable plastic chairs linked to table units in the chow halls, countless square feet of gray cement, indiscriminate yelling by inmates and guards, and drab looks on the faces of fellow prisoners.

What he hears and sees this morning as he enters the chapel stirs his soul: inmate musicians with instruments and voices joyously harmonizing; other inmates grinning and clapping to the beat; high ceilings framed by graceful wooden beams; straight-grained wooden pews, expertly cut and hewn, revealing skilled workmanship; a beautiful wood-paneled triangular wall behind the front altar area; fabric of vibrant colors adorning the altar; and a worship leader dressed in a suit coat and tie, smiling and reaching his hand out in welcome. As he moves toward the worship leader to shake his hand, Andrew steps onto padded carpet for the first time in three years.

Andrew feels like he's actually in church, somehow released from prison. He'll come back to this space that offers a feeling of liberation as much as he can.

He comes by the chapel often enough during his initial weeks at the Walls Unit that the chaplain, Ken Houston, tells Andrew that perhaps in the future, when there's an opening, he could work as one of his assistants. Andrew says, "Yes, sir—it would be an honor to do so."

The inmate commissary at The Walls carries a wide array of items: drinks, snacks, condiments, razors, soap, baby powder, nail clippers, reading glasses, shoes, long underwear, legal pads, stamps, art supplies—even protein powder for body-building inmates. Combination locks, to keep one's footlocker items squirreled away from curious or devious block mates, are a very popular item on the list.

Each inmate has an account that is supplemented by the wages he earns on the job and by any deposits made into the account by family or loved ones on the outside. No cash is exchanged at the commissary.

Andrew makes a special order at the commissary for the largest ticket item available—an electric typewriter. Only inmates who are enrolled as students, or doing legal work related to their own or a fellow inmate's case, are allowed to make the special purchase of a typewriter, as its purchase price of just under $200 far exceeds the permissible amount of inmate purchases per quarter.

He enthusiastically shows the commissary employee his receipt of class registration from Lee College and walks away with a new, white Smith-Corona typewriter. Back in his cell, he plugs the typewriter's cord into the wall and hears the motor kick in and purr. His heart swells, just like the first time he revved his old Camaro's engine back when he was in high school.

In March, Andrew receives the first promised packet of letters from Karen Gonsoulin's students. In his cell, he reads the very first one:

"Dear Andrew: I read the letter you sent to Mrs. G. and I've heard about what you did. What you did is making me think twice about what I do. I've driven while drunk and have ridden in cars with drunk drivers many times and I don't want to make the same mistake that you made. Forty years isn't worth it. Thanks for taking the time to write and explain to all of us about the mistake that you made."

The next one is from a girl who explains that her dad paralyzed himself in a wreck while driving drunk, and then, a few years later, her boyfriend and his little sister died in a wreck, victimized by a drunk driver. She tells Andrew that she had to go to their funerals on consecutive days. "I hope people will realize there are other ways to have fun. Drinking is not fun. It hurts people, and it just isn't fun to vomit and have a headache the next day. My family has many alcoholics, and they don't realize how much it hurts everyone to go through their ups and downs."

In another letter, a seventeen-year-old girl writes: "Your letter made me think about not driving drunk more than any advertisement, commercial, video, lecture, or assembly that I have ever seen or heard."

He will send every one of the twenty-three letters to his dad and stepmom, who will meticulously archive them in a plastic file box.

This night, Andrew hardly sleeps. The stories from the students confirm the words he's adopted as his personal mission statement: *I can communicate with people like me so these types of tragedies don't happen anymore.* His usual preoccupations when he can't sleep—barbed wire, growling dogs, and guards who treat him as if he was sub-human—are replaced by hopeful thoughts that dart through his mind. Perhaps, he allows, he is a person who is actually making a positive contribution to society.

In the morning, he tells himself it's the best night of rotten sleep he's had in a long time.

Chapter 33

A few months after the chaplain talked to Andrew about working as an assistant, an opening comes up. Andrew now reports to the chapel almost every morning, ready to take orders from his immediate supervisor, Chaplain Ken Houston. Andrew helps Houston set up the chapel for Sunday worship and for prison ministries events during the week. Houston is a bear-sized man who worked the Alaska pipeline and taught computer classes to federal prisoners before going to seminary. Divorce—his own—drove him into prison chaplaincy. He knew he'd have trouble finding another church to pastor after his marriage breakup, so he headed back to prison, not to teach, but to preach. He figured, as he told a colleague at the time, some of the inmates didn't deserve another chance at freedom because of their crimes, but all of them had a right to hear the gospel and turn their lives around.

Occasionally, Andrew is required to go into the execution chamber at The Walls to help the chaplains and the warden in their preparations on execution days. The reality is not lost on Andrew—it's a thin line between life and death. The chamber, where the State of Texas carries out the most executions of any civilized locale in the world, is located directly adjacent to the chapel.

Karen Gonsoulin continues her new practice in the letter-writing assignment, and soon response letters to Andrew Papke again clutter up her desk. She reads each one, and then files them away to send later to Andrew.

An older male student who's been in her class for three weeks without speaking or completing a single assignment approaches Karen's desk and tosses a multiple-page letter for Andrew onto it. He mumbles something about having been friends with Bethany Early. As he returns to his seat, Karen glances over his letter and sees that it's laced with profanity. She reads through it and calls the student to her desk. She tells him that while she appreciates his work, he'll have to rewrite the letter and leave out the profanity. He doesn't respond, other than to snatch back his letter with a quick swipe. He slinks to his desk, sits down in his chair, and starts to scrawl. For the next forty minutes, with his head buried in his notebook and his long hair curtaining off his activity from the rest of the class, he creates a sanitized version of his original screed.

The older student refers to Andrew as a "piece of trash" and precisely details moments from Beth's high school years and depicts scenes from her visitation at the funeral home. He's not making things up—he unquestionably said goodbye to Beth, a very good friend, as he looked at her heavily made-up corpse in the casket.

The mildly disinfected redo letter, five hand-written, angry pages, disparages Andrew and his actions. Beth, the writer says, pulled him in when he was new at their high school and introduced him to many of her friends. He's waited for this day to find out more about Andrew in order to give him a piece of his mind. Drugs, drinking, and jail have been a part of the writer's life, but, he says, he has never done anything as stupid as driving while under the influence. He closes his extended rant by admitting that everyone makes mistakes, including himself. He demands that Andrew ask for forgiveness and signs off with an expletive.

A few weeks later when Karen sends another packet of letters to Andrew, she includes the letter from the student who knew Bethany, with an attached note warning Andrew of its acidic but honest contents.

Using his new white typewriter, Andrew writes Karen Gonsoulin on May 29, 2000, for the first time. He's received two packets of letters from her.

"Dear Karen: Greetings and salutations! I hope this letter finds you in the best of spirits and health. I pray you will forgive me for taking so long to respond. I make no excuses because the work you do and whatever help I may have to offer is of the highest priority. I should have written sooner, but my recent transfer, college, paralegal school, work, A.A., and church keep me busy. I often find that I have little time to do anything extra. Ironic, isn't it.

"Today, I stood less than seven feet from a man they would execute in seven hours. I see them come in alive and somber (some are rowdy—I can't say I wouldn't be) and I see them leave peaceful and dead. They served their sentence and will never come back here.

"I cannot see any relief coming to the victims, regardless of the punishment. Some things just cannot be undone no matter how many murders take place. In fact, I think I would probably feel some guilt if I were a victim's relative in one of these cases. They killed three this week and have seven more scheduled for the next month. Seeing a walking dead man makes me think.

"Mrs. Gonsoulin, how many faces do you see in your classes that, fueled by drugs and/or alcohol, will walk that long mile to the death chamber someday? How many are a natural-born menace? Not many I suspect. Not many here either. Once again—bad choices in a horrible way ... If you think that lethal injection is peaceful and painless, then join the duped public; it is not.

"So, I think to myself, what can I say to your students to make them listen? What would have made me listen? I am not going to die in here—at least I'm not scheduled to. I could be out in twenty or so years.

"The responses from your students really gave me a lot to think about. I paid special attention to the ones with negative feedback. Sure, it stings to hear that stuff, but after further thought I am glad. Teenagers seem to base all decisions on status. If they hate me and think I am stupid and really uncool, then they are more likely to try not to be like me.

"I know for a fact, that in the early stages of my drinking career, if I had my friends telling me what a piece of trash I was for drinking, I would not have been so fascinated by it. There is a lot to be said for that. Now, here I am, a real 'cool' dude—no sex, no malls, no McDonald's, no anything. No life and a lot of guilt for the victims' families.

"This place is a hell where you relive your every mistake and every loss every minute of the day ... I don't want sympathy, I just want people to learn, because when you kill someone, your whole world ends (never mind prison).

"This is not like in the movies. This is real. The pain behind senseless acts far outlives the brief enjoyment of said senseless acts. What I thought was fun got people killed, and it holds true for any reckless act or omission of responsibility. When I looked into the eyes of the mothers whose children I killed, my spirit wilted. I don't want to see that happen. So, if I can help or share—I will. I want to.

"Karen, I am only twenty-three. I don't know much. All I know is what we have been doing is not very effective with teenagers. We have the right motive and intended result, but where is the breakdown?

"I just thank you for not giving up on kids. I thank you for all that you do. I want to do more for you. Any questions, suggestions, or requests you have, just drop me a line. I am always anxious for any ideas that may break through and create good."

Chapter 34

The chapel at The Walls is a freestanding structure located off the main prison yard. It's as if a giant crane dropped an old-fashioned, country church building inside the prison complex. A pitched steeple rises high above the steps that lead into the chapel through its west side doors. Andrew's responsibility is to keep these steps free of tree debris, garbage deposited there by the wind, and spit from inmates. The steps ascend from a breezeway shared with the building where Warden Jim Willett and other administrators labor for public safety and hope for prisoner reformation.

One summer day while Andrew sweeps the chapel steps, he banters with a fellow prisoner on the other side of the breezeway. Near the entryway of the admin building, Jack May is using his broom, like Andrew, against the same contaminating foes.

Jack's light brown hair is shaded gray, and slight wrinkles ring his neck. He's older and shorter than Andrew, but his bland prison white shirt drapes a barrel-shaped upper body that attests to the years he's spent pumping iron in penitentiary weight rooms.

"Who you snitching on today, Bible boy?"

"You, old hillbilly, for kissing up in the admin office."

They both laugh and flick pebbles in the other's direction with their brooms.

Andrew and Jack have gotten to know each other well in the past few weeks, their prison jobs similar, as is their understanding of penitentiary culture and how to survive in it. Jack is old enough to be Andrew's father and has taken him under his wing. The first time they talked, they discovered a mutual admiration of cars and mechanics. Jack's first job at The Walls was in the auto shop. Andrew has told Jack that he'd prefer turning wrenches to sweeping, but working for the chaplain is much better than other jobs he's had, like cleaning dishes or working in the laundry room.

Jack has told Andrew that working for C.O.s—correctional officers—is good but that it's a challenge to keep a balance between trust with administrators and acceptance among fellow prisoners. Too much coziness, he says, with the C.O.s—or with the chaplains—and other prisoners figure you're a snitch.

Jack's confided to Andrew that he's doing time for drug manufacturing and distribution. He's served more than ten years of a long sentence after getting busted with a whole lot of methamphetamines and cash in his possession in a rural portion of Southwest Texas. Sheriff deputies nailed him on his property, which was then confiscated after his conviction. Early on in prison, he's told Andrew, he saw the error of his ways. A revival tent meeting in the prison yard at The Walls helped him come around, and he's committed his life to God ever since. He participates in as many prison ministry opportunities as he can and encourages Andrew to do the same. "You gotta watch your back," Jack coaches Andrew, "but you also need to keep your hand on the plow and move forward."

Andrew's learned that Jack doesn't have a large family. When he was arrested, he left behind a two-year-old son that he's not seen or heard of since. Not a single family member has come to visit him for the duration of his time in the Texas penitentiary system.

Right after Labor Day, Andrew receives a fresh stack of letters from Karen Gonsoulin's new students. A few days later, Andrew walks by the mail room. The supervisor, whose staff has the responsibility of viewing the contents of every single letter that arrives at P.O. Box 99 in Huntsville, including the stacks that come from Karen Gonsoulin's class, calls to Andrew and motions him in. This prison employee rarely gives inmates the time of day, much less a smile or kind word. Mildly surprised, Andrew walks over, expecting to hear a comment that reinforces their full difference in status—free and incarcerated—looming between them like a force field.

"Hey, Papke," he says in a serious and quiet tone, "I want to tell you something about all those letters you get from students." It's a voice completely void of its usual superiority. Andrew steps in closer. Looking directly at the inmate, the man slowly nods his head up and down. He then says with persuasion, "Keep doing what you're doing."

PART V

BALM

Chapter 35

The hot Texas summer sizzles into mid-September. It's the time of the year when boys and young men, sweat spilling from their pores, grapple in pads and helmets on football fields all over the state. A former Texas footballer named John Sage travels from Houston to Huntsville to rendezvous with Raven Kazen, who's traveling from Austin. Sage and Kazen got to know each other at a Restorative Justice gathering two years earlier where Kazen introduced him to Ellen Halbert. The two women helped Sage transform some of his ideas about prison ministry into a working program. Sage and Kazen will meet with Chaplain Ken Houston in his office at the Walls Unit. The three of them will finish up preparations for the implementation of Sage's prison ministry, Bridges To Life, at The Walls.

All new prison ministries at the Walls Unit must be approved through the chaplain's office, with the blessing of the warden. For the past three months, Sage has been on the phone with Kazen, Houston, and others, soliciting their guidance with the piles of paperwork needed to obtain TDCJ approval for the ministry and clearance for its volunteers to enter The Walls. Sage's football days are a distant memory, but the same type of ambition that spirited him on the football field drives him to do whatever is necessary to get his ministry's foot inside the door of The Walls. For Sage, it's infinitely more important than football. He does it in memory of his beloved sister, Marilyn.

Sage pulls into the parking lot of Huntsville's main prison unit and sees the imposing red brick walls. A nervous fluttering in his gut, Sage feels just like he used to before the start of so many football games. His ministry, which facilitates offenders meeting face to face with surrogate or substitute crime victims, is barely two years old, but it has garnered a reputation for positively influencing all of its participants. Warden Jim Willett is concerned about putting offenders and their crime victims together because of security issues and the potential for re-victimization. But he has green-lighted the ministry for a one-time run at The Walls. Unlike the Victim-Offender Dialogue program, inmates sign up for this ministry on their own. Some who have signed up are longtimers at The Walls, and Willett will use their feedback to determine if this ministry will get a second opportunity.

Chaplain Houston, Sage, and Kazen discuss the inmates who will participate in the program. Kazen asks Houston if his young assistant, Andrew Papke, will be part of it. She tells Sage and the chaplain that Papke, an intoxication manslaughter offender who successfully went through the

Victim-Offender Dialogue program, could also benefit from this ministry. As Houston scribbles Andrew's name on a legal pad, Sage says he has a husband and wife team in his pool of volunteer crime victims who Andrew Papke can learn from.

Sage has recruited six crime victims to tell their stories for the initial session at The Walls. First-time entry into a prison is potentially alarming for anyone, whether a new inmate or civilian. But first-time entry into a prison for a crime victim is potentially traumatic.

Two of Sage's crime-victim recruits are coming to a prison for the first time. Sage has assured them of their safety, telling them that they will enter and leave the prison as a group. He warns them not to be overly alarmed by a sign they will see once they get past the penitentiary's entry point. The sign that says "NO HOSTAGE NEGOTIATIONS BEYOND THIS POINT" actually serves to protect them, Sage claims, from the possible danger implied. The warden, he promises, will see to it that nothing goes wrong on the day they visit the Walls Unit to share their stories with inmates.

Sage leaves the meeting with the assurance that his up-start ministry will debut at The Walls in two weeks with full institutional support. The butterflies in his gut have been replaced with the type of excitement he felt long ago when his football team had a comfortable lead at halftime. Over dinner he tells his wife that if Bridges To Life can have a helpful impact at the Walls Unit, the flagship institution of the TDCJ, Warden Willett will spread the word, and Restorative Justice just might have a fighting chance in the sprawling Texas prison system.

Chapter 36

Two weeks later, Andrew and twenty-one other male prisoners, all dressed in bland prison whites, gather in the chapel for the introductory session of Bridges To Life. A few of the older inmates' faces appear weary and unenthused. Andrew hears one of them say that he's seen every type of prison ministry come and go in his years at The Walls. Andrew knows that this particular inmate has been in the system for more than twenty-five years. His identification number, unlike Andrew's, consists of only five digits.

John Sage leads the opening session as the prisoners listen to his explanation of the program's goals. Eleven more weekly sessions will follow. They'll be together until January 2001.

"Gentlemen, the purpose of this program is to help you deal with conflict and troubled relationships, and at the same time help you strive for internal peace and reconciliation. If you're willing to work hard in a thoughtful and structured way, you can make some headway on the issues you're dealing with. This program draws on the Bible, experiences of offenders just like you, and the trauma and pain of crime victims. Together, these will provide you tools to bridge your current life to a new life where you are more at peace with yourself, your God, your loved ones, and society. This program is new, and it's had success bringing offenders and crime victims together in journeys of healing and peace."

At first glance, Sage, solid and broad-shouldered, looks like someone not to mess with. He starred as a defensive lineman for football-crazed Louisiana State University in the early 1970s. His manner, however, is gentle, and his way of speaking puts listeners at ease. He smiles easily and often.

Sage tells them the journey won't be easy because it will include meeting victims of crime face to face. These surrogate victims will have stories of pain and desperation strikingly similar to the stories the victims of their own crimes have suffered and continue to suffer.

The program, he says, will challenge the inmates to fully understand the impact their crimes have caused. The only way to healing is the path of accepting responsibility for one's actions and being accountable. He can't, he says, force anyone to be accountable. But for those who are willing to embrace the process of confession, repentance, and forgiveness—reconciliation and restoration are within reach.

Proselytizing or converting participants to a particular view of religion, he says, is not part of the program's philosophy. The main goals are that offenders' lives improve and that, once they are paroled, they don't come back to prison.

The meetings, consisting of large and small groupings, will last six hours on this first day. Sage reminds the offenders that because of the risks involved by bringing crime victims and offenders together, this program has been given only a tentative clearance from Warden Willett. He will evaluate Bridges To Life's pilot program at The Walls before giving it further clearance.

Sage concludes his introductory remarks and asks the twenty-two inmates to begin an honest reflection about their own life stories, and how they got to be where they are—imprisoned behind bars in Huntsville. He gives them twenty minutes to write in their notebooks before they break for lunch.

After lunch, John Sage stands tall at a wooden podium in the front part of the chapel. A few years past fifty, he grips the podium with hands large and strong enough to splinter the piece of furniture, if he so desired, in a matter of seconds.

"I've asked you to reflect on your own lives, and I want to tell some of my story.

"I used to live as if I was in total control. If I wanted something, I went for it and got it. I was an all-conference tackle on the football team at LSU and got drafted by the NFL. After graduation, instead of playing ball, I went into business for myself in my hometown of Houston. I also married my long-time girlfriend, Frances, a woman I adored. By 1984 when I was thirty-six, I had the world by a string. I was a millionaire entrepreneur with a devoted wife and two wonderful sons.

"Then came June 30, 1993. I was only a few blocks from home when my phone rang. It was Frances. 'Johnny, something horrible has happened! Marilyn is dead. Someone killed her!'

"Marilyn and I were only nineteen months apart, the fourth and fifth in a large Catholic family of eight children. We had been inseparable since we were toddlers. Marilyn did everything with me—building forts, playing football, climbing trees. We went to school together as kids, had the same set of friends, and got in trouble together. We were soulmates.

"She even picked out my lifemate for me. Marilyn and Frances were good friends at the all-girls Catholic school they both attended.

"But now Marilyn's life was over. A detective on the case told me that he'd been around murder cases for twenty-five years and had never seen anything this brutal. All for thirteen dollars and her car keys."

Sage pauses. Andrew notices that two inmates, previously slouching in their chairs, are now sitting up and focused on the speaker. Maybe, Andrew thinks, the two are getting more out of this session than a few hours of air conditioning.

"It took the police only forty-eight hours to make an arrest. Two nineteen-year-olds, a girl and a boy, confessed to the murder. They had been cruising the neighborhood where Marilyn lived, looking for a car to steal, and they saw Marilyn in the parking lot taking shopping bags from the trunk of her car. They snuck into her apartment behind her and attacked her. She never had a chance.

"I regretted I hadn't been there with Marilyn to protect her. What point was there to life, I wondered, if someone as good and loving as Marilyn could be taken from us? Her death triggered something in me and took me to a dark side of life I had never been.

"It was the only time in my life, in my internal man, where it really felt like I wanted to kill these people.

"At the trial for one of my sister's killers, I studied the young man at the defendant's table. He was dressed in a suit and tie and his hair was neatly trimmed. He didn't look like a monster. As the prosecutor played a tape of the young man's confession, I visualized myself wrapping my hands around the young man's throat and squeezing the life out of him. I was a mere twenty feet from him. I imagined strangling him, and it was as if my body started taking little steps to do it. I was beyond myself. This man had to pay for his crime.

"When the defendant got the death penalty, I finally thought I could move on with my life. Yet nothing felt re-solved. I had become a prisoner myself—of rage and depres-sion. 'When do I get my life back?' I asked God.

"In a Bible study group, I learned that Jesus said this to God: 'You have loved them'—all of us," Sage added—"'even as you have loved me.' God loved me? As much as he loved his own Son? I knew how much I loved my own two sons, but I could hardly accept the concept of God loving me. But there it was in black and white. Maybe that's what I had been missing all along—God's love.

"I continued with therapy, medication, prayer, and staying close to God's people. I enjoyed my family again. I moved on with my life. I tried not to think about my sister's killers.

"About four years after Marilyn's death, I got a phone call from a reporter with a national news magazine. 'Your sister's killer has an execution date coming up in a few months,' she said. 'Are you excited?'

"'No,' I said hesitantly, 'I'm not.'

"'But this awful woman deserves to die, and you can watch her execution. Won't it feel good?'

"'No, it wouldn't feel good,' I told her.

"'I can't believe you're not even angry!' she snapped and slammed the phone on me.

"To be honest, I was also surprised that I wasn't angry. Before, the only thing I could think about was what I wanted to do with Marilyn's killers, and it drove me to despair. Now it seemed as if that was another lifetime. I sat there for a moment with the phone in my hand and tried to resurrect the hatred I once felt. I couldn't do it. Sometime during the previous year, I had let go of my anger and desire for revenge and put my life in someone else's hands. How else could I explain my lack of reaction to the reporter's attempts to inflame me?"

It was at this point, Sage says, that he was introduced to a Restorative Justice prison ministry called the Sycamore Tree Project, which brought crime victims and offenders together. This introduction helped him envision and implement Bridges To Life.

"What helped me get to where I am today is faith and forgiveness. Talking to inmates like you has allowed me to see your humanity. And telling you a bit of my story helps me get on with my life. The healing we seek together in this place is as much for all of these victims here today as it is for you inmates."

Sage takes a seat. Chaplain Houston tells the inmates they have another twenty minutes to work on their own stories—how they ended up here in Huntsville. Then they'll reconvene in their small groups.

Chapter 37

Six chaplains, including Houston, facilitate the small group sessions as inmates listen to victims tell their stories. Today, six volunteer crime victims tell their stories of pain and travail, face to face with inmates. Twelve ministry volunteers also help in these small group meetings.

Andrew meets Kathy Connell and her husband, Bob, in his small group, gathered in the rear corner of the chapel. Kathy, a nurse, has blonde hair cut at her neckline. Bob is wiry, with a vertical scar covering his left temple, evidence of a dermatologist's knife. An aggressive form of skin cancer has plagued him for a couple of years.

Kathy starts their story by telling the small group—Andrew, three other inmates, two volunteers, and a chaplain—that she and her husband are East Texans, born and raised. They had six kids at the beginning of 1997 with the birth of their daughter, Emily.

And then it happened, she says, on October 18, 1997. "We lost four of our kids to a drunk driver as they were coming back from a football game in Centerville. Allen was nineteen, Laurel was seventeen, Lee was fourteen, and Sara was twelve. They were all good kids." It was a head-on crash only four miles from their house. Three of the four perished at the scene, she informs the group, and the drunk driver walked away relatively unhurt.

Andrew is struck by the similarities between this case and his own. He wants to reach out and express his sympathy to the Connells, but knows that he and the other three prisoners in the small group are listening right now, keeping their lips tight, their eyes attentive, and their ears open to their guests.

Kathy says that the evening started well. Allen's wife and child had gone to visit a friend of hers who just had a baby, so Allen was going to be alone that night. He called and asked his sister if he could ride to the football game with them. And she said, "Of course, c'mon."

"That was peace of mind for me as a mom ... you know, the big brother making the drive with the rest of them."

As she wipes a tear from her eye, Bob continues the story: "The four kids went to a church after the game for a youth event called the 'Fifth Quarter.' It was something the church traditionally did after football games to keep kids from going out drinking after the game. Our kids left the church at midnight." It was a thirty-mile trip to their home in Crockett, he says, and they probably didn't see but one or two other cars on the road, it being so late.

Kathy goes on: "I woke up around 12:30 and walked through the house. The lights were still on, and I calculated that by the time they got out of Fifth Quarter, they'd be home by 1:00.

"I went back to bed and back to sleep. It was out of the ordinary for me to fall asleep, because when you lie down and you're waiting for your kids to get home, you've always got one ear open, listening for them to come in, but it just didn't happen. I went to sleep as sound as I had ever slept."

Bob, who gives the impression he wouldn't flinch in the face of a tornado, continues. "The Houston County sheriff called our house about 4:30 a.m. He said he needed for us to come to the funeral home. Usually when it's something like that, they tell you to come to the hospital. We knew it was bad.

"When we got to the funeral home, and the knowledge sunk in of what had happened, the sheriff had to grab my baby daughter from my arms, because Kathy collapsed into me. We stood there for a while in complete shock."

After a long pause, Bob informs the group what they discovered about the horrible early morning wreck. "A drunk driver in a half-ton pickup crossed the median and basically ran over our kids in a little Toyota. And they were only four miles from home." Laurel was driving, he says, with the two younger kids in the back seat. Allen, who had been in the passenger seat, was taken from the wreck scene by helicopter to the hospital where he was later pronounced dead.

The drunk driver, Bob says, was only twenty-five years old. He was briefly hospitalized and then released, and told not to leave the area while the cops completed their investigation.

Andrew looks down at the floor. His heartbeat has been racing steadily since he heard Kathy Connell mouth the words, "We lost four of our kids to a drunk driver." He wonders whether the others seated near him can hear the pounding inside his chest. *This story is almost identical to mine.*

Bob tells the small group that all four of his children are buried on family property up by Thornton, Texas.

He takes his glasses off and wipes his eyes. It's the first time he's expressed emotion while telling their family's story. He puts his glasses back on and takes a deep breath: "Someone could have dug a fifth hole in the ground for me, and I would have laid beside them. The pain was more than we could stand. But there came a point when we had to decide if we were going to die along with them or if we were going to join the living." Bob and Kathy grab each other's hands and stare off in the distance. The silence hangs in the group.

The third anniversary of the wreck, Bob says, has just passed, and it's the toughest time of the year to deal with. Football, hunting, and the air getting cooler are simply signals that remind them of their loss. Also, he says, they've yet to go to trial because the DA's office messed up the perpetrator's blood sample with the first grand jury, and so a second grand jury has been convened to indict the drunk driver.

Kathy adds, "We haven't even spoken to the man. I really don't understand. We've not heard a word from him. He hasn't even sent a postcard or anything to say that he is sorry this happened."

The group takes a short break, and when they gather again, the chaplain asks Andrew to share his story. He looks at the Connells and says he's sorry for their loss. Unfortunately, he says, his story is in many ways similar to the story they just told. He emphasizes his guilty plea at his trial and talks about how initially he was ashamed to be alive.

"We do things in our lives," he says, looking at the Connells, "where stuff gets on your hands and it doesn't wash off."

He tells the group he's been very fortunate to be in contact with some of the survivors of one of the families he victimized. They've reached out to him, far beyond anything he deserved, and their actions have helped him see that his life still has a purpose. He's responsible now to live up to that purpose, even while in prison—and especially—if and when he gets out.

The initial six-hour session of Bridges To Life comes to a close. John Sage thanks all the volunteers who came, especially those who shared their stories. He instructs the inmates to continue to work on their own stories, focusing on the effects that their criminal activity has had not only on the victims of their crimes, but upon society as a whole. He knows that prison culture doesn't encourage inmates to admit to their crimes. But, he reminds them, there is no going forward in this program, or in life, without honesty.

Before going back to his cell, Andrew stops to say goodbye personally to the Connells. He again tells them how sorry he is for their loss. If there's anything he might be able to do, he says, please let him know.

Bob Connell thanks Andrew and tells him he's done plenty already. The three shake hands.

The next night in his cell, Andrew reflects on John Sage's and the Connells' testimonies and realizes that hearing their stories exercises his conscience. This experience touches him deeply, similar to the feeling his muscles and bones have after working out in the weight room with Jack May, his older friend and prison mentor. This is very hard work, he's beginning to understand, but it's necessary and even beneficial.

As his twenty-fourth birthday approaches, his understanding of his personal mission statement expands. "Communicating with those like him" also includes being responsible for the pain and chaos his deadly act created on June 29, 1996. He realizes that the heavy work it involves won't be going away anytime soon.

Chapter 38

n the fall of 2000, a few weeks after Andrew heard John Sage's and the Connells' stories in the Bridges To Life program, Howard Papke enters a South Austin church to share his son's story. It's the home church of his aging parents, and Howard has come to speak to the youth of the congregation on an overcast Sunday morning. The pastor invited Howard to talk to adolescents who will soon be driving. Sure, he would speak to the youth, Howard responded, out of duty to Andrew's desire to communicate to young people.

Ten teenagers seated in a circle listen to the man with gray-streaked brown hair and a drooping mustache. "My son got on the wrong track, and I might never see him out of prison. It's important to know the direction your life is taking."

The auto shop owner has brought an edited version of his son's open letter. Before passing out Andrew's letter to the youth, he tells them that his son was lost and aimless prior to the wreck. Now, however, he has much better direction in his life—but with two lives lost in the process. Howard reads them a poem that he says Andrew looks at every single morning:

"This is the beginning of a new day. I have this day to use as I will. I can waste it or use it for good. What I do today is very important because I am exchanging a day of my life for it. When tomorrow comes, this day will be gone forever, leaving something in its place. I want that something to be gain, not loss; good, not evil; success, not failure; in order that I shall not forget the price paid for it."

The kids ask Howard questions about Andrew—his activities when he was in school, where he worked, whether or not he went to church.

Howard answers their questions and then tells them with cold conviction that the decisions they make now can affect the rest of their days, just like has happened to his son. He hands out a copy of Andrew's open letter and tells them, after they read it to themselves, to write a letter to Andrew if they'd like.

A thirteen-year-old named Brian responds by writing:

"Andrew, I think you are a great person. You may have made a costly mistake and it hurt many people, but you are doing anything and everything in your power to help everyone else who could get in these kinds of situations ... Your dad made me also realize what can happen in the blink of an eye like your crash which you paid a big price for. I have your letter and I will keep it forever and whenever I feel like I need help from God, my parents, or you I will read the letter. It really means a lot to me and is very helpful. Thank you for sharing your experience and remember that God is always watching over you and can help."

The next day, Howard copies six letters from the youth onto one larger sheet, front and back, and sends it to his son. Andrew will read the two-sided letter, then place it with the other letters he safekeeps in the back of his footlocker.

Chapter 39

At Bowie High School, which Andrew, Krista, Robbyne, and D.R. attended, the principal stands outside and surveys preparations for a school assembly. Kent Ewing, in a white dress shirt, gray dress slacks, a red tie and suspenders, stands alone in the October morning sunshine on a hill toward the east end of the school's property that overlooks a two-lane road. Austin police have shut down and barricaded the two-lane road, and two wrecked cars are positioned on the road as if they have hit head-on. Theater class students with bloody makeup are set to role-play as injured drivers and passengers, and a firetruck, a sheriff deputy vehicle, an ambulance, and a hearse are at the ready, hidden behind a grove of live oak trees down the road. Principal Ewing has been plugging away the past two months to set up "Shattered Dreams," an assembly that features an extensive re-creation of a drunk-driving wreck.

Ewing has worked with police, EMS responders, MADD representatives, hospital personnel, counselors, and youth ministers to put the event together. Additionally, Bowie High School's P.T.A., its student council, and a group of its teachers and administrators have helped in the planning and staging of the assembly. Like other local high schools, Bowie has had a number of auto fatalities in the past few years, and Ewing has dutifully surveyed each post-wreck scene—including the Papke wreck in the summer of 1996. As he's told his staff, he feels compelled to do something about teenage drinking and driving.

The principal turns around and sees the first group of students and teachers walking toward him and the reenactment scene. Hundreds more students follow behind them. They've been told the assembly deals with drunk driving. As they approach and gather on the hill, some students point at the mangled cars. The hill accommodates all the students, making each one a witness.

A smoke bomb goes off behind one of the mangled cars, followed by screaming from within the cars. The smoke wafts away but the screaming continues. First responders spring into action. Firefighters converge on the wreck and retrieve a metal saw from their truck. As the saw whirrs and whines, some of the watching students cover their ears. The ambulance enters the scene, its siren clashing with the whine of the saw. After the firefighters successfully cut through steel, EMS responders extract a blood-covered crash victim from the wreckage on a spine board and transport him to the ambulance. Another crash victim emerges on a spine board but is not taken to the ambulance. The workers lower her to the ground and one of them covers her head to foot with a white tarp. A collective groan rises up from the gathered students.

A police officer confronts the driver of one of the cars. Walk a straight line, the officer commands him. The driver fails badly to do so. The officer, with a flashlight type of device, studies the eyes of the driver. Taking the young man by the shoulders, the officer turns him around and cuffs him.

After announcing loudly to the young man that he is under arrest, he walks him to his patrol car while reading him his Miranda rights. The officer places his hand on the driver's head and stuffs him into the back seat of his cruiser.

The black hearse, like a foreboding storm cloud, rolls into the wreck area. Two men in dark suits get out of the car and confer with sheriff deputies. As one of the dark-suited men writes notes on a small pad of paper, the other one opens the back swing-door of the hearse. Predictably, but shockingly, the two men lift the spine board that holds the still body covered by the white tarp and slide it into the hearse. The solid click of the swing-door shutting, as if a spell cast, stills the students. The hearse rumbles away with its shrouded cargo.

A collective murmuring hangs in the air after the departure of the hearse. A vice-principal with a megaphone breaks the low hum and informs the students that the reenactment is only the beginning of a two-day event to combat teenage drunk driving. The event he refers to as "Shattered Dreams" will continue throughout the day. He instructs the students to be observant and cooperative, and then dismisses them to return to their assigned classes.

Travis Thonhoff, now fifteen years old, is a sophomore at the school. He still plays baseball and marches with the band, but he also plays on the basketball team. Travis walks in from the reenactment with a buddy named Clint. The staged wreck scene, Travis confides to his friend, wasn't half as realistic as the actual wreck he saw one summer night as a kid. With that, Travis says to his friend "Talk to you later" and angles off to his next class. He'll see Clint later in algebra, their fourth period class.

Later, when Travis arrives in algebra class, he notices that Clint has changed shirts. His white polo shirt has been replaced by a black T-shirt. Clint's face has been powdered white, and when Travis approaches him and asks him what's going on, his friend makes no verbal response but gives him a red ribbon. His mouth slightly agape, Travis takes the ribbon. Again, Travis asks his friend what's going on, but Clint makes no response and takes his seat. He won't say a word for the rest of the class period or the remainder of the school day.

Unbeknown to Travis Thonhoff and the majority of Bowie's students, dozens of their classmates, including Clint, have been prepared to act as "silent messengers." Every fifteen minutes throughout this first day of the event, a heartbeat is heard over the intercom signifying a student death due to drunk driving. The dozens of messengers don't speak to fellow classmates after the intercom heartbeat announces their deaths, but only give out the red ribbons as a sign that a friend and classmate has been killed in a drunk-driving related crash.

One of the vice-principals, dressed as the Grim Reaper, also visits various classrooms throughout the rest of the day—in rhythm with the heartbeat—each time taking away a student victim, who returns to the classroom moments later clad in black and powdered white, silent and "dead."

Teachers have been instructed to be available to any of their students needing to talk, and to let students know that counselors and youth ministers will also be available for them the remainder of the school week.

The second day of Shattered Dreams features speakers representing the main participants in the reenactment—first responders, police, hospital personnel—as well as a speaker who has a deep personal connection to a fatal drunk-driving wreck.

Travis is one of more than two thousand students who file into the gym. He climbs the pull-out bleachers to find a seat. The gym is packed, and some students and teachers have to sit on the floor, leaning up against the walls painted red and black, the school colors.

Seated next to friends, Travis looks at the handout and reads some of the statistical information it offers: Texas roads had the highest number of alcohol-related deaths in the nation the previous year, eight young people die every day in the U.S. from alcohol-related crashes, most of the fatal crashes involving teenagers happen between 9:00 p.m. and 6:00 a.m. As he looks over the sheet and thinks about the reenactment he and his classmates saw the previous day, his thoughts go back to the wreck he witnessed when he was eleven years old.

Principal Ewing steps onto the makeshift stage and calls the students to attention. He reminds them, as he does every morning over the classroom intercom system, that they are the finest student body ever assembled. He asks them to give their attention to this second part of the two-day assembly. What they saw staged outside the previous day, he says, was not simply make-believe. The speakers know these situations personally, whether first responders or hospital personnel.

A police officer, a hospital nurse, and an EMS responder share their reflections with the students.

The next speaker who comes to the stage doesn't wear a uniform like the previous speakers. Dressed in a suit, he introduces himself and plainly states that his son died in a drunk-driving wreck close to where they are gathered, on South Brodie Lane during the summer of 1996.

Travis's stomach tightens as he hears the speaker say the names David and Bethany. This is the wreck, he realizes, that he and his mom witnessed. Vivid scenes come back: shattered glass and clothes and beer cans, first responders rushing about in the midst of blood and screams, the two covered bodies toward the ditch. The terrified looks on so many faces at the scene, including his mother's, take over his mind. The memories hold his attention like a trance until the speaker's voice breaks through to him again.

So many people are affected, the grieving father says, when a tragedy like this one strikes. Family members continually ask themselves "What if?" as they wrestle with what they possibly could have done differently to have changed the outcome of the fateful day. Grief, pain, and anguish give family members and friends of the deceased a new way to understand the world: before and after. The speaker tells the students that for him, the wreck didn't end on that summer night in 1996, as if it's all in the past. He thinks about it and despises its reality every single day. If they're not careful, he says, the choices that they make today have the potential to haunt them, and others, for life.

"This didn't have to happen," the speaker states emphatically to the students.

Travis hears that the speaker struggles with the relationship he has with the perpetrator, a relationship created by the wreck. The offender has written him a letter of deep apology and asks for forgiveness. The speaker holds up the pages of the letter. But as he places the pages back on the podium, he says that some days are better than others, and on most days he can't be sure how he can forgive someone who has taken the life of his child.

Travis Thonhoff didn't say anything to his parents after the first day of the assembly. Later this night, however, he tells his mom and dad about the program and how on the first day his buddy Clint "died" in a wreck. He also tells them about the speaker who was the father of the male victim of the wreck they saw on Brodie Lane in 1996. Kim responds to her son by saying that she hopes that all the students take Mr. Holland's message to heart.

The next day Kent Ewing phones a principal colleague at another high school and tells him that Shattered Dreams was a great success. Ewing tells him that the participant students, police, first responders, and hospital personnel were exceptional in how they carried out their duties. The speakers, he says, were extraordinary, and the students seemed to be very receptive and focused. One of the speakers, he goes on to explain, a man who lost his son in a wreck caused by a former Bowie student, was very impressive.

"I can't imagine the strength he had to stand up and talk so professionally about what had happened. He just laid it out for the kids. 'Use your heads,' he said, and 'Don't let this happen to you or your family, because things can change faster than you know.' He did a great job. I got the chills while he spoke."

Chapter 40

At the beginning of December, Andrew and the twenty-one prisoners participating in the Bridges To Life program gather for another of their weekly sessions at The Walls. John Sage has driven up from Houston to join the chaplain facilitators and the twelve ministry volunteers. Not one prisoner has dropped out of the program, now in its eighth of twelve scheduled weeks.

Ellen Halbert, the crime victim whom Governor Ann Richards appointed to the Texas Board of Criminal Justice, has driven to Huntsville from Austin to share her story with the inmates in the Bridges To Life program. Crime victims Ellen Halbert and John Sage are members of a club to which neither wanted to belong, but each has discovered that exercising the rights of club membership—sharing their stories—has brought them healing.

"In 1986 I was forty-three and living in a beautiful home overlooking Austin," Halbert begins. "It was Labor Day weekend. My daughter had just moved out to go to college and my son had spent the night at a friend's house. My husband had left early to play golf. I got up in the morning to take a shower. As I was walking to my bathroom in my robe, I spotted a man in a Ninja suit. He had these funny little boots and gloves and a turban. Everything was covered but his eyes. In his hand, raised over his head, was the biggest knife I had in my kitchen.

"I thought it was a joke, so I laughed. Then immediately I knew it wasn't a joke or a dream and that I was in deep, deep trouble. He said to me, 'Lady, you're going to have a terrible accident.'

"I told him to get out, but he knocked me over. He tied me up and blindfolded me. He took the knife and ran it across the bottom of my feet. He said, 'My knives are a lot sharper than yours.'"

Every man in the room is attentive to the speaker, who tells her story with confidence and a distinct lack of shame.

"For the next hour and a half, he raped me and stabbed me repeatedly. He laughed at me. I could sense him pacing the room, and he screamed at me continuously. He was so full of anger that I wondered why he hated me so much? He stabbed me in the chest and in the neck, and then I sensed his fist coming to the side of my head and striking it. It wasn't his fist, though, but a hammer."

The men shutter and collectively groan upon hearing Ellen's last word. She pauses momentarily before continuing.

"He beat me in the head with the hammer a few more times, hammered a knife into my skull, checked my pulse, and left me for dead—at least I thought so.

"After what seemed a long time, I looked up and there he was, watching me. He came over and hit me again with the hammer.

"He was a drifter. He had probably seen that we kept a house key under the outside front mat. I was the unfortunate luck of the draw. He finally left and was arrested later that day after trying to cash a check that he forced me to write for him. Besides that, my blood was on his person and he had my wedding rings in his pocket.

"My marriage didn't survive the attack and its aftermath. My daughter had to take that first year of college off to help care for me. And then the trial came. I was anxious to tell my story to the jury. I spent hours reliving every minute of the attack so I would be a competent witness.

"When it was explained to me that the law prevented my being in the courtroom except to testify, I was absolutely shocked. What kind of law is this? I didn't want to believe it. I had expected the trial to be a good experience, but instead, it added to my feelings of worthlessness.

"My attacker was sentenced to life in prison. He was all of nineteen years old, mentally ill, and into witchcraft.

"A while after the trial, I was driving to see my sister in Houston. I was consumed with anger and rage during the two and a half hours it took to get there. We were able to talk. After my conversation with her, I decided I needed to let go of the anger and rage. I knew my survival depended on my not being eaten up inside with anger. Rage was going to destroy me if I didn't forgive this man.

"I'm a big believer in forgiveness, but I don't believe that I have to go somewhere and say 'I forgive you.' It wasn't that I said those words, but it was the way I felt about what happened.

"I didn't want to carry the rage anymore. It was really amazing the way choosing to forgive made me feel inside. I was free. It's a process. I didn't do it for him. I forgave him for me."

After another slight pause, she takes on the tone of a preacher: "You can forgive and feel different about yourself.

I want to tell you that the rage you're carrying is hurting you more than it's hurting the person you're mad at.

"I had to pull on all my strength to heal from the attack and its aftermath, and eventually I was transformed. I'm proud of my healing journey—I like to talk about it because I think that maybe somebody else can catch it. But I realize that I can't expect everyone to heal the same way I did. I can talk about my own healing and how, by God, I survived and am stronger than I ever was before."

She steps back from the podium and the men join together in thunderous applause. Two inmates stand up, pounding their palms together. The other men follow suit.

An inmate approaches Ellen and explains that he's serving ten years for a drug possession charge and that his own mother tipped off the police. Ever since he's been in prison, he says, he's hated his mother for what she did and has been true to his vow to never talk to her again. But listening to Ellen's story has put everything in a different light. He tells her that he truly didn't want to be mad at his mother but felt like he had to because she disrespected him. If Ellen forgave the guy who attacked her, he says, he can certainly forgive his own mother and give her an apology for what he did in the first place. He says he'll write a letter to his mom immediately and thanks Ellen for sharing her story. Ellen smiles at him as he leaves. It's not the first time she's heard such a confession.

Chapter 41

few weeks after Ellen Halbert shared her story at
The Walls, one of Andrew's fellow inmates in the
Bridges To Life group approaches him for a private
conversation, out of the hearing range of any other prisoners
or guards. Typically, Andrew keeps his distance from him and
only occasionally talks with him. The man's reputation as
a hardened criminal—an experienced drug-runner between
Mexico and Texas and points beyond—gives him plenty of
sway in The Walls. Andrew's seen how he only needs to nod
his head and his inmate underlings jump up to carry out his
requests.

The man, in his early fifties, tells Andrew in a low voice
that he did a lot of bad things before coming to the pen.
Drugs, guns, counterfeit money, break-ins. At least, he says,
when he robbed houses he tried to do it when people weren't
home, because that way no one got hurt.

But now he sees some of the things he did in a different
light because of the Bridges To Life program. The woman
who told them about the attack and being left for dead, she
taught him something. When she spoke later in his small
group, she talked about being fearful for two or three years

after the attack and not being able to walk into her house by herself unless a family member accompanied her. It showed him how the effects of crime go out in ripple waves and affect other people. It wasn't just a crime against her, but against her whole family and her neighbors.

With an emotion-filled voice that surprises Andrew, he goes on to say that the program has challenged him to be more accountable and responsible for his actions. He says he still doesn't care much for the state institution that's punishing him for his crimes, but for the first time he feels a responsibility toward those he's harmed—and he's starting to understand he's harmed more people than he originally realized.

He tells Andrew that he's learning more about "manning up"—which he thought he already knew plenty about. Real men, he now understands, don't act like irresponsible little kids but are fully accountable for what they do. The man touches Andrew's shoulder, says thanks for listening, and walks away.

Two program volunteers for Bridges To Life set store-bought cookies onto paper plates and pour red punch in the rear of the Walls Unit chapel. The twelfth and final session—graduation night—has arrived. The graduation ceremony will feature an open mic where participants—volunteers and inmates—can stand before the whole group to share what the program has meant to them.

Andrew doesn't mind sharing his story when he writes it out. Speaking, however, is different for him. He remembers being beet-red embarrassed in front of a speech class in high school, the last time he's formally spoken in front of a group except for his trial. He's already decided he won't stand up to say anything.

Sage calls the session to attention and invites inmates to come to the podium and speak about how they've changed in the past twelve weeks and what will stick with them from this program.

An older convict slowly makes his way to the front. This program, he says, has taught him more about himself than anything he's ever participated in. He's done with trying to justify his own wrongs, he says, and that's what he'll take with him when he walks out of this room. The group claps as the older man limps back to his seat.

A young prisoner looks out and pauses before speaking, gathering his emotions. As a drug dealer, he says, he used to think there were no victims to his crime. He just sold drugs to people who wanted to get high. But now he knows that there are victims to what he was doing, including his own family. This program has impacted him, he claims, because it helped him see the other side of things.

Trust was hard at the beginning of the sessions, says another young inmate. But he's learned that he can open up and others will accept him. God, he says, can take ugly things and turn them around. He sees himself as being less prideful and judgmental now. He's feeling peace for the first time since he was a kid. He's got a big ol' bag of feelings, and Bridges To Life is helping him deal with them.

One inmate pounds his chest and points at Sage. "That gentleman over there," he says while looking at his fellow inmates, "thanks to him for having the courage to start this program for guys like us. Society thinks we're throwaways.

But God is working on us inmates and changing us in this prison."

After a lull, Chaplain Houston asks if anyone else would like to talk. Andrew raises his hand. He blurts out something about not having planned to say anything, but after having heard what the other guys shared, he's gotta talk.

"I was given two twenty-year sentences for what I did. But being in Bridges To Life has given me another kind of sentence—a life sentence. What I mean is that this program has helped give me my life back and given me something to use for the rest of my life."

A late January wind howls with bite from the north under a gray sky. The inmates milling around in the Walls Unit prison yard wear sweatshirts and prison-issued lined flannel jackets.

Warden Jim Willett makes a habit of spending time each week in the yard with the men under his charge. The long-timer with the five-digit I.D. number approaches the warden underneath a tree near the chapel. "Boss, I've been to everything y'all have offered to improve myself and try to make myself better if and when I get out of here. This is the first time it's done any good. This is a good program."

The next day Willett sends a letter to fellow wardens in the TDCJ, recommending a new prison ministry to his colleagues.

"I have been employed with the Texas prison system for going on thirty years and have seen a lot of programs offered to inmates to help with rehabilitation efforts. Without a doubt, the Bridges To Life program has made an impact on the participants more than any other with which I have been associated. It touched the inmates in a way that I have not ever seen before. It is my hope, both for inmates and potential victims, that this program can be expanded to include many more men in white."

Chapter 42

Martha Early didn't take the witness stand during Andrew Papke's trial, nor did she give a victim impact statement at the trial's conclusion. Adrian Early, Richard Holland, and Maria Soriano testified, giving Andrew a glimpse of who they were and how they had suffered—up until that time—because of the wreck. Helen Holland didn't testify, but because she was a well-known lawyer in Austin who had worked with MADD, Andrew had a sense of where he stood in her estimation.

From the trial, Andrew remembered Martha Early as quiet and petite. Other than that, she was a mystery to him. He wrote a long apology letter to the Earlys in 1998, as he did to the Hollands. With no guarantee that he'd hear back from either of these families so pained by his actions, he said that he was doing all he could to change his ways, along with trying to figure out better methods to combat teenage drunk driving.

Martha Early responded to Andrew. Her letter, written on June 3, 1999, revealed that she was a soft-spoken and unassuming woman with steadfast commitments to her Christian faith. Andrew cried when he read that she had already forgiven him, and then read on as Martha explained three faith convictions that helped her cope with her daughter's death: Bethany's life was temporarily on loan to her and Adrian as they raised her, Beth was now in heaven eternally with Christ, and her death was not in vain because he, Andrew, had since committed his life to Christ.

She fit a postscript sideways in the margin of the letter's last page: "There is not a mean bone in my body. I am not a vengeful person. I hope my letter gives you some peace."

Andrew responded with another letter in humble, hand-written words, expressing his gratefulness for Martha's acceptance of him. What happened next was beyond Andrew's wildest expectations. During the summer of 1999, as he tried his best to keep his head down at the Gladiator Farm, a flurry of letters and cards crisscrossed back and forth between him, the person responsible for Bethany's violent death, and Bethany's mom. Sometimes Andrew simply shook his head as he remembered David Doerfler telling him that "crime creates relationships." How improbable, yet true, that was.

During that same time, Martha Early called the Victim Services office of the TDCJ, asking for information about the mediation process so that she and offender Andrew Papke could talk face to face. Lisa Looger sent her an information packet that briefly outlined the steps and the process of the Victim-Offender Dialogue program.

Holding off on her decision to participate in the Victim-Offender Dialogue program, Martha kept writing Andrew, and he kept writing back. On Labor Day weekend, she wrote to him about a favorite Southern gospel hymn of hers, Bill and Gloria Gaither's "He Touched Me." "Shackled by a heavy burden, 'neath a load of guilt and shame," the song's opening line was so descriptive of Andrew and his situation. Jesus was the only one who could touch Andrew to make him whole, she wrote, and she would sing this song as a solo in church the following Sunday. "I will sing it for you—dedicate it to you in my heart. I hope I don't cry while singing it."

Through their first letters, Andrew learned that she was a stay-at-home mom while raising Beth and her two younger brothers. Adrian worked and continued with his studies, completing his Ph.D. in 1990 while the three children were still young. In 1991, Martha told Andrew, she was stricken with "hopelessness and darkness of the mind"—depression.

His own depression was severe, Andrew said, when he was first incarcerated. But meeting Chaplain Jameson, he wrote, helped him see some light. "I started praying and studying—you know that's the only thing that got me through that time when I didn't want to live." He wrote that he was still dealing with depression, but recently quit taking meds for it, telling Martha just like he told his doctor, that most normal people would become depressed if they had to stay in prison.

Andrew also learned that after Beth's death in 1996, and Adrian and Martha's divorce the following year, Martha had to earn a living. She found full-time work at a grocery store, doubling as a checker and a manager, which meant she sometimes worked the early shift and the late shift in the same week. Adrian lost his job during an economic downturn in 1998, which diminished some of his child support payments. Martha said she was exhausted most days after work, but thanks to her church and caring friends and relatives, she was able to make ends meet.

If her car or her son's car needed some work, Andrew wrote back to her, his dad was more than willing to help them. Martha said that she'd been wanting to go to the auto shop to tell his dad and stepmom that she had forgiven him, and besides, something was out of whack with the front end of her car.

"I wanted you to know," she wrote a few days later, "I had a wonderful two-hour visit yesterday with your dad and stepmom at their auto repair shop. A bond and friendship have formed, and I am really excited about it. We talked about me visiting you sometime, and if the Lord works it all out, I pray and hope it will be possible some day in the near future."

A month later, Martha told Andrew that she made an appointment to see Lisa Looger. The letter with that information was the last one Andrew received from Martha for a year and a half—until they would sit down face to face to dialogue in the presence of Lisa Looger in the Walls Unit on February 20, 2001.

This last letter from Martha reached Andrew just as he and Adrian Early completed their mediated dialogue in the presence of Lisa Looger. After the dialogue, Andrew and Lisa agreed that he would take a few months'

break from the 150-page manual that prepared participants for a mediated dialogue. The break lasted through Andrew's transfer to The Walls in February 2000. After settling into his new surroundings and signing up for college classes, Andrew contacted Looger to say that he was ready to dive back into preparing for the upcoming, but yet unscheduled, dialogue with Martha Early.

Over the next couple of months as he worked through the exercises in the manual, some of them for a second time, he noticed that two topics kept surfacing for him: his anger and Krista's abortion.

The anger that fueled his reckless driving and other poor decisions when he was a teenager—did it still reside inside him? In the strict environment of the past four years, he had learned to control and recognize his anger better. But why did he have so much of it, and where had it come from?

And Krista's abortion, a procedure that seemed to be such a problem-solver at the time, stayed in his mind and heart. Now as he reflected, he realized his regret about it was not fading with time. As if a bad seed buried and forgotten, it had taken root in his psyche and was threatening to produce bitter fruit.

I n the contact visitation room of The Walls just before Christmas 2000, Andrew sat across the table from Krista, holding both her hands, and told her he wanted to talk about a sensitive issue. It came up during the prep work for his dialogue with Martha Early. But, he stated, it was really his and Krista's issue—the abortion.

Krista immediately pulled her hands to her side of the table when she heard the ominous word.

Andrew explained that many of the exercises in the prep manual were adapted from Alcoholics Anonymous' twelve steps. Steps eight and nine encourage an offender to make amends—more than an apology—wherever possible. It was these two steps, he said, that made him write long letters to both victim families during his first year in prison. It's also why he wrote a letter to their own unborn child, expressing his pain and regret for the other life that was lost on June 29, 1996.

He didn't blame Krista, he was careful to say, but was taking responsibility for his own doing in the matter. It was something he simply had to do. Following these two steps, he said to her, makes living with the regrets of the past somehow more bearable for him. Should he send a copy of it to her?

Without saying a word, she reached up, regrasped both his hands, and nodded her head.

Chapter 43

I n the Walls Unit chapel, where Andrew has spent many hours in worship and contemplation, he sits across the table from Martha Early. It's February 20, 2001. Lisa Looger, as she did before with Andrew and Adrian Early, sits between them at the end of a wooden table. Looger's co-worker, Mark Odom, sits on a chair behind a tripod that holds a video recorder which quietly hums as a small red light near its eyepiece glows.

Andrew and Martha begin their conversation with small talk—about the day, the promise of spring weather, and the awe they share seated in a beautiful chapel with leaded glass and a soaring beamed ceiling reminiscent of older country churches. Smiling across the table at Andrew, Martha says she has some things she wants to show him.

She's brought pictures of Beth and David, a binder of letters and memorabilia that belonged to Beth, and her own well-worn Bible. Even though she misses Beth terribly, she says her focus is on the living—her sons and providing for them the best she can. She says her focus is also on Andrew and how he needs God's love and mercy. Even though some people are skeptical of jailhouse conversions, she knows that Andrew's is genuine and that his life has truly changed.

Andrew thanks her for her encouragement through her letters. He says he wants to answer any questions she has so that she can move forward with her life and feel that justice has been served. He admits to being nervous and thanks her again for taking time to see him and participate in this process.

She tells him that doing the prep materials was not easy. Her voice quiets and slows as she recounts the emotional difficulty of going back to that dark night when EMS personnel came to their door and told them the horrible news, and how she couldn't speak or yell or even cry. And how as parents they had to tell Aaron and Adam the next morning about their sister being killed.

Andrew nods his head and tells Martha how deeply sorry he is for what he has done, acknowledging that his words will never bring Beth back. He lives every day with the pain of what he has done and is not sure it will ever go away. "I have to keep telling you that I am sorry. Saying it for the rest of my life won't express how I truly feel."

Martha reaches across the table, touches his hand, and reminds him that she has forgiven him. "The two of us believe in the God who can bring good even from bad situations like this one," she says. And she tells Andrew that she believes they are equals in God's eyes.

Martha details for Andrew what the last year and a half has been like for her since they stopped exchanging letters, a requirement of the program's preparation process. Besides selling Avon products, she's now switched to working part-time at the grocery store and full-time across town at Dell Computer, where she sometimes has to lift fifty-pound boxes. Andrew's eyebrows flit as he hears this information from a woman who looks to weigh only slightly more than double the boxes she's required to lift.

Martha tells Andrew that recently, while she was working at the grocery store, "Circle of Life" from *The Lion King*, Beth's favorite movie, was playing on the store's speaker system. Martha was staffing a checkout line, and Elton John's voice made her tears flow while waiting on two customers. She was able to do her work while the song played out. But at other times, she says, completely out of the blue, acute sadness and pain cover her like a blanket. She doesn't mind crying for her daughter, she tells Andrew, because it reminds her that she had a wonderful and beautiful daughter, and she doesn't ever want to forget Bethany.

"I miss her and still ask God sometimes why she had to die. I miss what life was like when she was still alive. When she left this earth, our family's life changed forever."

Andrew nods, maintaining the silent pose of listener while Martha dries her tears.

She says she wants to change the subject. She so appreciates, she tells him, that his dad and stepmom have worked on her and her sons' cars. Things were so bad she thought she would have to sell her house. The second and third jobs, though, have helped her keep the house. Aaron has joined the Marine Corps, and Adam is finishing his junior year of high school and works at a restaurant close to their house.

Andrew says he hopes Beth's two brothers are doing okay. Martha suggests that Andrew write letters to them. He says he will.

When Martha drives by the wreck site almost every day on her way to work, she says a prayer for Andrew. He shakes his head and says he doesn't deserve it, but he's grateful all the same.

"Andrew," Martha says, "when Beth was killed, I knew I had to be strong. I had two teenage boys that needed their mom. The preparation paperwork that Lisa gave us to do brought me back in touch with emotions I had initially suppressed. I needed to do that work."

Coming here today, she says, was a great test of her faith. She knew she had forgiven him in her heart and on paper in the letters they had exchanged. But she wasn't sure if she would feel that same forgiveness when they sat across the table from each other. Martha pauses, and then says, yes, she has forgiven him and can feel it. "This whole experience has strengthened my faith."

"You are truly a woman of God," Andrew says to her while opening his hands, palms up, as they rest on the table. He looks at his hands and explains that while he was in the shower house this very morning, it occurred to him that the hands he was washing were the same hands that held the steering wheel that killed Bethany. How Martha is able to do what she's doing—meet with him face to face, pray for him, reassure him of her forgiveness, and even hold his hands—is a true testament, he says, to her faith.

Martha asks Andrew about his artistic abilities. In one of her earliest letters to him, she mentioned that she liked cherubs. Andrew drew little angels hovering around a rose bloom in his next letter to Martha. She loved it and has since claimed images of cherubs as a positive reminder of Beth. Somehow, she says, their innocent expressions make her think of Beth when she was thoroughly bored or perturbed about something.

"I'm glad you're drawing, Andrew. It's a good outlet for you that can bring satisfaction and a sense of accomplishment and help you express your inner thoughts." Andrew asks if it would be okay if he drew a portrait of Beth. Of course, she says, it would mean a lot to her if he was to do that. She slides a photo of Beth that she brought with her to his side of the table.

Thank you, he murmurs. As he takes in the face of the young girl, his jaw tightens shut and his eyes dampen.

After a short break, Andrew says, "I don't want the lives of David and Beth to be lost in vain." Martha knows about Andrew's attempts to reach out to youth through his open letter and the video work he's done with an insurance company.

"Perhaps," he wonders, "we could write a book together someday?"

Martha stares at him with big eyes and covers her mouth with two fingers. After a long pause, she begins expressing her initial thoughts about Andrew's idea: what a powerful story it could be—a story of forgiveness, of God's sustaining power and ability to reach down into a bad situation and produce some good from it. Yes, she says, the idea of writing a book together intrigues her.

Andrew tells Martha that as he worked through the preparation manual a second time, he had to confront an issue he's been suppressing: his anger. He learned from Adrian Early about his unsuccessful attempts to manage his anger immediately after Beth's death.

Andrew quotes a line from the manual: "What do you do when you can't change the past? Grieve." He says that he's learning to feel, more than think, his way through his grief. He's been discovering that he harbored hard feelings about his childhood, specifically about his parents' messy divorce. Writing down those feelings—anger, hurt, disappointment—in a grief inventory in the manual somehow diffused their powers.

These are the feelings, Martha nods, that we turn over to God so they don't run or ruin our lives.

After lunch, Lisa Looger suggests they work on their affirmation agreement. As was the case a year and a half earlier when she sat between Andrew and Adrian Early, Looger hasn't had to intervene or prod either Andrew or Martha this day in The Walls chapel. They continue to talk and write on the forms Looger's provided. They both commit to stay in touch and pray for each other. Any future letters will need to go through Looger's office. With a loving wink of her eye, Lisa also asks that they pray for her, too. Martha turns her face to Lisa and with a warm smile promises that she'll always pray for her.

Earlier, Andrew showed Martha some of the letters he received from students in Karen Gonsoulin's correctional class, commenting that he's made good connections with the students for over a year. Andrew will continue to reach out to students, they also agree, in his attempt to educate them about the dangers of drinking and driving.

For the final addition to the document, they both write down their dream agreement—to one day write a book together.

Andrew and Martha, joined by circumstance and faith, put down their pens to stand and pray. Mark Odom, quiet as a mouse for more than three hours, shuts off the video recorder. The two employees of the TDCJ stand nearby the victim and the offender who join together in prayer. Then they reach toward each other in a full hug as Martha is grasped and encircled by the arms of her daughter's killer.

Later that afternoon, Mark Odom drives back to Austin with Lisa Looger as his passenger. Having participated in multiple mediated dialogues, the two Texas criminal justice employees talk about how committed to forgiveness Martha was with Andrew. Even so, Odom points out, she did a good job of asking tough questions and making Andrew see the pain that she's gone through and continues to go through.

Lisa observes that Martha did a great job with the preparation, and to forgive in person is not the same as forgiving on paper. She was able to do both, Looger says, because she dared to accept the idea that all of us—including Andrew—are connected as equals.

Sweeping the steps outside the chapel a few days later, Andrew sees his friend Jack bound out of the admin doors.

"Hey, Andy, give me a hand with some chairs and tables."

"Is the coffee hot?"

"C'mon."

Jack and Andrew regularly help each other with tasks, whether in the admin office or the chapel. Jack makes sure the coffee pots are kept full in the admin office. From a prisoner's perspective, this coffee is not only hot, but good. The instant coffee available to inmates from the commissary, supplemented in their cells with warm water, is routinely referred to as "floor scrapings."

If Andrew plays his cards right, Jack tells him, he can someday have Jack's job of helping in the admin office. Jack says his release date should be coming up in the next three or four years, and this job would be a good one for Andrew.

The next day, Andrew sits down with Chaplain Houston in the chapel at the same table where he talked with Martha Early. The supervisor asks his charge about his second time through the Victim-Offender Dialogue program. Andrew reflects that it was emotionally draining but incredibly powerful, just like his other mediated dialogue and experiences in Bridges To Life. "The whole process for me, chaplain, is a balm of healing."

PART VI

REUNION

Chapter 44

Two newspapers, from Austin and Houston, arrive every day to prisoner common areas at The Walls. The crossword puzzle pages and Sports sections disappear quickly, but Metro sections with their descriptions of crime and court cases do not. Through the newspaper accounts, Andrew follows other intoxication manslaughter cases in Texas and beyond. Howard Papke and his wife Cathy, similarly vigilant, keep a plastic file box at their house where they neatly store documents related to Andrew's trial and imprisonment along with newspaper clippings of other intoxication manslaughter cases. Father and son have paid close attention to a drunk-driving wreck in Austin notably similar to Andrew's.

From brief exchanges with his dad and stepmom, but mostly from his own investigations by reading the *Austin*

American-Statesman, Andrew knows the details of the drunk-driving wreck caused by an eighteen-year-old high school student named Reggie Stephey in the early morning hours of September 19, 1999. Stephey, alone, drove his Chevy Yukon truck home from a party on Austin's west side, and at 4:30 a.m. crossed the center line of a two-lane road and struck an Oldsmobile coming from the other direction that carried five passengers. Just like Andrew's Acura, Stephey's Yukon left no skid marks on the asphalt.

The smashed Oldsmobile caught fire and the flames lit the pre-dawn sky. Two of its passengers died on the scene, and three survived. Stephey, able to walk away from his truck unscathed, called 911 as the Oldsmobile burned. One of the victims, Jacqui Saburido, a Venezuelan exchange student, was pinned in the car while it burned and was eventually salvaged unrecognizable from the wreck. Barely clinging to life, she was transported by helicopter from the wreck to Brackenridge Hospital in Austin. She would survive with burns on more than 60 percent of her body and was left completely disfigured with stumps for fingers, no ears, no eyelids, no eyebrows, no hair.

Stephey was indicted five months later for, like Andrew, double intoxication manslaughter and additional related charges.

In April 2001, during a visit with Andrew at the Walls Unit, Howard Papke mentions that Reggie Stephey's trial is finally coming up, more than a year and a half after the wreck. Andrew wonders out loud how the accused might plead. As far as he can tell from what he's heard, Howard says, Stephey will plead not guilty.

On June 27, 2001, Andrew's dad opens the *Austin American-Statesman* and reads that Reggie Stephey has been sentenced to seven years imprisonment for the drunk-driving wreck that killed two people and permanently disfigured Jacqui Saburido. The previous week as he closely followed the trial, Howard was not surprised to read that Stephey pleaded not guilty to the charges. The same Travis County DA's office, that four years earlier helped convict Andrew, successfully presented the evidence that guided the jury to convict Stephey. The trial featured moving testimony from Saburido, who lives close to the specialized burn unit of the University of Texas medical school in Galveston. In the nearly two years since the wreck, the twenty-two-year-old has had more than forty surgeries to repair her skin and restore the function of some extremities, lost when, astonishingly, she dodged death and survived an inferno.

The elder Papke also reads how Saburido's father, Amadeo, moved to Texas from Venezuela to care for his only child. Currently they're searching for a specialist who can help rebuild an eyelid for Jacqui to prevent her from losing all sight in her left eye, for which she wears a specially constructed goggle.

"If I could have died before living in this situation, I would have," Amadeo Saburido told the newspaper's reporter. "But for me, dying is a luxury I don't have. My daughter needs me."

Howard tells his wife Cathy that because of the great disparity between Andrew's and Reggie Stephey's sentences, he's going to spend additional time researching the Stephey case. Because of Andrew's situation, Howard is on a first-name basis with the county clerk, the keeper of trial and other pertinent documents, and is well known to employees at the DA's office. The similarities between his son's and Reggie Stephey's cases are many, but their sentences are worlds apart. Howard Papke wants to know why there is a thirty-three-year difference between "Guilty" and "Not Guilty" pleas in Travis County, for the same exact conviction.

At The Walls, Andrew reads the Austin newspaper account, as did his dad, that details the Stephey conviction. Although the jury didn't take long to convict Stephey, Andrew reads that they took parts of two days to determine his punishment. Stephey's lawyer asked the jury to give his client the minimum sentence, noting that Reggie had no prior run-ins with law enforcement and could become an effective speaker to warn teenagers about the consequences of drinking and driving.

Andrew shakes his head and smirks. He imagines that every single DWI defense lawyer in the country uses this same line with juries, nothing more than *quid pro quo*—you scratch my back and I'll scratch yours.

The *Statesman* article details something similar to Andrew's encounters with Adrian and Martha Early. Andrew scans the article. While the jury was determining his punishment, Stephey called for a "roundtable meeting" with the victims and their family members. The meeting was unofficial and had nothing to do with the verdict or the pending sentence.

According to the newspaper account, Stephey told the group that the jury's guilty verdict convinced him that he was at fault and that he was extremely sorry. Stephey then listened to his victims, including Jacqui Saburido, tell of the pain and anguish he caused them. The meeting lasted one hour. The article quoted the positive response after the meeting from a father of one of the deceased in the wreck. Stephey, he said, gave him a cross and they shared tears and a hug. "Every time I can, I will pray for Mr. Stephey. He will have enough time to think about what he did, realize he made a big mistake, and promise himself he will never do it again."

The parents of another victim refused to come to the meeting. They equated Stephey's not guilty plea with lying about the incident, calling it "an additional offense," and didn't want to have anything to do with him. The mother simply said that Stephey had caused so much pain by lying that she couldn't bear anymore to look at him or listen to him.

On the second day of deliberation, the jury came back with a sentence. Seven years in prison for each of the two charges, to be served concurrently, meaning Stephey would be eligible for parole in three and a half years.

Two weeks later at The Walls, Andrew looks across the visitation table at his dad and stepmom. They talk briefly about the Stephey case, discussing the disparity in the sentences handed down by two different juries.

Andrew looks at his dad and asks him, "Did I do the right thing when I pleaded guilty?"

"Yes, you did, son, but your sentence was too long."

Chapter 45

Two and a half months later, on a beautiful mid-November morning, Andrew strolls past the prison yard's rose garden toward the chapel, the fresh air inviting him to breathe deep. Seeing the clump of trees outside the chapel, he smiles as he thinks of a tree fort he and his brother Dave shared at their dad's house as kids. He walks into the chapel and greets Chaplain Houston, and then asks if it's all right if he helps Jack May in the admin office today. Jack has responsibility for preparing a lunch for a correctional officers' meeting and setting up the conference room. Houston nods his head and says he'll be at that lunch and that it better be good. "Guaranteed, boss," Andrew calls out as he straight-arms the chapel door.

While they place folding chairs at tables for the lunch meeting, Jack mentions to Andrew that it's been six months since he's last heard from his mom. Even though his mom has never visited him in the twelve years he's been under the thumb of the TDCJ, she's been a support for him. Jack has usually been able to talk to her on the phone every other month—one of the perks he's garnered as a trusted inmate working in the admin office.

Jack has told Andrew how he upset what little family he had—a younger stepsister and a couple of cousins—when he got busted for manufacturing drugs. He said that their attitude toward him was "you lie down in the bed you make." He accepts their opinion and says he can't get too mad at them for not coming to see him; they'd warned him he was going down the wrong road before he got arrested.

A letter he received from his mom, his last communication with her, made Jack's jaw drop. He told Andrew about it the next day. His mom responded to a knock on her front door and opened it. There stood a young man, and as she wrote to her son, "I thought it was you." The letter stated that it was a fourteen-year-old teenager who looked exactly like Jack—his son who was two years old at the time of Jack's arrest and conviction. Neither Jack nor his mom had heard anything about the boy, named Chad, since his mother disappeared with him and cut off connection with Jack's side of the family after his arrest.

Back in the kitchen adjacent to the conference room, as they stack freshly sliced tomatoes next to cheese and cold cuts, Jack tells Andrew that he's worried about his mom and his son that he's known nothing about all these years. Something must be going on, but he has no idea what it might be.

Two weeks later, Jan hangs up the phone on her side of the visitation booth at the Walls Unit and stomps away. Krista, standing nearby while waiting for her second turn to talk to Andrew, watches her mother-in-law brush by and sighs. She slides into the vacated seat across from Andrew on the other side of the glass. Krista left San Antonio in the early morning darkness, picked up Jan in Austin, and the two drove up to Huntsville together. It's the last Saturday in November 2001, Thanksgiving weekend.

Krista picks up the phone and asks what's going on.

He says not to worry, that his mom knows if she walks out the door she can't come back in. His brown eyes are calm and clear as he tells Krista that Jan is just worked up with the Christmas season approaching.

Krista says that on the drive up, Jan commented that it's now been five Thanksgivings. Andrew nods his head, well aware of how many Thanksgiving days he's chalked up behind bars. His mom was reminiscing, Krista says, about when Andrew and his brother Dave were little kids playing baseball and chasing around together. But then, Krista says, Jan quieted down for a long time before asking: "What parent ever expects their kid to grow up and end up in the penitentiary?"

Andrew changes the subject and asks Krista how her studies are going. She's pursuing an undergraduate degree in criminal justice at the same university in San Antonio that she started at right out of high school. She tells Andrew that her forensic science class is her favorite. It's an upper-division course that she couldn't take until she finished her required classes. Andrew tells her to keep at it and says he'll let her know if he needs help with his basic courses. It will take about three more years, he says with a laugh, at two classes per semester for him to complete his associate's degree.

After a while, Krista tells Andrew she'll check if his mom is ready to talk again. He winks at her and blows her a little kiss.

Jan reappears, takes the booth seat again with a slight smile, and picks up the phone. She tells Andrew she's sorry, but that it's just still so hard to see him on the other side. Is there something else, she asks, she could send him this year for Christmas? She says she'll see him just once more before Christmas and will bring the usual bag of change for the vending machines. But she'd like to do something other than go to Office Max and have them send him, according to prison regulations, the usual pencils and notepads like she's done for all the earlier Christmases.

Andrew repeats what he's always said, that he doesn't need anything and doesn't want anything. Jan mumbles something about Andrew being just like his father.

Okay, he says, since she's being so insistent, there is something different she can do for him this Christmas. He nudges his nose close to the glass and stares at his mother: "I want you to bring my friend's mom here to visit him. She hasn't ever been here, and it's been more than twelve years." Andrew leans back and looks at his mom with the confidence of a poker player about to rake in all the chips.

Jan looks at her son with her eyebrows scrunched and eyes like slits. She asks him if he's serious.

"Yes, Mama, I am."

As Jan and Krista drive back to Austin this afternoon, the mood of their conversation swings between skepticism and excitement about the task Andrew has given them. At first, Jan was beside herself with the request—tracking down a woman they don't know and bringing her to

Huntsville for a prison visit—but Andrew insisted that she and Krista could pull it off together.

Andrew shared other additional details as Jan and Krista tag-teamed on the visitation phone with him before they left. Jack's mom, an older woman who lives somewhere in Southwest Texas, doesn't drive anymore except to her Baptist church and the grocery store. Andrew said he'll figure out exactly where she lives, but he doesn't want Jack to know about the visit. It will be, he said, a Christmas gift for Jack. Andrew also told his mom and wife about the family members, including a teenage son, whom Jack May hasn't seen in the multiple years he's been behind bars. Jack occasionally exchanged letters with a few family members, but after all this time, he feels that he doesn't know them and they don't know him.

They have no idea, Andrew said, that Jack is a changed man.

Two days later, Andrew and Jack mirror each other, their swishing brooms on their adjacent posts spitting up dust and dead leaves into the warm winter air. Andrew asks Jack if he has any update on the situation with his mom. Jack says he doesn't because his supervising correctional officer is out for the week and so there's been no chance to call his mom. Andrew motions for Jack to follow him, and they enter the chapel.

Andrew briefly explains Jack's predicament to Chaplain Houston and wonders if Jack could have permission to use the phone and call his mom. The chaplain says yes, that can be done.

Jack dials his mom's number at her rural Southwest Texas home and gets through to her. Andrew purposely overhears the conversation and takes some mental notes. Later, after Jack leaves the chapel, Andrew tells Chaplain Houston what he's planning to do. Thirty minutes later he leaves the chapel, skipping down his clean steps with a dual accomplishment: he's asked Chaplain Houston to update Jack's meager visitation list with the name Betty Jo Haynes. And he left a message on his own mom's answering machine, telling her Jack's mom's name, phone number, and address.

From Austin, Jan makes phone contact with Jack May's mother. She lives in a small town fifty miles west of San Antonio. Jan's explanation of her phone call and its request is met with a coughing fit on the other end of the line. Eventually, the older woman says that she's sick and doesn't think she can make it all the way to Huntsville, five or six hours away by car.

Jan promises to come and get her and make the trip as smooth as possible. Betty Jo admits that she should try to see her son and that they can give it a try. They agree to make the trip on an upcoming Saturday, the fourteenth day of December 2001.

The agreed-upon Saturday arrives with a forecast promising a high in the 70s for Central Texas and clear skies for the one-way trip of 300 miles. Jan, Krista, and Betty

Jo travel east toward San Antonio just after sunrise. Jan and Krista have learned that Betty Jo has cancer and has been told she might not have much time left. She was in a minor car accident toward the end of the past summer and had to check into the hospital at nearby Hondo, Texas. They kept her overnight, and the next day a doctor she didn't know entered her room and told her in a matter-of-fact tone that she had cancer.

At 1:00 p.m., offenders Jack May and Andrew Papke are called up and asked to report to the contact visitation area. Andrew's heard his name called dozens of times for Saturday visits, but not Jack. They meet in the room on the prisoner side of the visitation area, and Jack looks at Andrew, wondering what in the world is going on. He has never received a visit. Andrew plays his cards close to the vest and says they'll just have to see.

Andrew and Jack are called to enter the visitation room together. There, seated on the far side of the table are Jan, Krista, and Betty Jo. Jack walks in first, sees his mother, and stops in his tracks. Andrew comes up from behind, puts his arm around Jack, and brings him up to the table. As Jack hugs his mother, Andrew smiles at his mom and his wife, mouthing a thank you to each of them before giving each one a hug.

Introductions go around the table, and Betty Jo tells her son that the two kind women seated beside her drove her the whole way. Jack says he recognizes Krista from pictures that Andrew has shown him. As Jack slaps Andrew on the back, he tells Jan that he's very pleased to meet her. Even though her son is a young guy, he says, he's all right. Especially on a day like today.

The five laugh, smile, tell stories, and get along as if contented family. The conversation takes on a serious tone when

Betty Jo, who worked a few years as support staff for the Drug Enforcement Agency in South Texas, tells her son how disappointed she was in him when he was arrested. Jack tells his mom that he understands her feeling that way, but thankfully, those days are long over. He's given his life over to the Lord, he says, and he ain't ever looking back. Betty Jo smiles at her son.

Jack asks his mom about his son, Chad. She tells him that he lives a couple of towns over from her and has always been told that his father is dead. Chad happened to be in a store one day and overheard someone talking about Jack. The boy inquired when he heard the name Jack May, because he thought he was dead. The reply came: "He's not dead, son. He's in prison." Within a week, the boy was knocking at his grandmother Betty Jo's door. Betty Jo shakes her head as she tells Jack, like she did in her last letter, that the boy is a carbon copy of him.

Betty Jo says it's the last she's seen or heard from him. Maybe, Jack responds, he can track him down somehow.

None of them pays attention to the clock. The C.O. in charge of visitation allows them to visit for four hours, double the usual allotted time. The only uncomfortable moments of the visit are when Betty Jo hunches over in her chair, coughing into a discolored handkerchief.

The next week, when Jan and Krista talk on the phone, Jan remembers how she worried about Andrew when he was at the Gladiator Farm with all the young inmates in the Ferguson Unit. Recalling the violence and the presence of prison gangs, which Andrew told her about, she says it was the only time in her life when she doubted God's existence. She tells her daughter-in-law how pleased she is that Andrew spends so much time with Jack, who seems to be a very good man—almost like an uncle or a father to Andrew. She thought Andrew's special Christmas request was crazy, she says, but she's so glad to have met Jack and Betty Jo.

Christmas Day, a Tuesday, settles upon the Walls Unit. It's been a warm December, but a chill arrived a few days earlier and has stuck around. The guys assigned to work fields won't go out today, but Andrew's on duty to ready the chapel for Christmas worship. Jack gives him a hand with extra chairs from the admin office as a larger than normal crowd of worshipping inmates is expected by Chaplain Houston.

With all the extra chairs in place, Jack thanks Andrew again for setting up the visit with his mom. It was sure good to see her, Jack says, but he's worried about her cancer, especially with her coughing on and off throughout the visit. Now he knows why he hadn't heard from her in the past six months, Jack says; she didn't want him to worry about her. Andrew says he'll ask Chaplain Houston to include prayers for Betty Jo during the church service.

That would be good, Jack says, because Christmas Day is her birthday. He does the math. "She's sixty-four years old today."

Waiting outside an assistant warden's office in the admin building at The Walls, Jack May has readied himself for a day-long furlough to a small town in Southwest Texas. He's still a ward of the Texas criminal justice system, but he's traveling with a guard and a maintenance worker on this crisp, bright day in the middle of January to be at his mom's bedside. Instead of prison whites, he's dressed in a dark, button-down shirt and khaki slacks. The warden has approved a request that offender May see his mom one more time before she dies. Word arrived to Jack's C.O. that Betty Jo was confined to bed, under the care of a hospice nurse, and wouldn't have much longer to live.

Jack spends fifty-five minutes at his mom's side before getting back in the car to return to Huntsville. As they drive, he thanks his traveling companions for taking him. He stares out the window at dormant fields where dried up corn and cotton plant stubble stick out of the bleak winter dirt.

Wiping a tear, Jack mentions losing his dad years ago. Now that his mom's about to pass on, he says, he's about out of family.

A little more than a week later, on January 26, 2002, Betty Jo Haynes dies.

Jack will be granted another furlough to attend his mother's memorial service, two weeks after her passing, in the same small Southwest Texas town where she lived. Arriving from Austin, Andrew's mother Jan will attend the service to express her condolences to Jack.

Two weeks after Betty Jo Haynes' memorial service, Jack and Andrew stand and talk at their posts in the breezeway. Jack tells Andrew that Jan, his mom, is pretty special, and that he really appreciates all she's done. He pauses and then tells Andrew that he wants to ask him something. Jack knows that Andrew's mom and dad divorced years ago. But he wonders, does Jan have a boyfriend? He says he thinks he has feelings for her, but he doesn't want to do anything that would mess up the friendship he has with Andrew.

After staring at the ground for a long moment, Andrew raises his head and nods at his friend with a smirk. "Well, I guess you have just as much right as anyone else to be miserable, if that's what you want." After an initial silence, they both begin to laugh. The laughter builds, and they fall into each other in mock battle, like two sumo wrestlers. Smiling, they push away, and Andrew says that if it's meant to be, there's nothing he can do to stop it.

Later in the day, Jack writes a letter to Andrew's mom to thank her again for all she's done and expresses his interest in pursuing a meaningful relationship with her.

A few weeks later, when Jan confirms to Andrew in a letter that she's interested in his friend Jack, he writes to her: "Mama, please don't break his heart."

Chapter 46

Many months later, Jan rakes up two large plastic bags worth of brown leaves in the front yard of her home in southwest Austin. After taking off her gloves in the garage, she walks into the kitchen and answers a phone call from a young man who identifies himself as Jack May's son. He says his name is Chad and wonders if he could come up and live in her house in Austin for a while. He says he doesn't like his high school and really just needs to start fresh in a new place. Startled, Jan tries to talk, but doesn't know what to say. After the young man asks if she's still on the line, she clears her throat and grabs a pencil. She takes his phone number down and tells him she'll get back to him as soon as she can.

Five days later, on the first Friday night in November, Jan stands in downtown Austin's crowded bus station awaiting the arrival of Chad May. Just as she's wondering how she might recognize this teenager she's never seen before, she spies a younger version of Jack May walking toward her—short and well built—and waves him over. As she introduces herself, she sees he has the same watery blue eyes and dimpled chin as his father.

The next day, a Saturday visitation day at The Walls, Jack May is called up to the contact visitation area. Once again, Andrew is with him as they wait to enter the larger room. They both know exactly what's happening for this visit. The past summer, Jack tracked down a mailing address for his son and reestablished contact with him. Chad replied and said that things weren't so good in the rural Southwest Texas town where he lived. Jack wrote him again and gave him Jan's phone number, suggesting he call her if he needed to. Jack added Chad to his visitation list.

Early this morning, Jan drove up from Austin to Huntsville with Chad. Arriving right before noon, they grabbed lunch and then turned in to The Walls' parking lot. As they ate in the car, Jan said to Chad, "This is the place where my son and your father are. Both are good men who made serious mistakes when they were younger, but now they're trying to make up for it," she continued.

More than twelve years have passed since Jack has seen his son. As he waits with Andrew to enter the visitation room, Jack fidgets with his hands and paces. A guard tells him to take a deep breath, because it's time for them to enter the room.

Jack walks into the room with Andrew at his side. Once again, as he did when he saw his mom in this same room ten months earlier, he stops in his tracks when he sees Jan and Chad seated at the table. Andrew says, "Come on, buddy," throws his arm around Jack's shoulder, and walks with him to the table. Jack grasps his son's right hand firmly, places his left hand on his son's shoulder, and tells him that it's great to see him.

After Andrew and Jack each hug Jan, they all sit down. Jack takes off his glasses and wipes his eyes with a handkerchief. He says he didn't used to cry like this when he was younger—he wouldn't allow himself to do it. But now he just lets it out, and he doesn't care who notices. He looks up with a smile and says that he's really happy to see his son.

Rain falls for a third consecutive day in Austin, delaying the onset of the monotonous summer heat. It's Friday, June 6, 2003.

In an Austin municipal courtroom before a justice of the peace, Jan stands next to Jack May's son, Chad. The judge leads them through a marriage-by-proxy ceremony. Within five minutes, the judge pronounces Jack and Jan May legally bound to one another as husband and wife. Earlier in the year, with Texas bluebonnets and Indian paintbrush blanketing the sides of the roadways from Austin to Huntsville, Jan, seated across from Jack in the contact visitation area at The Walls, said "Yes" to Jack's proposal that they marry. He was scheduled for release before the end of the year and told Jan he wanted to be with her.

As Jan and Chad leave the municipal court, Jan's ring finger displays a gold ring capped with a diamond. Jack sent it to her from prison the previous month. A note in the mailing said the ring was made by Jack's good friend, Big Mitch, in the prison's metal shop. Big Mitch completely surprised him with the ring, Jack said in the note, and also made a matching gold ring for him. His ring fit great, Jack wrote, and he hoped Jan's fit just as well as his did.

The following day, a Saturday visitation day at penitentiaries all across Texas, dawns gloriously sunny in Central Texas with no rain clouds in sight. Jan drives east from Austin to Beaumont, where Jack has recently landed after receiving transfer orders. They make their first official visit as husband and wife and compare their rings. Jan's fits just right. There's no wedding cake to share, but they celebrate the occasion with candy bars and Cokes from the vending machines.

Jan and Jack also talk about plans for Jack's upcoming release, scheduled for the end of the year, six months away.

After spending six months and a few weeks at the Stiles Unit in Beaumont, Jack May is transferred back to the Walls Unit on the second day of 2004. He's scheduled for release on January 5.

Since Jack spent most of his fourteen years of imprisonment at The Walls, he's placed back into the regular population for his final weekend of incarceration. He and Andrew greet each other with a hug in the prison yard, close to where they used to sweep their adjacent entryways. Andrew congratulates Jack on his marriage, saying that now when he calls him "old man," it will have additional meaning.

After some more laughs about their new relationship, Jack tells Andrew that he has a few things to say to him before he gets released and that he might as well say them now.

Jack tells Andrew to keep his head up, to watch his back like he showed him, and to stay out of trouble. He also tells him that he'll come and see him as often as he can and that

God will watch over him. Andrew's so good with all the reading and writing he does, Jack says, that he must keep on studying and improving himself. Then Jack grabs hold of Andrew's shoulders, looks at him straight on, and tells him to keep moving forward, because someday he'll be walking out of here, too.

Chapter 47

Years later, Andrew paces toward his cell, holding in his left hand a reply letter from a publishing company in New Mexico. Moments earlier he took it from the guard who called out his name during mail call. He's anxiously awaited a response from the book producer. He sent the publisher a manuscript of his story—231 pages—that he banged out during the past two years on his well-used Smith-Corona typewriter. After Andrew received his bachelor of business administration degree from Tarleton State University in 2009, writing his story in book form became his primary academic activity. He enters his cell at the Hughes Unit in Gatesville, Texas, with the letter postmarked June 17, 2011, tightly grasped in his hand.

Martha Early met Andrew again at the Walls Unit for a second mediated dialogue in October 2003. Lisa Looger, as she did previously, sat between them at the dialogue table. Martha told Andrew that she had dreams about Beth. Sometimes she saw her in her casket, and other times she saw her as vibrant and pretty as ever. Perhaps, she said, it was reassurance that her spirit was alive and she was happy.

Their main agenda item for their second time through the Victim-Offender Dialogue was to discuss an outline for the book they would write together, a story of God's redemption, honoring the lives of David and Beth. It was a story they wanted to share with the world.

They left the mediated dialogue with high hopes. Neither, however, made much progress with writing after the meeting because they were both busy. A year later, Martha wrote to Andrew, "I haven't started our book yet. I feel it will never happen. 'Our book' will probably end up being 'your book.'"

Andrew continued his junior college studies, and Martha continued working two jobs, while enjoying a new church community with her new husband.

Lisa Looger passed away unexpectedly at the end of 2004. She was only fifty and left fellow journeyers in the recovery community grief-stricken, as well as many co-workers in the criminal justice system. More than four hundred people—including Raven Kazen, David Doerfler, Ellen Halbert, Mark Odom, and Martha—attended her memorial service in Austin. Later Martha would say that Lisa's death hit her very hard; somehow it broke part of the link that connected her with Andrew.

Andrew was transferred from The Walls to the Hughes Unit in Gatesville, forty miles west of Waco and just north of the Fort Hood military post, after earning two associate degrees from Lee College in 2005. His new unit offered the opportunity to continue his college studies through a program offered by Tarleton State in nearby Stephenville, Texas.

His first job at the unit was as a ranch hand in the horse stalls, grooming, feeding, and shoeing the animals that carried rifle-bearing high riders during work days at the unit. Later he was assigned to care for the prison pack dogs, used to track down escaped prisoners. He also worked in the leather shop, applying his artistry to belts and wallets.

In 2006, his first parole hearing resulted in a "set-off" of three years, meaning his petition for parole was denied and wouldn't be reconsidered by the parole board for another three years. Martha Early Moffett, Adrian Early, Chaplain Ivan Jameson, Chaplain Ken Houston, Warden Jim Willett, and Krista were among a dozen who wrote letters of support for Andrew to the parole board.

Krista visited him the Saturday after they learned his parole was denied. Both had hoped for a favorable decision, but as Andrew said to her, his denial was no different than the results of most first-time parole hearing cases. Their disappointment was raw, but they managed to crack a few smiles and share a few laughs. Her face scrunched sour when she told him how her stomach would turn every time she drove by a Kentucky Fried Chicken restaurant or saw one of its commercials on TV—reminding her of that night, and of the food no one touched, as they waited in Sam Ireland's office for the jury's sentence. Krista also commented how she wrote to the parole board that most prison marriages had an expiration date of two to three years, but she and Andrew were still together almost ten years into his imprisonment.

Better days waited ahead, they promised each other, when they would pursue their dream of sharing a home together, with Andrew educating youth about the dangers of drinking and driving. Krista told him something else she wrote the parole board—that she planned to be with him every step of the way for the rest of their lives. The board's denial, she told him that day, didn't change a thing for her.

Two years later in 2008, Krista began working at a forensic lab. The full-time job required her presence Monday through Thursday, allowing her to continue her frequent Saturday visits with Andrew. Closing in on their mid-thirties, Andrew and Krista had been together for more than half their lives but had been separated most of that time. Despite their commitment to their relationship, he feared that his remaining incarceration time had the potential to separate them even further.

The formula for determining days served by a prisoner in the Texas criminal justice system consists of calendar days served, half a day credit for work days satisfactorily performed, and a full day of credit for good behavior. Being written up for poor behavior has the potential to wipe out an inmate's credited days. All aspects of the formula are a strong incentive for a hard-working and clean-behaving inmate who can earn more than two days credit for each day served. Andrew's conviction of intoxication manslaughter, however, requires a minimum of fifty percent actual days served, meaning ten years of calendar time for a single twenty-year sentence.

In 2009, his second attempt at parole was successful. His good work and behavior records pushed his accumulated time served beyond the time required for the sentence of David's death. Serving the twenty-year sentence for Beth's death awaited next. If he were to make parole for her sentence, his earliest possible release date would arrive in 2019, when he'd be in his early forties. With another set-off or two, he wouldn't get out until well past his fiftieth birthday.

Earlier that year, he walked the Hughes Unit chapel stage in a blue robe to receive his degree from Tarleton State. Howard, Cathy, Jan, Jack, and Krista clapped and then ate cake with him and the other graduates and their loved ones in the chapel. Andrew planned to continue his education and applied for a transfer to a unit near Houston where he could study for a master's degree in English. A paperwork snafu, however, meant he wouldn't be able to start the program until 2011.

He decided to stay at Gatesville. A master's degree in English wouldn't come his way, but he would take on an alternative assignment in the same category of study. He pulled off a maneuver on his Smith-Corona, still white but scuffed and smudged after a decade of use, for the biggest writing job he'd taken on as an inmate. In order to get two run-throughs from his $6 replaceable ink ribbons, he wedged an ice-cream stick underneath the ribbon cartridge so the keys would only type on the ribbon's bottom half. When the ribbon ran through, he flipped it over, wedged the stick in again, and typed on the unused half of the ribbon. Doubling the ribbon's life helped make up for the dozens of pages he ripped out of the typewriter, crumpled, and tossed toward the far corner of his cell as he labored through the writing process.

The pounding of the Smith-Corona keys eventually produced his life-story manuscript. It was a two-year process from start to finish. After sending the 231-page manuscript to the publisher in New Mexico, he knew that the dream he and Martha shared was now his alone.

n the relative privacy of his cell in the Hughes Unit, he holds in his two hands the letter from the publishing company. After taking a deep breath, he opens the folded letter. He immediately sees that their response consists of three concise paragraphs. His eyes dart left to right.

The first paragraph congratulates him on compiling a working draft that has "good potential." The second paragraph expresses their interest in going forward with the project, but with one non-negotiable condition: He must remove all words and ideas related to God. The head publisher likes the storyline, the paragraph concludes, but won't publish anything as "openly religious" as his manuscript. The third paragraph instructs him to respond within two weeks.

He rereads the second paragraph with its requirement to strip out the "God language."

He crumples the letter in his hands and throws it toward the toilet: *No chance.*

n the manuscript, Andrew has told his story with greater detail, using the same style and chronology as he did with his open letter to the students at Bowie High School, readers of the *Austin American-Statesman*, Karen Gonsoulin's pupils at the correctional school, Bob and Kathy Connell in the Bridges To Life program, and the prisoners he's spoken with over the years—starting with June 29, 1996, and his reckless behavior.

A movie he saw early on in prison, *The Mission*, has been influential in the writing of his manuscript. Andrew identifies with the plight of Robert De Niro's character, Rodrigo Mendoza, an eighteenth-century, Spanish slave-trading mercenary, who kills his brother in a fit of passion. Above the law in his own city, Mendoza sinks into depression under the heavy guilt of his transgression. There's nothing he can do to bring back his brother, but he accepts a challenge to perhaps renew his own life. He returns to South America with a group of Spanish missionary priests who have a mission settlement in a Guaraní village. The head priest challenges Mendoza to ask forgiveness of the Guaraní people whose family members he previously forced and sold into slavery.

While making the trek to the isolated and mountainous Indian village, Mendoza drags behind him a rope sack containing the wares of his previous life as a slave trader—swords, a helmet, and the rest of his armor. After an arduous journey, the sack of penance still burdens Mendoza as he presents himself, head bowed and hands behind his back, to the Guaraní. They can kill him, justly, if they wish. A Guaraní leader accosts the vulnerable Mendoza, pulling his head back by his hair as he threatens his naked throat with a long shiny blade. Mendoza's face shows no fight—he knows he deserves to die. The priests can only watch as the slave trader's life dangles on the edge of the blade. The Guaraní leader loudly asks his people what to do with the kneeling, defenseless, and guilty man.

Andrew knows that in cases like his and Mendoza's, it's the people who've been wronged who have the power to give life back. He understands what it feels like for Mendoza when the Guaraní leader uses his knife to slice, not Mendoza's throat, but the rope that carries his heavy burden. Mendoza, his life restored by the grace of the Guaraní, takes religious vows and commits his life to work alongside them. Similarly, Andrew has taken a self-imposed vow to tell his story so that the suffering he caused three families doesn't happen to other families.

The parents of his victims, Andrew has written, taught him about taking responsibility. He will not forget what they said to him during their victim impact statements, with agony deeply etched upon their faces. He's written about sitting at tables across from Martha and Adrian Early and hearing them talk of the pain he caused them, even as they both offered him forgiveness and challenged him to make something good of his life.

He's written that, ironically, David's and Beth's deaths have given him his life's purpose—to reach out to kids who have the potential to do, before they do it, what he did.

Writing the manuscript wasn't a big stretch for Andrew. After the *Austin American-Statesman* published his open letter on December 31, 1999, he wrote a number of articles and letters during the next decade that were published in other periodicals. A common theme emerged in all these writings: Andrew admits to daily having to confront his past. Somedays, he writes, he looks in the mirror and sees the enemy. That load of guilt and shame, just like Mendoza's rope sack, is easy to pick up again and drag around.

"Denial is attacked through self-awareness." He writes that he read this truth in the victim-offender preparation manual before meeting with Adrian Early. Getting stuck is not only easy for crime victims, but for criminals as well. Andrew writes that Restorative Justice principles—with the pragmatic goal of healing through honest disclosure—saved and shaped his life after his horrendous misdeed. Anger and resentments, rooted in his childhood, no longer fuel each other as they did when he was a teenager. He's been introduced to the virtues of understanding, empathy, and compassion by a community of healers, initially wounded by criminals like him. These healers have helped him rewrite his own story and helped him make sense of it.

After two days of stewing about the letter from the publisher, he writes them a response, saying that he can't change what he's written. He will look for a different publisher.

Later in 2011, a change at Krista's lab requires her to begin working a conventional Monday-Friday week. As a homeowner, dog-owner, and committed volunteer at a local animal shelter, her Saturday treks across Texas highways diminish. It's been fifteen years since the wreck, and the days that Andrew and Krista spent together swimming in rivers, camping on the beach, and romanticizing about their future family seem a lifetime ago.

Andrew and Krista still maintain their status as husband and wife. But for the first time since he's been incarcerated, a two-month stretch passes where he doesn't see Krista's gentle face communicating her love and support.

Chapter 48

I n the 331st District Court of Travis County, Judge Bob Perkins looks at the court reporter and asks if she is ready to record the proceedings. "Yes, your honor," she replies with a nod. It's February 25, 2014. Adrian Early, Martha Moffett, Aaron Early, and Jim Willett are present in the courtroom, ready to testify for a motion brought to the Court on behalf of Andrew Papke. Buddy Meyer, Travis County Assistant DA, and Grady Tuck, representing Andrew Papke, are seated at what are normally the prosecution and defense tables. This day and its gathering are different though. Howard and Cathy Papke, and Jim Willett's wife, Janice, are also seated in the gallery.

In 2010, Judge Perkins decided not to seek re-election to the Court he had presided over since 1982. Even so, he continues to be active on the bench, substituting in this courtroom where he served and in others. But revisiting a case over which he presided, as he's doing today, is as rare as snow in South Texas.

Lawyer Tuck, on behalf of Andrew, brings a motion to reform the sentence from the case that the State of Texas carried out against his client in 1997. The Travis County DA's office, now led by Rosemary Lehmberg, has been swayed by the opinion that Andrew Papke's sentence of forty years is too severe. The DA's office has communicated to Perkins that it doesn't oppose, but rather supports, the motion from Andrew's lawyer.

The DA and her assistants know that Reggie Stephey's sentence, representative of a trend in other intoxication manslaughter convictions throughout Texas, was much lighter than Andrew's. Andrew was and is guilty—the verdict is not in question—but the stacking of the two twenty-year sentences is. Perkins indicated to the DA's office that he would entertain the motion.

Second-term DA Lehmberg was arrested for DWI in 2013, pleaded guilty, and received a stiff forty-five-day jail sentence. While in jail, she wrote a detailed apology letter to the citizens of Travis County, confessing to immense shame for her behavior that not only broke the law but the trust between her and the community. Asking forgiveness and announcing that she would not seek re-election, she pledged to complete her term of three remaining years. Discharged from jail for good behavior after three weeks, she entered an out-of-state treatment facility and completed its thirty-day rehab program.

Returning to Texas, she faced ferocious political pressure from Governor Rick Perry and a civil case seeking her dismissal, brought by the Travis County Attorney. In December 2013, eight months after her arrest, her civil trial played out under intense media scrutiny. Her attorney, Dan Richards, the son of Ann Richards, the late Texas governor who was herself a recovering alcoholic, said in his closing argument, "I'm a believer in redemption ... and I'm a believer in recovery." The judge agreed, dismissing the charge against Lehmberg.

After Lehmberg's acquittal, a long-time newspaper columnist in Austin wrote that, because of the DA's travails, the people of Travis County were perhaps better off because they were being served by a top prosecutor who confronted, rather than ignored, her drinking problem: "We could have a DA who's now a better person than when we elected her."

Lehmberg telephoned one of the guards at the Hughes Unit in late January to personally verify that Andrew Papke was a model prisoner with a clean record. Satisfied, she gave Buddy Meyer the go-ahead to consider the reformation of Andrew's sentence, in the same court, with the same judge who stacked his sentences seventeen years earlier.

Judge Perkins swears in the four witnesses, and then instructs Grady Tuck to call his first witness. It's 2:06 p.m.

Adrian Early testifies that he is in favor of reforming Andrew's sentence. Martha Moffett testifies similarly. Each talks of Andrew's remorse, his college education while incarcerated, and his commitment to faith—knowledge personally garnered by each through the TDCJ's mediated dialogue program. Aaron Early, who patrols highways in Texas as a state trooper, also testifies that he's in favor of the sentences against Andrew being served concurrently. A nineteen-year-old kid destroyed three families that night in 1996, he says, but everyone in this room probably did a thing or two that wasn't so smart at the same age. Having worked a couple of intoxication manslaughter cases as a trooper, he hasn't seen a sentence given out as harsh as Andrew's.

Tuck reminds the Court that Andrew first served the sentence for David's death and is now serving the sentence for Bethany's death.

Jim Willett, the former warden at the Walls Unit, crosses the bar and approaches as the final witness. He explains that he's been retired after having worked thirty years for the TDCJ and that he's never taken the witness oath before to testify on behalf of an inmate. Howard Papke, he says, asked if he would come and testify on Andrew's behalf. He thought about it and determined it was the right thing to do.

"I saw a young man who did the things that we asked him to do while he was in prison and did other things on his own to try to improve himself. I like the way that he tried to live a Christian life. And everything I can understand since I was around him is that he has continued to try to improve himself. And so I think he would be a good member—a productive member—of society. I think a lot of people might benefit by him being out."

Grady Tuck presents his closing argument and says he can understand the pain the Earlys and Hollands deal with, as he, too, is a parent who's lost a child to a drunk driver. Unfortunately, nothing can bring back David or Beth, he says, but after seventeen years of incarceration, perhaps justice has been sufficiently served to the person responsible for their deaths. He urges the Court to give Andrew Papke a second chance at freedom.

Perkins reaffirms that the stacking of the two sentences at the time of the trial was the correct decision. But, he says, now that Andrew has made parole on David's sentence, and Bethany's family members are opposed to Andrew serving additional time, he'll certainly consider reforming the structure of the sentence from "consecutive" to "concurrent." He says he'll need some time to research the issue and stands the Court in recess.

Meanwhile, Andrew remains at the penitentiary in Gatesville.

Howard and Cathy Papke visit Andrew on the first Saturday in March and detail for him the proceedings of the February gathering in front of Judge Perkins. Andrew thanks them for all the work they did to produce the hearing but says he doesn't want to get his hopes up. As far as he's concerned, he tells them, he still has multiple years to serve on his sentence, and that's what he plans to do—one day at a time—unless he hears otherwise. Only contact him about the decision, Andrew says to his father, if it's good news.

Tuck phones Howard four and a half weeks later. He tells Howard that he has just received great news. Judge Perkins has ruled that Andrew's sentence will be reformed to be served concurrently, meaning that he'll most likely be eligible for release from the custody of the TDCJ as soon as all the paperwork is signed. Howard tells Tuck, his long-time friend, that he doesn't know how to thank him.

Howard, at home, dashes to his computer and logs onto the TDCJ's JPay website that, for a fee, transforms emails into printed letters for inmates. He nervously pecks out a short note to his son, and then maneuvers the cursor on the send icon. He can't click the mouse fast enough, but finally succeeds. Momentarily paralyzed, he stares at the computer screen until it becomes a watery blur. His shoulders start to heave.

During the next evening's shift change, Andrew hears the guard who's just come on duty bellow out his name. He reaches out to take the JPay letter. He's received only a few JPay letters before, all of them updates on legal issues from his dad. Upon seeing the envelope, his throat immediately tightens and his heart hammers. He retreats to his cell, sits on the edge of his bunk, and with eyes closed mouths a short prayer.

He takes the letter from the envelope and opens it. Seeing his father's name at the top of the page, and the date "April 2, 2014," his eyes race to its short message below: **"All will be O.K."**

Images bombard his mind: his grandfather breaking down on the last day of his trial, his brother reaching out his hand to take a bloody cross Andrew pulled from his own neck in the hospital emergency room, Adrian Early telling him to forgive himself, his father pointing to the parking lot sign outside of the Travis County Jail. Shaking with chills, he collapses to the cement floor and the decisive voice of his father rings in his head: "Andy, all will be O.K."

He knows he'll be going home—soon.

Chapter 49

little more than three months later, he's transported
to the McConnell Unit in Beeville, Texas. For many
years, the TDCJ scheduled all prisoner releases from
The Walls. Now, however, the prison of release is matched
by geographic proximity to the assigned parole area for the
inmate, which for Andrew Papke is San Antonio.

Andrew is housed in isolation at the Beeville Unit in far
South Texas. The TDCJ reasons in its new policy that there's
no sense in putting a prisoner scheduled for release in the
regular population. There are two sides to the security coin—
for the prisoner himself, and for the prison administration
that has the task of releasing the correct prisoner. Andrew
knows from brief previous experiences that isolation is no
picnic. It's up to twenty-three hours a day in a small cell with
no outside window, no knowledge of whether it's night or
day, constant guard presence and handcuffing whenever he
leaves the miniscule cell, and no radio or fan, only a toilet.

The fourth day of his confinement arrives with a breakfast
plate of powdered scrambled eggs and stale toasted bread
handed through the bean slot in his cell door. His sweaty hand

grabs the plate, but he won't touch the food. It's Monday, July 14, 2014, the day of his scheduled release.

Twenty minutes later, the guard looks in at him through a slim vertical rectangular window on his door and motions to him that he can shower if he likes. Yes, sir, he responds and backs up to the door, on his knees, with his hands behind him at the level of the bean slot. Andrew strains to reach his hands through the slot and the guard cuffs him. Andrew rises to his feet, steps forward, and faces the back of the cell. The guard who cuffed him opens the cell door, accompanied by another guard. They take him to an isolation shower cell, 2' x 3' x 8', uncuff him, and lock him in the stall. As the lukewarm water spills on his face, he fears that somehow a last-minute glitch will take his hopes, like the water, down the drain.

Back in his cell, he hears his full name called out loudly by a voice he hasn't heard in his four days at Beeville. The same voice commands him to put his prison ID through the bean slot. He's told to stand back and face the cell door. The street-clothed supervisor checks his ID, looks at Andrew's face through the cell door window, and then tells him to pack his belongings and prepare to be cuffed. The supervisor leaves, and the two guards who accompanied him to the shower, after cuffing him again, stride on either side of him, escorting him to his next destination. One of them carries Andrew's tow sack of belongings.

They arrive at the front admin section of the unit. Andrew steps into the enclosed room and a wave of air conditioning makes him shudder. He's told to sit, and he notices ten other prisoners seated in the same area. He sees three smartly dressed civilians behind a table at the front of the room with a placard that says "TDCJ Parole Board Representatives."

Again, he hears his name called. A guard uncuffs him and points him to a window where a female prison employee asks him to give his full name, date of birth, and prisoner ID number. As further instructed, he rubs each of his index fingers in a black ink pad and leaves his prints on a form that prominently features his name and the words, "Release Date: July 14, 2014." As the clerk points in the direction of a bin draped with used clothing, his hopes rise. *My God, I can't believe this is actually happening.*

Even though it's the middle of July in South Texas, he picks out a dark shirt with a collar and work pants with a heavy zipper and a big button to secure the waist. The guard escorts him into a restroom and tells him he has two minutes to change. He wants to say he won't need anywhere close to that long, but keeps his mouth shut. He emerges and places his bland prison whites in a hamper next to the bin.

The guard points for him to return to the clerk's window where he receives a check for $50. He's told to report to his parole officer in San Antonio tomorrow before 5 p.m., where he'll receive an additional check for $50. She instructs him to sign his name on what she refers to as his "walking papers." As he signs his name, he reads: "The State of Texas hereby grants parole and release to inmate Andrew Papke, #791425, who agrees to comply with all the conditions implied herein ..."

All those close to Andrew—Jan and Jack, Krista, Howard and Cathy, their daughter Luci, Dave, and Chad—wanted to be at the gate of the Beeville prison to welcome Andrew back to the free world. Andrew was resolute: only his dad was to come and get him. Howard Papke, alone in his pickup, left Austin this morning just as the sun nudged the eastern horizon.

At a side door of the admin office, four guards line up the eleven inmates in alphabetical order according to last names. Then, with two guards at the front of the line and two others at the rear, the eleven men are marched to the front gate, a threshold that promises to shed them of their inmate status, as if snakeskin, so that they might emerge on the other side as parolees.

One final test awaits each of the eleven, however—the TDCJ's last chance to make sure that it releases the correct inmates to the general public. Two guards at the front gate hold eleven travel cards, slabs of cardboard with a recent photo and detailed information about each inmate's personal and incarceration record. The information is specific enough to disclose where each inmate's tattoos are located.

Andrew has watched the seven men in front of him successfully exit. Under the close watch and direction of an armed guard, the brand new parolees stepped off the curb, and like vapor, disappeared into the front passenger seat of a waiting vehicle. No hoopla, no hugging, no carrying on— in perfect clockwork order, the released inmate to the next vehicle in line. Andrew also sees a high rider on horseback with a rifle, working in tandem with the armed guard. Two new parolees not picked up by a vehicle turned to their right and entered a van destined for the Greyhound bus station in Beeville.

Andrew steps up to the guard who holds his travel card.

Responding to the guard's inquiry, Andrew gives his original date of incarceration, highlights his inmate work history, and correctly states his mother's maiden name. When he replies to an inquiry about his tattoo and points back at his left shoulder blade, saying that it's similar to the team logo of the Atlanta Falcons, he hears the words "Step forward." He crosses the threshold.

He watches as his dad, on cue from the armed guard, pulls forward in his pickup truck. Andrew opens the door, steps up, and ducks inside, followed by a clean click of the door.

"Hey, Dad, what took you so long?"

Howard only looks at him with a wry smile, lets his foot off the brake, and slowly pulls forward.

A few weeks back, Andrew told his mom that she could host a gathering for him in Austin—he insisted to her that it wasn't a party—in exchange for her accepting his request that only his dad come down to Beeville to pick him up. Howard has told Jan that they'll arrive at her place— Jan and Jack now live outside Austin city limits—sometime that evening, depending on what Andy wants to do.

Sixty miles southeast of Beeville lies Port Aransas, a popular Texas beach location that Howard frequented with Andrew and Dave when they were boys. Andrew told his dad that he might want to drive straight to the coast to gaze at the wide-open blues and greens of the Gulf of Mexico on his release day.

"Where we going?" the father asks the son as their truck nears the edge of the McConnell Unit's property. "Port A?"

Andrew, looking out the window, says he doesn't think so. "Let's just drive toward Austin."

"Are you sure about that?" the father asks. "Yes, sir," the son responds, "let's go home."

The straight north drive from South Texas is mostly silent—not much talking, no radio.

As they get closer to Austin, Andrew starts to see familiar spots. Everything—buildings, roads, landmarks—looks smaller than he remembers.

They arrive in San Marcos, twenty miles south of Austin, and decide to grab a bite at an Outback restaurant. Before getting out of the truck, Andrew changes into new Wrangler jeans and a western shirt that his mom sent along with Howard. He slides his legs out of the pickup and pulls on his cowboy boots that he sent home to his dad before he left Gatesville. While walking into the restaurant, he cinches tight a leather belt and shakes his head at the thought of how he used to take twine from hay bales to hold up his elastic waistband prison whites while working with the horses in Gatesville.

Andrew mentions to his dad that he needs to sit in the back of the restaurant where he can see everything that's going on.

Looking at the menu, he tells his dad that everything looks good, but he has no idea what to order. Howard orders steaks for both of them. When the server brings the steaks, Andrew digs in with his knife and fork. For more than seventeen years, he's attacked the food on his plate with nothing more than a prison-issued plastic spoon. After a few moments, Howard tells his son to slow down. No rush, he says. They have all the time in the world, and there's no need to worry that some prison guard will show up and issue them orders to move on.

Father and son head into South Austin. Andrew says his gathering can wait. First, he wants to see his grandfather, Howard's dad. The eldest Papke celebrated his ninetieth birthday the previous fall. A World War II veteran, he worked as a machinist until his eyesight deteriorated in his eighty-fourth year. That same year was also the last time Grandpa Henry and Grannie Delores drove up to visit him at Gatesville. Andrew knows that his grandfather's health has been failing. He's been hospitalized numerous times in the past year for congestive heart failure.

Howard walks up the driveway to the house where his parents have lived for almost forty years. Andrew follows him. They walk past the garage where Henry has his extensive collection of tools. Andrew remembers when his dad taught him and his brother to put tools back in their proper places. Howard said he learned the very same lesson from his father. As Howard knocks on the front door and announces their arrival, Andrew also remembers the stories he heard from both his dad and grandfather about how the two used to drag race each other at a track east of Austin.

Inside, Henry and Delores Papke stand to greet their grandson. Andrew hugs each of them. Yelping and jumping, a boisterous Jack Russell terrier adds to the excitement. Grandfather Henry says that it's sure great to see him, especially because they weren't sure if they'd get a chance to do so. The older man hands his grandson a card in an envelope and says that they've been saving this for him, and what's in the card is intended to help him out with whatever he needs.

They sit in the living room and talk briefly about how Austin has changed from what it used to be.

After saying their goodbyes, Howard and Andrew drive out to Jan and Jack's place. Andrew mentions to his dad that

Grandpa Henry looked better than he anticipated. Howard says that it's the best he's seen his dad in a long time.

The July sun burns strong into early evening as Howard and Andrew slowly motor up the long gravel drive leading to Jan and Jack's house, set on a hill southeast of Austin. Dogs shadow the truck's advance and howl. Many have gathered to welcome Andrew—his mom and Jack, Dave, Chad, Grandma Dunlap, Cathy and Luci Papke, Krista, and a slew of cousins, aunts, and uncles he's not seen in more than seventeen years. Everybody hugs him and says welcome home.

Andrew remembers this property from the time he was a child, called the "country place," owned by his mom's side of the family. He and Dave lived here with Jan for a time shortly after the divorce. The air, just like he remembers it, is fresh and clean and smells like home. He looks to the north past the horse pen and sees a hazy silhouette of downtown Austin, much more built up than it used to be.

Barbequed brisket and chicken, potato salad, three kinds of beans, cakes and brownies, and all sorts of fixings meet his eyes as he walks into the house. He's not hungry but grabs a plate anyway and helps himself. He catches his mom watching him from the corner of the kitchen and smiles at her.

Jack approaches him and holds out a set of keys. He explains that he picked up a '65 Chevy truck the past year and has been fixing it up for him. Taking the keys, Andrew smiles and shakes his head. Then Jack reaches into his pocket and produces a cell phone. As he hands it to Andrew he says, "This is a smart phone." He smirks and says, "Good luck with it."

Andrew and Krista made it through the early rocky years of Andrew's incarceration by sheer will, and then later, as they matured, by a mutual devotion to the cause of his parole. It was a shared existence as husband and wife that tightened their bond, even as they were separated by razor wire, watch dogs, bulletproof steel doors, and countless personnel ably upholding a well-established system of law and order.

But the last three years, with his possible parole still years away, they've drifted apart. Krista completed her schooling and bought a house that turned into a home, filled with four beloved dogs. Andrew and Krista still loved each other, but what was the point? Did they still have a future together? She hasn't visited him much in the past three years, but they claim a deeply shared history and a union as husband and wife.

Judge Perkins's order that Andrew's sentences be served simultaneously caught Andrew—and Krista—by surprise. From the last update of his prison record, his future parole habitation was listed at Krista's address in San Antonio. Right before he left the Gatesville prison, he tried to change his preferred parole location to Austin. He was told he'd have to extend his stay if he wanted it changed. He and the prison clerk who gave him the information both laughed. San Antonio it would be.

His final destination this night, July 14, 2014, is Krista's home in San Antonio, a one-hour drive from Jan and Jack's place outside of Austin.

The late-night drive to San Antonio is mostly quiet. Andrew's eyelids are heavy. During the previous night in the tight, solitary confinement cell, he barely slept. When they do talk, she tells him about new tasks she does at her job at the lab. She says she likes her work and hopes to advance farther in the field. He always knew she'd make it, he says, from the time she graduated from high school.

Krista's four dogs raise a ruckus with the entrance of the visitor. A bag of doggie bacon bits sits on the kitchen counter. She tosses it to him and says that it might help his cause.

After the dogs settle down, she tells him she needs to be at work before 8 a.m. and points down the hallway to the extra bedroom where he'll sleep. Walking there, he passes a framed picture of him and Krista from high school days, enters the bedroom, and tosses his tow sack on the bed. She stands in the hallway by the door. He turns and says thank you, and from a distance, they bid each other good night. The dogs follow Krista into her bedroom, and she closes the door.

Andrew showers, long and hot, and then dries off with a cotton towel so plush that he imagines he's floating in clouds. Coming back to earth, he sees himself in the mirror and notices that his brown eyes are weary, yet clear. He tells himself it's been a long day, but a good one, and that he needs to get some sleep.

As he walks back into the bedroom and eyes the lamp on the bedside table, he wonders how dark the room will be when the lamp switch clicks off. Sliding under the covers, the coolness of the sheets jolts him, and he shakes with chills. With a jittery hand he reaches up and turns the lamp off. In the inky darkness and still quiet he's not known for seventeen years, on a bed so soft, he shuts his eyes.

His mind races and his ears twitch upon hearing the slightest noises that break the stillness.

Ten minutes after having switched the lamp off, he turns it back on, gets up, and yanks a blanket from the bed. He throws it around his shoulders, kicks his tow sack to the corner, and lies down on the floor. Its carpeted firmness reminds him of his metal rack of a bed.

He's more comfortable now, but his mind continues to race. He thinks of only one thing and all the things related to it—the night of June 29, 1996.

EPILOGUE 1

Andrew and Krista

The next day, after a mostly sleepless night rehashing the details of the wreck, Andrew rides a bus toward a downtown San Antonio parole office for his orientation. Each time the bus stops and its doors swing open, he welcomes the burst of summer heat that enters and watches people get on and off the bus—freely of their own volition—and wonders if he'll ever be able do it as nonchalantly as they do.

His parole officer leads him to a small room and instructs him to sit at a stall outfitted with a computer screen. A video will require his attention for the next twenty minutes. All parolees are required to watch the video produced by the Texas Department of Transportation, highlighting the stories of participating subjects Jacqui Saburido and Reggie Stephey, to counter drunk driving. It's a story with which Andrew is intimately familiar.

His dad picks him up after the orientation. They drive to Austin where Andrew and Howard meet with Grady Tuck. Andrew thanks Tuck for his work to help get his sentence reformed, and Tuck offers Andrew a part-time job as a legal assistant in his office.

Two weeks later, Henry Papke, whose health has taken another turn for the worse, is admitted to a hospital in Austin. Henry is put on oxygen but is still lucid enough to converse between labored breaths. Andrew goes up to the hospital and sits at his grandfather's side for hours at a time. During one of their conversations, Henry tells his grandson about a recurring dream he's had all his life, based upon actual experience: being stuck in foxholes during World War II while exploding shells and gunfire blazed above, about, and around him. Andrew does the math in his head and realizes it's more than seventy years since his grandfather fought for the Allies in France.

Andrew tells his elder that it's good to be out of prison, but the wreck and its consequences haven't gone away. Nodding his head to his grandfather, he confesses that it's been almost twenty years, and his nightmares about the wreck that took two peoples' lives, messed up his friend, and severely damaged three families haven't gone away either. As he looks at his grandfather struggling to breathe, Andrew makes a mental note that his own nightmares might accompany him all the days of his life.

Splitting his time between Austin, where he visits his hospitalized grandfather and works for Grady Tuck, and San Antonio, where he checks in with his parole officer and sees Krista and her dogs, he has one main worry. He gets along much better with Krista's dogs than at first, but he's not sure what type of future he and his wife will have together.

The afternoon of October 16, 2014, Papke family members and others gather in the shade of outspread live oaks at a cemetery in southwest Austin where Henry Papke, who always had a ready smile and a kind word to share, has been laid to rest. Andrew tells the pastor who officiated the funeral service that he was grateful on the day of his release from prison to see Henry at home. After that, Andrew continues, he saw his grandfather only in the hospital where doctors and nurses tended to him during the last two months of his decline.

Andrew stands tall in cowboy boots, Wrangler jeans, and a dress shirt under a black Stetson hat. Krista, the sun's rays reflecting off her long, straight, blonde hair, stands attentive at his side as they converse with the pastor in the same cemetery where David Holland was buried more than eighteen years ago. The pastor, who more than a decade earlier had invited Howard Papke to share Andrew's story with youth at his church, asks Andrew if he would come to the same church and share his story with a new group of young people. Without hesitation, Andrew responds, "Absolutely."

In March of the next year, Andrew drives up from San Antonio to tell his story to the teens, most of them learning to drive, at the Austin church. Fifteen adolescents arrange their folding chairs in a semi-circle around Andrew. A number of adults, mostly parents of the youth, quietly listen to the former prisoner from the back of the room. Andrew's telling is calm, confident, fittingly honest, and appropriate for the emotional level of the young group. He makes special mention of the Victim-Offender Dialogue program, commenting that it helped restore his life. After speaking for an hour or so, Andrew takes questions. Each one in the youth group has a question or a comment.

Standing and listening with the parents in the back of the room is a young lawyer named Brian Sullivan. Almost fifteen years earlier at the same church, he listened to Howard Papke share the same story. From Brian's positive response to Andrew's story in 2000, Andrew gained the knowledge that his message was appropriate for all sorts of teens and not just those going down the wrong road, like him and many of Karen Gonsoulin's students.

Shortly after his grandfather's death, Andrew and Krista decided to start dating again—one dinner, movie, or walk in the park at a time—both of them open to their relationship going wherever the process led. It didn't take them long to rediscover the deep commitment and love that had held them together through many trials and tribulations. In the spring of 2015, right before Andrew came to speak to the young people at the church, they recommitted themselves to their marriage.

Four years later Andrew and Krista are still together. They share a home with the beloved dogs that kept Krista company during the latter part of Andrew's prison sentence. Krista continues to work as a forensic scientist, and Andrew is now employed full-time in a different line of work. Both stay busy with their jobs and try to enjoy the outdoors as much as they can—biking, hiking, boating and fishing, and walking their dogs.

They stay close to Howard and Cathy, as well as to Jan, Jack, and Chad, and Krista's mother, and enjoy seeing them and other family members at gatherings.

Andrew kept exact count of Krista's visits during his time as an inmate at two jails and five penitentiaries in Texas: 426 visits, almost two per month. Andrew comments that their marriage ceremony-by-proxy facilitated contact visits, but, more importantly, an abiding love bound them to each other through the seventeen years and seven months of his incarceration.

It still does as of this writing.

Andrew carries the same sense of responsibility that he did in prison, wanting to find ways to help young people. His assistance to the author in the writing of this book was open-ended and thorough. Now that the book is published, he responds to speaking requests on a case-by-case basis. For him, rehashing the events of the wreck and its consequences, as it is for the victims of his crime, is still an emotional experience.

He tries very hard to strike a balance between the future and the past in how he lives in the present. As stated on the dedication page of this book, he does not want to and will not in any way profit financially from the telling of his story. He does not want to do anything to add to the pain of the victims of his drunken behavior on that terrible night in June 1996.

But he has also been humbled and encouraged by the numerous persons through the years who have told him how his writing and speaking have touched and changed their lives and perspectives. He walks humbly with the past, while being willing to quietly share with others if it reshapes their future for the good.

"Doing time was the easy part," he says. "Prison went away, but the other stuff is still there." Sharing his story continues to be part of his mission, a responsibility he has chosen in an effort to wrest good out of something deeply catastrophic.

EPILOGUE 2

Others

This book is not just about Andrew Papke. Many others, long before he landed in prison, cleared the path that he and some of his victims would later take, leading to restoration and healing. The path is anything but easy, and not many offenders and victims choose, or are able, to take it.

The transformation of an offender is an individual story, but it necessarily involves a group or community. Andrew Papke benefitted from many individuals who reached out to him from a variety of groups and communities.

From the moment he decided to plead guilty at his trial, he took responsibility for, as much as possible, righting the wrongs he committed. This is an individual decision, but it is not solitary work. The practices of Restorative Justice placed him in communal settings and provided him with methods to chip away at his unenviable task. Healing, a beneficial by-product of this process, touched him then and continues to guide his steps and decisions today.

He's eternally grateful to those who offered him their acceptance, forgiveness, guidance, and love.

Howard and **Cathy Papke** are retired and reside in Austin. Howard enjoys seeing Andrew when he can. They occasionally find time to go fishing, and when they do, they talk about cars and trucks.

Jan and **Jack May** continue to live on their property outside of Austin. After Jack's release from prison, his son **Chad** lived with them there until he finished school. Jack is a fixture on the classic car show circuit in Texas. He has a bevy of ribbons and trophies he's won for his 1937 Ford.

Adrian Early lives near his son Aaron in Central Texas. The elder Early's wife **Kathy** passed away from cancer in 2009. The last time Adrian saw Andrew Papke was when they embraced after their mediated dialogue in 1999. When told of Andrew's claim that the Victim-Offender Dialogue program was "life-saving" for him, Adrian was moved to tears. He says Andrew's contrition, during his trial and two years later during their face-to-face dialogue, was a "great gift."

Martha Early Moffett lives with her husband Harrell in the same house from which she waved goodbye to Beth at the kitchen window on June 29, 1996. Now retired, Martha says she still gets tears in her eyes during the holidays when she thinks of her daughter, whom she trusts to see someday in a heavenly future. "Andrew has been given a precious gift from God. He has been given another chance." She says that she was glad to stand up for him at the hearing for sentence reformation in February 2014. She's also confident that God will be honored as Andrew speaks to young people through this book to change many lives for the better.

In the early 2000s, brothers **Aaron** and **Adam Early** served in the United States Marine Corps during the Iraq and Afghanistan wars. Aaron has worked as a Texas state trooper since 2007. Many times, he's pulled over drivers whom he suspects are under the influence of drugs or alcohol. Every time he does so, he remembers his sister and tells himself— and sometimes the driver—that this stop might prevent another family from having to deal with the type of tragedy his family knows intimately.

Maria Soriano moved to New Mexico a few years after David's death. **Benjamin** and **Lucas Holland**, David's brothers, both live in Los Angeles.

Richard and **Helen Holland** continue to reside in Austin, enjoying family and retirement.

Davis **Doerfler** coordinated the TDCJ's Victim-Offender Dialogue program for eight years before resigning in 2001. He continued to work in the field of Restorative Justice as a consultant, sharing the gospel of victim empowerment and offender self-awareness with faith communities, county jurisdictions, and state criminal justice systems, until his retirement in 2013.

During his tenure as coordinator of the Victim-Offender Dialogue program, Doerfler searched for the drunk driver responsible for debilitating his daughter Meredith. He didn't want revenge but wanted the driver to know about the ripple effects his actions had upon his family, especially upon Meredith. The pursuit was unsuccessful.

Raven Kazen retired in 2008 after a career spanning more than thirty years in Texas's criminal justice system, the last fifteen years as TDCJ State Director of Victim Services.

When crime victim trailblazer **Cathy Phillips** passed away in 2009 at fifty-seven years of age, Raven Kazen was at her bedside. She conducted Cathy's funeral service and commended her tenacity, which was the greatest force in the creation of Texas's Victim-Offender Dialogue program. "Cathy Phillips," Kazen says, "more than anyone else, taught me that the victim is always right."

John Sage continues to lead Bridges To Life, which has expanded its reach to ten states beyond Texas and to four countries outside the United States. Sage and his prison ministry staff claim more than 40,000 offenders as program graduates and mobilize a volunteer core of more than 750 men and women. Sage argues that Bridges To Life program graduates have significantly helped reduce recidivism rates in those states where the ministry operates, consequently lessening the tax burden and improving public safety.

The Texas Board of Criminal Justice held its annual Governor's Criminal Justice Volunteer Service Award ceremony in Austin on April 6, 2017. John Sage received the Carol S. Vance Volunteer of the Year award, the ceremony's most prestigious honor. Andrew Papke was among more than 500 persons who applauded Sage as he accepted the award. After the ceremony, Sage and Andrew posed for a picture together in front of the TBCJ blue and gold seal. It was the first time Sage and Papke had seen each other since the early 2000s.

Ellen Halbert remains active as a crime victim advocate and Restorative Justice proponent. She retired from the Travis County DA's office after fifteen years of coordinating its victim services witness program, assisting crime victims, and overseeing a mediation process based on Restorative Justice principles for pending prosecutions of criminal cases. She says, "Most of the time I told crime victims, 'This offender needs to hear what you have to say to them.' There were rules about not screaming obscenities or carrying on in an inappropriate way. But there wasn't a time when I finished a mediation that I didn't walk about two feet off the ground because of what it did for these two people in the room."

While she was working in the DA's office, Halbert discovered that her assailant, still imprisoned, had had a difficult childhood in a highly dysfunctional family. A brother-in-law of the assailant told Halbert by telephone that he had been threatened by the assailant months before Halbert's attack. Halbert's assailant-to-be then left the northeast state of his residence and disappeared. The caller also told Halbert that he had seen her picture, and that she and the assailant's mother looked very much alike. That detail revealed for Halbert the likeliest reason for the perpetrator's attack upon her. A type of psychological transference—seen in other criminal cases—was the most likely culprit, making Ellen the substitute recipient of the attacker's rage against his own mother. The assailant is still incarcerated at the time of this writing. Ellen Halbert's question of "Why?" has been answered without her having to meet with her attacker.

Bob Connell continues to live near Crockett, Texas. He works for the TDCJ, supervising prisoners working in agriculture. He says he wouldn't be able to do this type of work without having participated in the Bridges To Life program.

Bob and Cathy Connell eventually reached a plea agreement, almost four years after the wreck, with the county DA for the drunk driver who killed their four children. The man pleaded guilty, apologized to the Connells, and served prison time.

Cathy Connell passed away in 2014 after a couple of years of failing health. She remained active in Restorative Justice and victim services outreach before her illness, sharing her story with fellow crime victims, giving them a glimpse of light from her experience to combat the dark emptiness that crime creates.

Karen Gonsoulin, the teacher who used Andrew's open letter with her correctional school students, taught public school for more than thirty-five years. Of the letter exchange she carried out with Andrew—for six years and numbering more than 300 letters—she says, "It was the most important thing I did as a teacher, period."

Kim and **Bob Thonhoff** live in the same Austin neighborhood close to the wreck site. Twenty years earlier she encountered Andrew belligerent at the wreck and seemingly unmoved during his trial. Hearing that he was out of prison and committed to telling a story of transformation, she smiled. "Every time I drive by David's and Beth's cross I say a little prayer for all involved. To hear that Andrew has turned his life around is like an answer to prayer."

Travis Thonhoff, the eleven-year-old witness of the wreck, says that the memory of the crash has never left his consciousness. "There's a time in everyone's life where they figure out their own limits, and I know that being a witness

to the wreck made it more real for me to understand consequences of actions." When he was in college, and now as a
young professional, he has taken away car keys from people
who have been overserved at parties or events. He says it's
not easy to do, because a lot of the time the people holding
the keys become argumentative. "I remind them that it's not
about tonight, but tomorrow."

Reggie Stephey served every day of his seven-year
sentence and was paroled in 2008. Like Andrew, he
pursued a college degree while incarcerated. **Jacqui
Saburido** as of this writing lives in her native Venezuela and
has endured more than 100 corrective surgeries.

Judge Bob Perkins and former **Assistant DA Buddy
Meyer** both say that the reformation of Andrew's sentence in 2014 was "the right thing to do." Perkins remains active as a substitute on the judicial bench.

Meyer retired in 2016 after serving in the Travis County
DA's office for more than thirty years.

Prominent Restorative Justice academician Mark
Umbreit of the University of Minnesota interviewed
David Doerfler numerous times during the early
days of Texas's foray into state-sponsored Victim-Offender

Dialoguing. Doerfler aptly summed up his work for the researcher: "We help people face their darkest hour and prepare for the dawn."

Twenty years after its inception, the **TDCJ's Victim Services Division** still provides national leadership in its field. Current Director Angela McCown says, "Texas continues to be the leader in **Victim-Offender Dialogue** because we started one of the first programs in the nation. We have one of the largest paid staffs, and we have the dialogue process guaranteed as a victim's right in the Texas State Constitution." In 2017, the TDCJ initiated eighty-three new Victim-Offender Dialogue cases and conducted thirty-one cases to completion.

As of this writing, more than thirty other state criminal justice systems offer a replica or variation of the Texas model.

EPILOGUE 3

Author's Note

I first met Andrew Papke at his grandfather's funeral service. Henry Papke and his wife Delores were longtime members of the church I pastored, St. John's/San Juan Lutheran Church, in Austin. Howard Papke, their son, was my auto mechanic. Years earlier, I had invited Howard to come to our church to speak with the youth and, after Henry's funeral, for Andrew to do the same.

Over the years, Howard had told me some of the details of Andrew's wreck and its aftermath. He'd always add that he feared never being able to see his son out of prison. Henry flatly told me he wouldn't see his grandson ever again. Both also told me that Andrew had paid a hefty price for what he did in June 1996 but was trying to live a life, even while incarcerated, that was worthy of the respect due to the two lives lost in the wreck and the harm done to their families.

When I heard Andrew tell his story to the youth at my church, including the centerpiece about the Texas prison system's Victim-Offender Dialogue program, I knew the story had to be shared on a wider scale. In response, Andrew told me about his manuscript but said in the same breath that it was lost. Prison cells don't have storage units, he smiled and said, and he hadn't had any luck tracking down the only copy of the manuscript that he had sent to a friend while still at the Gatesville Unit.

By summer's end in 2016, almost two years after I shook Andrew's hand for the first time, we met at a Mexican restaurant north of San Antonio. I asked him if he'd allow me to write the story that started with the tragic and unnecessary loss of life, continued with the admission of guilt and the acceptance of responsibility, and gravitated toward restoration and healing. I told him I'd be honored to tell the story.

Andrew promised to think about it and respond within a week's time.

Forty-five minutes later, he texted me: "Write it. I don't need any more time to think about it."

A few months later, Andrew and Krista sat down with me, and I turned on my phone's recorder app for one of the many interviews I'd do for this book. It was an emotionally draining retelling, but one that Andrew has been committed to sharing ever since he wrote his open letter late in 1997 from the Holliday Unit. "Being able to tell my story gave me some release. I couldn't be down there in prison and not have anyone learn from this."

Toward the end of the interview, Andrew told me about the recurring nightmare that he had while in prison and that continued since. "I have these dreams where I'm in that car again, and I'm in that turn again on Brodie Lane, and I know what's going to happen, and I try to turn the wheel but the wheel doesn't respond, or something happens ... regardless, I cannot avoid hitting the Volkswagen head-on again.

"I'm there—sometimes Krista is with me in the passenger seat, or my dad's with me, or other people are with me in the car. It's different variations of it but always the same result that I can't stop. And I wake up sweating and crying and kind of reach over and grab Krista.

"I've had the dream back-to-back. I fall asleep after waking up and have it again. So many things trigger it—the time of year, the holidays, the anniversary of the wreck, a song on the radio, if I see a black Acura or a red VW Beetle. I get sweaty hands. I'm getting sweaty right now just talking about it.

"The only reason I'm doing this is so that hopefully somebody will be helped by it. Period. Otherwise I'd just let it go, let it stay in the past, and go on with life.

"People assume that because you're free again, you've paid your price for what happened. But it's never going to be over. Ever. Maybe someday in the hereafter, maybe it's over then. But I never know ..."

Early the next morning, my phone buzzed with a text message. It was Andrew.

"I was in the car again last night. This time you were with me. We were in the turn on Brodie Lane, but this time it was different. Instead of struggling to steer right to miss the VW, I just yanked the wheel to the left and went with it. We missed the crash! I don't remember any more details, but I got out. We were in the ditch, but everyone was okay."

A new dream. Or the same old dream with the nightmarish beginning, but with a completely unexpected ending.

The new dream doesn't bring back Beth or David or diminish the pain borne by their families and loved ones, but it is further confirmation for Andrew to keep telling his story. Sometimes healing does come from the vulnerable sharing of one's pain. I've seen this happen in pastoral ministry. But researching this project and speaking with dozens of crime victims and Restorative Justice advocates, many who are a part of this story, have made me aware of a whole new level of healing that is, frankly, astounding and unfathomable.

"Every time I tell my story, I heal a little bit more." Ellen Halbert's statement, appearing as an epigram opposite the title page in this book, reveals a deep truth based in the experiences of both crime victims and perpetrators. The stories highlighted in this book speak of healing from life-altering trauma and are shared to encourage and inspire healing for those dealing with similar tragedies.

"There is a balm in Gilead to make the wounded whole;
There is a balm in Gilead to heal the sin-sick soul."
Nineteenth-century African-American Spiritual

Acknowledgments

Although I'm a pastor, I've always said that people in the recovery movement have taught me more about spirituality than church folks. That's not a knock against church folks. But the commendable character traits specified in the Serenity Prayer—the acceptance of things that can't be changed, the courage to act upon those circumstances which can be changed, and the wisdom to know the difference between the two—are qualities I've noticed over the years in people in the recovery movement.

Since the first time I met Andrew Papke, I've consistently seen those same traits in him. I thank Andrew, first and foremost, for his honesty and lack of defensiveness in retelling his story. I also thank his wife, Krista, for her support in the telling of this painful yet redemptive story. Her deep reservoir of quiet strength, I suspect more than anything else, helped Andrew survive his incarceration.

I'm also grateful to Adrian and Aaron Early, Martha Moffett, and Benjamin Holland for speaking with me, with extra special thanks to Martha Moffett for her permission to use all the letters she wrote to Andrew. I deeply appreciate their cooperation in the telling of this story, even though it shines a spotlight again upon the horrific events of June 1996, and its lingering pain.

The other crime victims who openly told me their stories taught me the truths, many of which I was unaware, of their burdensome experiences. Special thanks to Ellen Halbert, John Sage, and Bob Connell. Another crime victim, Linda White, and a sheriff's deputy traumatized at a crime scene, Al Reyes, whose stories did not make the final edits of this book, gained my utmost respect by sharing with me how crime and its effects did not bury the rest of their lives in resentment, pain, and rage.

My gratitude extends to three writer friends in Austin, each one schooling this latecomer in the ways of the story-telling craft. Longtime scribe and high school creative writing teacher Michael DiLeo engendered in me a confidence from the moment I shared with him that I was going to write this story. Like the experienced editor and writer that he is, he laid out various options of voice—highlighting their pros and cons—to tell this story.

University of Texas journalism professor and award-winning author Kevin Robbins gave me pertinent reading assignments on writing and took the time to review them with me. He also fielded my numerous calls and emails about other writing issues with great patience, exhibiting (on the surface, at least) a confidence that his oldest student would eventually find his way.

Pastoral colleague and multiple-selling author Peter Steinke encouraged me to stay on the path marked by the sign "Narrative" and not to deviate. I met with these three separately, but their advice felt synchronized. They offered suggestions, but none ever told me how they would write the book if they were in my place. Rather, their collective wisdom pushed me forward and led me to choose the definitive voice for the recounting of this tale.

Thanks also to each one, whether connected to Andrew's story or to the development of Texas's foray into Restorative Justice through its criminal justice system, who met with me and shared their expertise and wisdom, providing the sinews and tendons that hold the two stories together.

I'm indebted to the publishing and editing team of Merle and Phyllis Good. Thanks to them for taking a chance on a relative newcomer and working with me to transform my sometimes meandering manuscript into a polished narrative, capable of emitting a light strong enough to overcome darkness.

The deepest gratitude I offer to my spouse, Denise Anderson, who steadied our economic household for the fifteen months that I worked on this book. The length of my self-imposed sabbatical away from church work, originally estimated to be no more than six to nine months, was severely underestimated. I thank her for her patience and unwavering support. Not once did she question the validity of this project or my investment of time in it. Her endurance allowed me to meet some incredible people—wounded healers each one—and to hear their harrowing yet redemptive tales. I'm honored and humbled to tell these tales in this book, for the related purposes of healing and the construction of a better society.

Notes

This book consists of two main stories: Andrew Papke's transformation and the development of the TDCJ's Victim-Offender Dialogue program.

The interviews I conducted with Andrew Papke and others serve as the main sources for the construction of this double narrative. The trial transcripts from his 1997 and 2014 cases, respectively, *The State of Texas v. Andrew Papke*, 331st District Court, Travis County, Texas, Causes 96–4199 and 96–4200, and *The State of Texas v. Andrew Papke*, 331st District Court, Travis County, Texas, Cause 96–964200–A, provide much information about his particular story, as do the letters that he and Martha Early Moffett wrote to each other over a period of fifteen years. Interviews (all occurring in 2017 or 2018) of more than forty persons connected to either story—and sometimes both of them—helped enlarge the narrative. Articles from the *Austin American-Statesman* (abbreviated below as *AA-S*) and other periodicals, and other sources help shape the double narrative. Howard and Cathy Papke kept an archive of material that Andrew sent to them from prison, along with material they gathered that related to Andrew's case. This will be referred to, below, as the Papke family archive.

PART I—THE ROAD TO HUNTSVILLE

Chapters 1–2

The chronology of the events from June 29, 1996 comes from interviews, the 1997 trial transcript, and documentation from Dr. Linda White who provided me a copy of her dissertation *Hope in Process: A Qualitative Study of Victim-Offender Mediation/Dialogue in Texas* (December 2001), in which she details her extensive interviews of Andrew Papke and Adrian Early after their participation in the Victim-Offender Dialogue program. Interviews: Andrew and Krista; Kim, Bob, and Travis Thonhoff; Adrian Early; Jan May; and, Linda White.

Chapter 3

The remembrances of David and Beth are constructed from interviews with Early and Holland family members, David Sweet, and Martha

Early's letters to Andrew. Two *AA-S* articles provide pertinent details, "Austinite charged in wreck that killed 2—Intoxication manslaughter charges filed after accident killed teens on way home from date," Bob Banta, July 1, 1996; and, "Funerals and Memorials," July 3, 1996. Some of the remembrances come from Early and Holland family member testimonies given during the 1997 trial. The Lucas Holland quote is from an interview he gave on "The Kevin Gill Show" podcast, November 28, 2016.

Chapters 4–7

The 1997 trial transcript provides quotes and most of the storyline for the wreck scene and Andrew's initial time in the Travis County Jail system. David Sweet and Jason Harrell provided additional documentation, as did the Papke family archive. *AA-S* articles featuring coverage of the wreck scene and its aftermath include: "Driver charged in fatal crash had history of legal scrapes—Drunken driving suspect has had speeding convictions, marijuana charges," Bob Banta, July 2, 1996; "Mother's deed's couldn't shield stepson from tragedy—Teens' deaths bring home horrors of drunk driving to MADD supporter, victim's brothers," Bob Banta, July 3, 1996; "Keel, former prosecutor, to represent defendants—Keel to join criminal defense firm," Stuart Eskenazi, November 26, 1996; and, "Parties are putting cap on alcohol," Abby Kaighin, December 18, 1996. The Papke family archive contains June 29, 1996 wreck scene photos. Interviews: Andrew and Krista, the Thonhoffs, David Sweet, Adrian Early, Aaron Early, Jason Harrell, Chris Snoeberger, Buddy Meyer, Bob Perkins, and B.J. Hassell.

Chapters 8–11

Two *AA-S* articles, in part, tell of Jamie Balagia's transformation from cop to lawyer: "Officer found not guilty of weapons charge," Berta Delgado, October 10, 1989; and, Stuart Eskenazi, previously cited, November 26, 1996. Testimony in the 1997 trial transcript details Andrew's time on bail before the onset of his trial. Interviews: Andrew and Krista, Jan May, Adrian Early, Buddy Meyer, Bob Perkins, B.J. Hassell, and Ken Baldwin.

Chapters 12–17

The 1997 trial transcript provides the backbone narrative for these chapters. Three *AA-S* articles provide trial coverage, its background and development: Bob Banta, previously cited, July 2, 1996; Bob Banta, previously cited, July 3, 1996; and, "Jury assesses 20-year sentence for intoxication manslaughter—Andrew Papke, 20," Dave Harmon, April 25, 1997. Austin lawyer Gordon Karchmer gave me descriptions of conditions of the Travis County Jail and of procedures in the District Court 331 courtroom. A University of Texas *Voces Oral History Project* interview from 2014 provided background information on Bob Perkins. Interviews: Andrew and Krista, Buddy Meyer, Ellen Halbert, Bob Perkins, the Thonhoffs, Adrian Early, B.J. Hassell, and Jan May.

PART II—AN OPEN LETTER

Chapters 18–19

An *AA-S* article tells of Maria Soriano's creation of the wreck site memorial for David and Beth: "A sign of remembering," Dave Harmon, May 12, 1997. Documentation in the Papke family archive includes the original copy of Andrew's open letter from November 1997. Interviews: Andrew and Krista, and Jan May.

PART III—FACE TO FACE IN TEXAS

Chapters 20–23

David Doerfler provided significant information about the development of the TDCJ's VOD program. Restorative Justice proponent Jon Wilson's in-depth interviews of David Doerfler in 2000 also provide important information concerning the development of the VOD program. Restorative Justice academician Howard Zehr records some of Ellen Halbert's story in his book *Transcending: Reflections of Crime Victims* (Good Books, 2001). The PVAC website details Nell Myers' advocacy of crime victims' rights, as do two *AA-S* articles: "Crusader for rights of victims gets honor," Andy Alford, July 23, 2000; and, "Daughter's murder changed housewife into activist," David Hafetz, September 28, 2000. An HBO documentary on Cathy Phillips, *Confronting Evil: American Undercover* (January 19, 1993), details her story and records part of her dialogue with prisoner Anthony Yanez. Interviews: David and Cindy Doerfler, Ellen Halbert, Raven Kazen, Adrian Early, and Andrew Papke.

Chapters 24–27

An article in *The Austin Chronicle* by Michael May, "What Is Justice?", August 24, 2001, provides rich detail of both stories and includes quotes from Papke, Early, and Holland family members and David Doerfler. Doerfler's VOD manual, the 1997 trial transcript, and an *AA-S* article by

Bob Banta, "Vandalism renews families' suffering," June 7, 1999, provide additional information. John Bridges provided photos for me to study from *AA-S* archives. Interviews: Andrew Papke, David Doerfler, Raven Kazen, Ellen Halbert, Adrian Early, Linda White, and the Thonhoffs.

PART IV—MORE LETTERS

Chapters 28–30

Martha Early's letters; Michael May, previously cited, *The Austin Chronicle,* August 24, 2001; Austin Bowie High School's *Lone Star Dispatch,* October 22, 1999; Linda White's dissertation; and, Bob Banta's previously cited *AA-S* article from June 7, 1999, provide the storyline. Interviews: Andrew Papke, Michael Reeves, Bob and Kim Thonhoff, Raven Kazen, and Adrian Early.

Chapters 31–34

Andrew Papke's letter, "Letter from prison: a night of drinking, a life of regret," was published in the *AA-S* on December 31, 1999. Karen Gonsoulin and the Papke family archive have all the letters sent during the six years of exchanges between Andrew and Karen's students. The Papke family archive also contains the letters and cards sent to Andrew in response to the *AA-S* publication of his letter. The *AA-S* published Karen Gonsoulin's inquiry in Jane Greig's column, titled "Good news, cowgirl—we found your dream hat," February 14, 2000. Jim Willett's book, co-written by Ron Rozelle, *Warden: Prison Life and Death from the Inside Out* (Bright Sky Press, 2004), was helpful in its descriptions of conditions and procedures at The Walls. Interviews: Andrew Papke, Karen Gonsoulin, John Bridges, Ken Houston, Jim Willett, Jan May, and Jack May.

PART V—BALM

Chapters 35–38

John Sage has given his testimonial speech hundreds of times, in and outside of prisons. Sage's speech is reconstructed here from my interview with him, along with the following documentation: *Guideposts*, "A Deeper Surrender," John Sage, August 2000; and, a recorded presentation by Sage, "Forgiveness: from hate and rage to love and joy," given at St. Theresa Catholic Church, Houston, Texas, on March 24, 2011. Bob and Kathy Connell's speech is reconstructed from my interview with him, and from an interview of them on an episode of *The Montel Williams Show* from 2001, on which Ellen Halbert also appeared. Additional background information on Ken Houston comes from an article by Jennifer Lee Preyss, *Victoria Advocate*, "Former death row minister reflects on service," February 2, 2018. Interviews: Andrew Papke, John Sage, Raven Kazen, Ellen Halbert, Bob Connell, Ken Houston, Jim Willett, and Brian Sullivan.

Chapters 39–41

Ellen Halbert, like John Sage, has given her speech hundreds of times. It is reconstructed here from my interviews with her; my witnessing of Halbert as she gave her speech to male inmates at the Kyle Correctional Unit, TDCJ, Kyle, Texas on August 15, 2017; along with the following documentation: Zehr's *Transcending: Reflections of Crime Victims*; CNN Transcripts, *Larry King Live*, January 12, 2005; and, her own article in *The ICCA Journal on Community Corrections*, August 1997, "I Can Remember a Time … A Crime Victim's Journey to Restorative Justice." I also attended Bridges To Life graduation ceremonies in two other Central Texas prisons to get a sense of the emotion present in those meetings. Jim Willett's recommendation letter was provided to me by John Sage. The Austin Bowie High School yearbook from 2001 describes some of the "Shattered Dreams" assembly. Interviews: Ellen Halbert, John Sage, Travis Thonhoff, Clint Harnden, Kent Ewing, Celester Collier, Kim Thonhoff, and Jim Willett.

Chapters 42–43

Michael May's *The Austin Chronicle* article, cited above, August 24, 2001; and, Linda White's dissertation provide details for Martha and Andrew's mediated dialogue, as do Martha's and Andrew's letters to one another. Interviews: Andrew Papke, David Doerfler, Raven Kazen, Mark Odom, Linda White, and Ken Houston.

PART VI—REUNION

Chapter 44

Dave Hafenz's extensive piece on Jacqui Saburido and Reggie Stephey in the *AA-S*, "Chasing Hope," May 12, 2002, provides ample detail for this chapter. Other *AA-S* articles include: "Two die, three hurt in fiery wreck on RM 2222," Bob Banta, September 21, 1999; Dave Hafetz, "Tearful Stephey says he is sorry," June 26, 2001; and, Dave Hafetz, "Stephey gets

7 years for deadly wreck," June 27, 2001. Interviews: Andrew Papke, Linda White, B.J. Hassell, and Al Reyes.

Chapters 45–46
Interviews: Andrew and Krista, Jan and Jack May, and Ken Houston.

Chapter 47
Martha Early's letters provide chronological detail. Interviews: Andrew and Krista.

Chapters 48–49
The 2014 trial transcript and Martha Early's letters provide the chapters' structure. Documentation in the Papke family archive includes the JPay letter of April 2, 2014. These *AA-S* articles document Rosemary Lehmberg's story: "Top local stories of 2013," December 29, 2013; and, "Lehmberg seeks another chance," Jazmine Ulloa and Ciara O'Rourke, December 11, 2013. The Dan Richards quote comes from the above-cited *AA-S* story of December 29, 2013. The long-time *AA-S* columnist quoted is Ken Herman in his article of December 11, 2013, "DA gets new view of court from witness stand." Interviews: Andrew and Krista, Buddy Meyer, Bob Perkins, Adrian Early, Aaron Early, and Jim Willett.

EPILOGUES
The Victim's Informer, TDCJ Victim Services quarterly newsletter, June/July 2008; *Criminal Justice Connections*, TDCJ newsletter, March/April 2016; Martha Moffett's letter to me dated January 16, 2017; Umbreit, Vos, Coates, and Brown, *Facing Violence: The Path of Restorative Justice and Dialogue* (Lynne Rienner Publishers, 2003); and, the Papke family archive provide pertinent information and quotes. Michael Morton's book, *Getting Life: An Innocent Man's 25-Year Journey from Prison to Peace* (Simon & Schuster, 2015) provides a high-profile incident of psychological transference, similar to Ellen Halbert's case. Interviews: Andrew and Krista, Adrian Early, Aaron Early, David Doerfler, Ellen Halbert, Raven Kazen, John Sage, Bob Connell, Jim Brazzil, Karen Gonsoulin, the Thonhoffs, Jon Wilson, B.J. Hassell, William Petty, and Angela McCown.

About the Author

T. Carlos Anderson is a writer, community activist, and pastor living in Austin, Texas. He has served thirty years as a bilingual spiritual leader with a special focus on social, economic, and restorative justice issues.